*For Mary
with lo*

# WHATEVER HAPPENED TO CT STUDD'S MISSION?

*Richard Barclay
Xmas 2013

Both grandchildren of
C T Studd*

# WHATEVER HAPPENED TO CT STUDD'S MISSION?

## Lessons from the history of WEC International

Evan Davies

WEC PUBLICATIONS

**Copyright © Evan Davies 2012**
Published 2012 by WEC Publications,
Bulstrode, Oxford Road, Gerrards Cross, Bucks, SL9 8SZ, UK
www.wecinternational.org.uk
ISBN 978-0-900828-90-4
Cover design by Chris Lawrence
Typesetting by WEC Media and Communications Office, Leeds, UK

British Library Cataloguing in Publication Data
A CIP catalogue for this book is available from the British Library

Printed by Lightning Source UK Ltd, Chapter House, Pitfield, Kiln Farm, Milton Keynes
MK11 3LW UK

READ MISSION    WEC PUBLICATIONS

# CONTENTS

The author and publishers wish to thank the following for permission to reproduce copyright material:

Articles from *International Bulletin of Missionary Research* (1998; 2008).

Christian Focus Publications for the following books by Stewart Dinnen: *Faith on Fire* (1997); *Learning about Union with Christ* (2001); *Real Guidance* (2003).

Lutterworth Press for the following books by Norman Grubb: *C T Studd: Cricketer and Pioneer* (1993); *Christ in Congo Forests* (1945); *After C T Studd: sequel to the life of the famous pioneer-missionary* (1945); *Once Caught, No Escape: my life story* (1969).

Regnum Books for *The Story of Faith Missions* (1994) by Klaus Fiedler.

# ACKNOWLEDGEMENTS

This book was started as a result of a discussion with former International Director, Dieter Kuhl. He suggested it would be a good idea for someone to write a history of WEC. We left it there, but as the years went by and I moved towards stepping down from leadership myself, the thought began to grow in me that this needed to be done. The result would be a legacy passed on to my colleagues and a future generation of WEC members, as well as to a wide spectrum of people who needed to know what has happened, through the lives of ordinary people who trusted in an extraordinary God.

The story of WEC International has dominated my life. Born in the Congo of WEC missionary parents, brought up in a home for missionary children in Scotland, resident for a while at the New Zealand base, trained and then staff member at WEC's Missionary Training College in Tasmania, related to many who served with WEC and eventually part of the International Office, all gave me a glorious kaleidoscopic overview. People and events, principles and experiences remain on a broad canvas in my mind.

Thankfully I was able to undertake a course of study at Tabor College in Adelaide, of which a central requirement was a ministry thesis. The Director of the Postgraduate Department, Rev Dr Graham Buxton, and my supervisors, Rev Dr Mark Worthing and Dr Richard Hibbert, were of invaluable help. The bulk of this book is the result of that thesis.

Writing about WEC is all about people. Many members of WEC and various friends have been very kind in sending me materials and making comments about the project. Among these some have stood out—Judy Raymo, Jenny Carter, Leslie and Jill Brierley, Mike Brogden, Jonathan Chamberlain, Traugott Böker, Glenn Myers and Dr Brian Woodford.

I have been blessed to have access to a good collection of WEC literature and magazines which has made my job more straight-forward. Norman Grubb was an enthusiastic storyteller of the early days of WEC, and produced a succession of books that flowed with a record of the work of the Holy Spirit. Stewart Dinnen, a mentor and friend, wrote further narratives of more recent events. Helen Roseveare in her lovely style filled in gaps in WEC's history in her volume *Living Stones*. I am grateful for their contributions.

Although I am deeply indebted for the contributions I have received from many in WEC, past and present, I hasten to admit that, unless specifically acknowledged, the opinions and conclusions expressed are my own.

Most of all I must thank my wife, Jenny, who continually encouraged me, and took time to read and comment. She is a special gift from God and a wonderful co-worker in a life of faith.

It has been an exciting venture, even, to lift the lid on part of the story. There is so much more that could have been shared.

Evan Davies
Tanunda, South Australia
November 2010

# INTRODUCTION

It was 2009 and the computer spilled out the news. A fortune teller in Thailand had started coming to church after facing a family tragedy and suicidal thoughts. A South Korean couple was joining a missionary team in Japan at the same time as Carla from Brazil was moving to the city of Nagahama to improve her Japanese language. In Timor Leste, the Esperança team was starting two new programmes: a reading club three mornings a week and a Friday evening special for teenagers. In North Africa a teacher urged a foreign student to give him an Arabic Bible, and then eagerly read it aloud saying this was better than food. Maud from Northern Ireland came home from one of her regular visits to a remote town in the Congo, where she helped to rebuild the medical facilities and provide encouragement to the church and its leaders. From Asia came news of several baptisms among a largely unevangelised ethnic group, in spite of state hostility and repression. What was the connection between all of these?

WEC International is a Christian organisation with a history going back to 1913. It started as a small group led by Charles Thomas Studd, who had served as a Christian worker in China and India and then felt directed to initiate a new work in the Belgian Congo. Studd was controversial and, at that time, a public figure who dominated the structures and ethos of the infant organisation. Through books about him, he has become widely known. Many Christian people will, when asked, acknowledge the identity and impact of CT Studd, but not so many would claim to have any understanding of WEC International, the mission he founded.

WEC is what can be called a 'faith mission', that is one of the Christian associations which arose in succession to the China Inland Mission founded by Hudson Taylor. These societies grew out of the Protestant tradition, but also out of the independent and non-church streams into what have become known as inter-denominational agencies. They embraced the concepts of evangelical theology with the ideas of individual responsibility to God and a determination to trust him for their support by faith rather than by reliance on denominational generosity. As Andrew Walls has said, the unique voluntary and evangelical societies, which arose at the end of the 19th century and beyond, took 'the modern, Western form of a movement which had reappeared from the early period of Christian history'.[1]

By 2009 WEC International, originally one of these western-style agencies, had a total membership of 2,195 members, of which 1,819 were active workers from 50 nationalities serving in more than 80 countries.

How WEC has survived calls for exploration. What was the context in which WEC grew? What personalities, theological views, spiritual initiatives and values shaped it? Will any of these hinder its future growth? To acquire the best background, CT Studd's life and the things that influenced him ought to be examined. Subsequently it is important to look at those who succeeded him and the various issues that affected the society, shaped it and enabled it to develop and achieve its stated objectives. Supremely the concern will be to call attention to significant principles that need to be articulated, for the benefit of present and future members of WEC and a wider public.

Many new organisations do not reach beyond their tenth year or make the transition from a localised operation to being multi-sited over many regions and nations.[2] WEC had very uncertain beginnings and faced considerable opposition. The founder of the society was radical and unpredictable, and by the time of his death he had alienated the home constituency and was left with inexperienced representatives. The whole venture was seen by some as wild and irresponsible.

Effective organisation is a crucial achievement. To assess a Christian organisation is not the same as evaluating a commercial business, yet there are similar criteria that need to be borne in mind.[3] The opinions of those who are intimately connected with the organisation, as well as other competent observers, are valuable indicators. The quality of its services, the increase in its membership and the changes in its objectives over the years, can be seen as measures of its growth. Job satisfaction, motivation, morale, cohesion, consensus and share in decision-making can all give indications of the members' estimation and respect for the organisation. Has it maintained stability in times of pressure? What training is available for its members? These issues highlight whether the organisation has been successful in attaining its stated objectives and whether it has had the ability to reinvent itself or refine its goals as circumstances change.

When terms are used like 'progress', 'effectiveness' and 'growth', what is being conveyed? Is the company fulfilling its key strategic initiatives? Are its interim or key result areas being achieved, and are there ways of assessing these?

WEC's objectives are expressed in its *Principles and Practice*:

1  *To fulfil as quickly as possible the command of our Lord Jesus Christ in Matthew 28:18-20 and Acts 1:6-11 by a definite attempt to evangelise the remaining unevangelised peoples of the earth before His return. By 'evangelise' we mean to present Jesus Christ in the power of the Holy Spirit so that people may come to a living faith in Him as Lord and Saviour, be discipled and serve Him in the fellowship of His Church.*
2  *To plant local churches according to the pattern of the New Testament and establish them in the knowledge of the Word of God and spiritual power, and also to minister to existing churches when invited to do so.*
3  *To develop bases worldwide for the training and sending out of personnel, to further the work of evangelisation according to Acts 1:8 and the planting of churches.*

These are supplemented by a list of agreed 'Activities'.

'Effectiveness' describes WEC's ability to meet its own objectives.
'Progress' shows whether WEC remains on target with its expressed expectations and stated goals. In some ways the task in its essence remains almost impossible to measure, for CT Studd, the founder of WEC, had said, 'Write down WEC as a failure till every soul has heard of Jesus' and 'Our objective is the evangelisation of all

the unevangelised regions of the world'.[4]

'Growth' in broad terms refers to increase, in line with WEC's objectives, in the number of bases, workers and fields where WEC is working, of the unevangelised people groups which are being evangelised, and the development of the church in the places where WEC workers have served.

This chronological history sets out the background and follows the stories of all the international leaders of the mission and of key events that have shaped the society to the present day. Analytical consideration on the central questions and a separate chapter collate the findings of the story. Some practical suggestions for future action are made. The literature of the association, archival material, wider references, correspondence and interviews with leaders and members of the organisation and other groups which know WEC, are all utilised to give the broadest view of its development.

In summary, our aim is to present a coherent history of WEC for those unfamiliar with it, and to try to find answers to the questions that follow.

1  What are the factors that have contributed to the survival and development of WEC International, including values, personalities, decisions, pivotal events, catalytic ministries and structures?
2  What are the developments that could hinder its progress?
3  Are there significant principles that are worth articulating for the future guidance of sincere global-minded Christians?

Additionally, in view of its centenary in 2013, these topics are important to enable WEC to reflect on the past and plan sensitively and strategically for the future.

# CHAPTER ONE
## CT STUDD'S EARLY LIFE (1860-1907)

### Who was CT Studd?

*Some want to live within the sound of church and chapel bell.*
*I want to run a rescue shop within a yard of hell.*[5]

The founder of WEC International, Charles Thomas Studd, liked to write rhyming verse, and his poetic attempts are indicators of his values. The lines above, which came to be well-known in contemporary Christian circles, reflect his passion for practical Christianity and disdain for comfortable religion.

Tedworth Hall in Wiltshire, UK, the fine mansion and home of Edward Studd, was a strange place to birth 'a rescue shop', which would impact hell and extend the work of the Kingdom of God in all the inhabited continents. Mr Studd was a retired and wealthy Englishman who had owned two indigo plantations in India and possessed a fine string of racehorses. In 1860, one of his sons, Charles Thomas, was brought up at Tedworth Hall. Through God's providence, 'CT', as he became known, would become the founder of the Christian missionary organisation provisionally called by Studd 'Heart of Africa Mission' (HAM) and 'Christ's Etceteras' in 1912. Officially founded in 1913 the society's name was changed to 'Worldwide Evangelization Crusade' (WEC) in 1919 and eventually renamed 'WEC (Worldwide Evangelization for Christ) International' in 1982.

Studd enjoyed all the privileges of class and wealth. His future son-in-law, Norman Grubb, described how CT had an excellent upbringing, attended Eton private school and went on to Cambridge University. He was well known in the sporting world for his cricketing skills, playing for Cambridge and England with the legendary Dr W G Grace. As a key member of the English side which went to Australia and recovered the Ashes, CT was 'acknowledged as the most brilliant player of his day.'[6]

The young CT's whole way of life was deeply affected by a spiritual transformation his father experienced. Edward Studd was intent on pursuing a life of horse training and racing ,and had little time for anything to do with religion other than a dutiful acquaintance with Christianity. He was encouraged, very much against his will, to visit the Drury Lane Theatre in London in 1875 where the American evangelist, Dwight Lyman Moody, was speaking. Edward was so moved by the message that he decided to hear Moody again. On the next occasion he experienced a radical Christian conversion. This overturned Edward's life, causing him to abandon racing and, for the last two years of his life, deliberately target his wide circle of friends and family, with the intention of bringing them to a similar commitment.

His efforts paid off when, on the same day in 1878, a visiting speaker managed to corner three of Edward's sons separately about their relationship with Christ and each came to a personal experience of faith. As a result the brothers commenced a Bible study group at Cambridge University, led by the eldest, Kynaston. However CT continued to concentrate on cricket, with Christianity taking a back seat until, confronted by the severe illness of his brother George and the preaching of the evangelist Moody, he dedicated himself to God. The change was dramatic. His burden now was to share his faith with his friends at university and on the English cricket team. At the conclusion of the cricket year in 1884, he felt he must face his future. Was it to be the law or Christian service? After an experience of Christian consecration he made himself available for service for Christ. Impressed at the devotion of his Cambridge colleague, Stanley Smith, and after hearing a missionary from the China Inland Mission (CIM) describe the needs of China, Studd received a call to serve as a missionary in China. His application to CIM was accepted.

One of the most remarkable influences on CT Studd and the future WEC came from Hudson Taylor, the founder of the CIM.[7] As a young man of 21, Taylor sailed for China as the first missionary with the Chinese Evangelization Society in 1853. But things did not go well because it seemed that the English board of the mission tried to control the field activities without much understanding of the actual situation or the needs of the workers. After great heart-searching, Taylor felt God wanted him to start a new organisation with a vision to reach the inland areas of China. The goals of CIM were clear and spelled out in the missiological distinctives of the mission.[8]

The principles were different from accepted practice. People in China who had not heard about Christ were to have priority in the way that mission was to be conducted. Taylor was not content to live in the famous 'Treaty Ports' with their secure environment and protection by foreign military presence, but was keen to move inland. Faith in God to provide the needs of each worker was to be the missionaries' way of life, with no appeal for funds and a corporate sharing of what moneys were received. Taylor's slogan was 'God's work, done in God's way, will never lack God's supplies.' All of the Christian workers were to identify with the local people by dressing in Chinese clothes. Policy was to be determined by those on the field, without interference from the councils that had been set up in their home countries. Volunteers from all walks of life were welcome, not solely those with much education or ordination. Single and married women were to serve as full team members and as the equals of men. Taylor was known for a rapid encouragement of an authentic inter-denominationalism in the mission.[9] The churches were to be self-supporting, self-governing and self-propagating. These principles, originally formulated by Rufus Anderson and Henry Venn, were radical for the time and carried influence far and wide in the years to come.[10] They formed a serious background to what Studd eventually would import into WEC.

Amazingly, among those volunteering for service with CIM were seven young men, including Studd, from wealthy homes who had connections with Cambridge University. Some were well-known in the sporting world. The challenge of the lives of The Cambridge Seven, as they were called, and their public meetings throughout Britain had a profound impact on hundreds of students and the general public. Their farewell service in Exeter Hall, London on 4 February 1885, attracting a distinguished and packed audience, left a great impression on many and was spoken of as a meeting unique in

England.[11] CIM and other missionary societies were deluged with applications.

## The context

Studd sailed for China on the day the British General Gordon was killed by followers of the Mahdi in Khartoum. Although certainly a time of transition, the world in which he was brought up was rather different from ours. Victoria was Queen of England; Britain still 'ruled the waves', and colonialism was in its heyday; China was going through major upheaval; India was still under the domination of the British Raj; the Crimean War was recent history; European countries were arguing among themselves and redrawing the map of Europe and the colonial world; the influence of the Ottoman Empire was fading; the United States of America was still recovering from the deep trauma of the Civil War; female suffrage was but a daydream; electric lights, motion pictures, photography, powered air flight and steam-powered ships were in their infancy.

In the second half of the 19th century, Christianity was experiencing a period of great controversy. Biblical studies were exercising the minds of many in Germany. Their viewpoints were to have a profound critical influence and, in the end, moved many Christians away from acceptance of the supernatural and historical orthodox theology. The church in England was not exempt: the place of the Bible was under question, Darwinian viewpoints were being hotly debated, and the Oxford Movement had recently exercised influence on and caused division in Anglican Church life. There were increasing numbers of independent and Baptist congregations, burials in churchyards could be conducted by non-conformist ministers, and Oxford and Cambridge universities were freed from Church of England control.

Revivals of religion and organised evangelistic campaigns affected thousands of people. Independent evangelical organisations were developing under the influence of the American evangelist, DL Moody. Charles Haddon Spurgeon, Baptist by conviction and a convinced Calvinist, was attracting vast audiences to hear his forthright preaching. In Britain and America new denominations appeared and the total membership increased significantly. This was coupled with a period of decline in other major religions.

Advances and growth were not confined to the heartlands of Protestant Christianity. Pioneering individuals and new societies were taking the Christian message to people who had no knowledge of Christ and his gospel: 'The Great Age of Missions' or 'The Great Century' were in full swing. Worrall has stated that the history of the 19th century missionary movement represented one of the wonders of Christianity.[12] William Carey (1761-1834) had alerted the Protestant Church, especially the English-speaking part, to the challenge of the world outside western civilisation. In 1792 he produced a small book called *An Enquiry into the Obligation of Christians to use Means for the Conversion of the Heathen*, which was pivotal in its aim to prove, by research, the extent of the unfinished task facing the church. The major denominations started taking an interest in the missionary task in India, China, South East Asia, the South Pacific, West Indies, round the coasts of China and in Africa. Furthermore in the late 19th and early 20th centuries, inter-denominational and non-denominational societies made their appearance and targeted the inland areas of the major landmasses, notably Africa, South America and China.

## Studd in China

What was the young CT Studd like? In the book, *The Cambridge Seven*, Pollock recorded that, in the meetings addressed by Studd before he left, CT came across as a gentle character with burning words, although not classed as eloquent. He was a man of eager intensity and quick reactions, intolerant of any delay in obeying God. His mother spoke of him as 'erratic and needing to be with older and more consistent Christians.'[13] He was uncomfortable with the thought that he had the trappings of wealth, while there were many poor in England and millions overseas who were struggling to survive. Cecil Polhill-Turner, one of his companions, described him as given to a rigid austerity in the early days in China and that he would choose rather to sit on a bench seat than one with a back.[14] Many of these characteristics would be evident throughout his life.

China was an adventure and a challenge. The country was going through political upheavals; there was conflict within the royal household, and intrigue among the foreign powers eager to gain the ascendancy in China. CIM had grown to one hundred and fifty when the new and famous members arrived. The Cambridge Seven were well-known and their reputation preceded them. Meetings among the foreign community in the coastal cities were impressive, but the young missionaries soon moved inland to learn the culture and language, and to open up new areas for evangelism. For each of them their lives were to be devoted to unceasing and influential service.[15] After initially trying to wait on God for the gift of languages, Studd realised that the secret for him was hard labour and disciplined effort.[16] In fact, this gave him the opportunity and time to understand the culture and the Chinese people.

When CT received word in 1886 that he had inherited a considerable fortune from his father's estate, he determined to give it away. With joyful heart he sent gifts to a number of Christian organisations including the Salvation Army, Dr Barnardo's orphanages, George Muller's orphanages and DL Moody.[17] It was a period of significant evangelical activity. Lord Shaftesbury (1801-1885) was a leading social reformer with a considerable influence throughout mid-19th century England. William and Catherine Booth had commenced in 1865 what was to become the Salvation Army when the Methodist New Connexion Churches, with which Booth was serving, had limited their evangelistic ministry. Within a short time the radically aggressive, evangelistic and social work of the Salvation Army had thousands of full-time officers and centres of operation around the world and plans for a far-reaching social experiment. George Muller, of German descent, had contributed to the development of the Open Brethren churches. He also started a series of orphanages in Bristol which, during his lifetime, housed over 10,000 children, and ran on the basis of no appeals for finance, but were supported through answers to prayer alone. For this incredible venture, part of a much wider philanthropic and missionary ministry, it is estimated that the sum total of money he received in answer to prayer was nearly one and a half million pounds.[18]

CT Studd retained a substantial amount of his father's inheritance for his future wife as a wedding present, but when she challenged him to give all to God, he gave the balance to the Salvation Army. His wife Priscilla had an Irish Anglican background and had been greatly moved by and involved in the work of the Salvation Army. She arrived in China in 1887 to work with CIM. Through a remarkable concurrence they worked together for a period in Shanghai and found their vision, passion and temperaments very much in harmony. An enthusiastic correspondence followed, which resulted in engagement and eventual marriage. They had five children in China; four were girls and one, a boy, died at birth.

The city of Lungan (now Changzhi) in Shanxi province was their centre of service for several years. The Studds found it hard to make spiritual headway with the significant Muslim population. CT and Priscilla were radical in the way they handled the different culture and made evangelistic forays into the town. Hudson Taylor was alarmed when they tried Salvation Army methods, and felt they needed the wisdom of CIM leadership to keep them on track rather than causing unnecessary opposition to the gospel.[19] Results came through the development of a drug rehabilitation centre to reach opium addicts, and through preaching and visiting the surrounding area. Initially the Studds remained as CIM associates, but eventually became autonomous workers. They were pioneers and appreciated the opportunity to work independently. However CT's increasing asthma attacks and Priscilla's regular bouts of ill health caused them to return to England after 10 years in China. Hudson Taylor met up with them at the time of their departure and found them in 'beautiful spirit.' Studd presented CIM with the considerable property he had obtained for the work.[20] They fully intended to return to China, but this never happened.

In the early period of his life, Studd's remarkable influence was seen in the call of a great number to Christian service, among them key leaders like Dr Wilfred Grenfell, pioneer to Labrador, Bishop Mowll of China and Sydney, and Bishop Brown of Jerusalem.[21] Others, like the famous Baptist preacher FB Meyer, were stirred to a new commitment in their Christian walk.[22] Many students were emboldened to think about Christian service, through the burning words and obvious example of the wealthy young sportsman and his colleagues who had renounced all to follow Christ.

## Return to England and open doors in America and India

On their return from China, CT along with Priscilla and their daughters were able to live with CT's mother. They needed time to recuperate, for both had been sick and CT had nearly died a year before. He recovered, but Priscilla was diagnosed as having an incurable heart disease. Before long CT was keen to do something, and commenced an itinerant ministry around Britain, to share what God had done in China and to challenge people with what he felt God wanted to do in the lives of Christians.

Following the departure of the Cambridge Seven, CT's brother Kynaston had responded to an invitation from the American evangelist DL Moody to share the missionary burden across America. Consequently he was a part of the leadership team at a conference in 1886 organised by Moody at Mount Hermon, Massachusetts, which resulted in the founding of the Student Volunteer Movement (SVM) in 1888. With its slogan 'The evangelization of the world in this generation' under the leadership of John R Mott, SVM had an incalculable effect on the whole missionary cause. At a time when interdenominational mission societies were being founded and growing, it contributed thousands of educated young people into a movement that already contained many unordained tradesmen. It is stated that the SVM resulted in 25,000 students going into Christian service overseas by 1945.[23] As an outcome, the birth of the future WEC organisation was to take place in a western Christian atmosphere which stimulated a youthful passion for world evangelism.

At this juncture in his career, CT was able to take up the challenge of moving around the United States for eighteen months, with a passionate message for his mainly student audience to know God's forgiveness for past sins, to ask for and receive the Holy Spirit, and to be fully surrendered to the divine will. It was a busy period of great opportunities to speak and counsel. He spoke to many people and numbers were affected by his ministry. On the other hand it was difficult for Priscilla, who found relationships at home stressful and wished to join her husband, although she was often very ill. CT himself was prone to asthmatic attacks, and the strenuous schedule contributed to a lack of good eating and adequate rest. Later, both of them made a short visit to America, where Priscilla's ministry was greatly appreciated. Studd was impressed at his wife's preaching. 'She was an extraordinary personality. Wherever she went everybody seemed to confide in her.'[24]

For years CT had been burdened for India and with the need to redress the impression his father had conveyed, as a businessman who was only eager to make money. Studd believed that someone from the family should go and share Christ with the people who had known Edward in his unconverted days. The opportunity came when he was invited by a family friend to take a tour of meetings. Not only were many people converted, but CT was invited to become the pastor of the Union Church at Ootacamund, South India. The family moved there in 1900. This was a profitable time for them all, remembered with joy by Priscilla and the four girls who enjoyed the freedom and experienced spiritual growth. Although CT struggled with ill health, his ministry had an effect on a wide circle. Eventually he had to return home to England in 1906 or he would have died in the moisture-laden cold winter climate of the hills.

Once they were back in England, the question was, 'what would CT do to keep his passion flowing and make his life continue to count for God?'

India                    – 1906

# CHAPTER TWO
## CT STUDD AND THE FOUNDING OF WEC (1908–1931)

CT Studd founded WEC in the Belgian Congo in 1913 when he was fifty-three. Within a comparatively short time the fledgling mission grew in numbers and influence and the young church exploded into life.

Studd was a radical character and strong on the teaching of holiness. Even though he was an Anglican by background, his theology was unashamedly biased towards the Arminian and Methodist view, with an emphasis on their doctrine of sanctification. His emphasis was 'If you have the Holy Spirit in you, you live a holy life.'[25] He believed any church should show, by its fruit, that the gospel of grace was real and lives had been totally transformed. He could not tolerate the doctrine of 'once saved always saved.' The scandal of seeing members in the young Congo church abandoning their original commitment to God so deeply disturbed him that he took the unprecedented step of banning the celebration of baptism and the Lord's Supper until people learned that practical holiness was more important than ceremonies. In fact the sacraments were not restored to the life of the churches for ten years until 1937 when Studd was dead and Jack Harrison was the field leader. He expressed the essence of what he was aiming for by saying, 'I want to see Jesus running about in thousands of black bodies and purified hearts.'[26] Grubb described the situation that faced the founder of the young mission.

> It was not an emotional issue to Studd but a biblical one. A practical holiness of life as contained in the Commandments, not merely an imputed holiness through the righteousness of Christ, is as binding under grace as under law... As a matter of fact grace demands a far higher standard of living than law (see Matthew 5:17-48). Hence the Scriptures combat the statement so widely

*taught today, that a man can be living in sin and still claim to be a child of God ... God has not altered His commands and standards one jot from the days of Sinai, but now He makes absolutely perfect provision through Christ and the Spirit for living an absolutely holy life.*[27]

Studd strongly conveyed his feelings to the missionaries and insisted that the life of holiness should be a reality for them too. At one stage in 1925 when funds were low, discouragements abounded, people had left the field and there were constant misunderstandings with the home committee, CT called his immediate team of eight missionary co-workers together for a time of seeking God. As they searched the Bible for guidance, they studied Hebrews 11 collectively and discussed ways that could best describe the kind of heroism that was needed. One of the team said that the way soldiers gambled with their lives in World War I was a powerful illustration; they 'couldn't care a damn for their lives' as they fought for king and country. The combined reaction of the group of missionaries was that those who wanted to live for Jesus should be those who 'Don't Care a Damn' (DCD) if they lost their lives in the process. The transformation was immediate. When they left the room that night, there was a fire in their souls and a holy resolve to practice the teachings of Jesus and take the message of the transforming power of the gospel of Christ to people everywhere whatever the cost. So the DCD vow was birthed.[28] A dramatic change in their lives was apparent to the churches, colleagues and visitors.

Needless to say this was scandalous to the well-educated and cultured Christian people in the home constituencies, who heard tales of the vow and its scurrilous name. In an attempt to balance the picture, Studd personally produced a booklet called *The DCD*, replete with pictures of chivalrous knights and skull and cross-bones drawings, in which he told the story of its adoption and meaning. In forceful language he explained that God was looking for people who would be totally abandoned to God and, if willing to be DCDs for him, they would made a strong impression on the world and glorify Jesus. He exclaimed 'Oh, let us not rust out – let us not glide through the world and slip quietly out, without having blown the trumpet loud and long for our blessed Redeemer.'[29] The impression on the friends of WEC and many Christians generally was shock, horror and a feeling that, by using this kind of language, Studd had gone too far this time. But the way the Congo church and foreign team alike responded was, to Studd, evidence that he was on the right track. In many ways this was a turning point in the history of WEC and stamped the society with a uniqueness and determination to be utterly devoted to Christ in spite of what others may think. Writing about that event, Helen Roseveare has commented, 'From that time on, throughout the mission, there was a new love, unity and joy in sacrifice and zeal for souls. No one murmured if funds were short; no one wanted to go on furlough.'[30]

This was not different from the experience of many similar organisations. As Karl Fiedler says, 'In almost every case, following the start of a faith mission, a severe crisis followed, in which the climate, insufficient equipment, lack of experience and personal peculiarities played a role.'[31] But to really understand the background, we need to look back to the beginnings of WEC.

## 'Cannibals want missionaries!'

The launch of the society was to spring from a remarkable encounter. While walking down a street in Liverpool in 1908, the 48-year-old Studd saw a sign advertising an address by the German explorer and concerned Christian, Dr Karl Kumm, the founder of the Sudan United Mission and husband of Lucy, daughter of Dr Henry Grattan Guinness.[32] The startling announcement 'Cannibals want missionaries!' appealed to Studd's sense of humour and love of adventure. He had returned from missionary service in China and India due to ill-health. Kumm had just completed a major journey of exploration across Africa and was deeply impressed that there were many tribes which had never heard the gospel of Christ. Explorers, traders and scientists had gone there but there were no missionaries. Kumm's talk struck Studd like a thunderbolt and instead of contemplating a return to India, he felt God challenging him to become involved in Africa and its needs.

Kumm invited Studd to join him in a further journey of

exploration from Forcados in Southern Nigeria to Khartoum in
Sudan. CT set up a committee to support him which agreed on
condition he received medical approval, but at the last minute his
doctor refused to give permission. Interestingly Kumm's journey in
1908-1909 took him just south of an area in Chad where WEC
workers would work in the future.[33] On his return in 1910, Kumm's
experiences were front page news in the British press. His burden
was to build a chain of mission centres across Africa to stem the
advance of Islam. This vision would be shared with many people and
on 9 June would involve three other famous missionary-minded men
on the platform of the Sudan United Mission Annual Meeting, Lord
Radstock, Samuel Zwemer and CT Studd.[34] The next day Kumm
went to Edinburgh to share in the opening addresses at the famous
1910 World Missionary Conference. This conference had been called
by John Mott of the Student Volunteer Movement and its descendent
the World Student Christian Fellowship. Stephen Neill wrote that it
was an impressive gathering, the like of which had never been seen
before in Christian history.[35] Cleverdon said that even the
newspapers asserted that whatever of that conference passed into
oblivion, the speech by Kumm would never be forgotten.[36] Studd
received a copy of the report[37] and was deeply moved by the
passionate appeals from many presenting the needs of the world.
Mott showed the amazing way new means of communication were
transforming Africa with greater opportunities now available for
missionary work.[38]

Following the 1910 conference, CT tirelessly presented the needs
of Africa throughout the UK and another committee agreed to back
him again on the condition that he had medical approval. When this
was not forthcoming, he undertook to go without it, believing God
would provide and take care of him, even if his wife and friends did
not approve. The necessary money came from various sources and
on 15 December 1910 CT sailed for Port Said to make an exploratory
trip to Khartoum in Sudan. He was greatly stirred when, in the
loneliness of his cabin, he felt God said to him 'This trip is not merely
for the Sudan, it is for the *whole unevangelized world*.'[39]

Studd's health was a source of concern for much of his Christian
service and especially during the latter period of life. He suffered

from asthma and an incessant sense of weakness. In addition he was concerned during this exploratory trip for his wife, writing to her again and again to assure her of his love and prayers, and challenging her to fulfil some role for God in this new venture. Eventually he came to the belief that God could heal her, and use her and the girls as a powerful example of God at work. He was convinced that the genuine cautions he received from doctors and his friends were ultimately stopping him from accomplishing what God was calling him to: a new 'crusade' for Christ.

Joining with Bishop Gwynne of Khartoum and Archdeacon Shaw of the Church Missionary Society (CMS), CT made an exploration to the south of Sudan, and realised that the task there could be left to CMS. But, having heard of thousands across the border in the Belgian Congo who 'depraved and destitute' had never heard about the gospel from a Protestant missionary, he sensed that this was where God was calling him to go. Delayed by ill health, he returned to Britain in the middle of 1911 to report on his findings and recruit reinforcements for the immense task facing him.

CT's little booklet *The Heart of Africa: The launch of an assault on the devil's den* encapsulates his thinking at this stage. He was still influenced by Kumm's passion to see Christian missionaries enter countries and areas that were at risk of being influenced by and converting to Islam. He was convinced that a dedicated and even simplistic plan was better than none. In this document he revealed his desire to go and work in the north-eastern Belgian Congo with the African Inland Mission (AIM), another new interdenominational society, and pleaded for more recruits to join the four already intending to go. Initially he was to go as the field director for AIM's new field in the Congo.[40]

In a very satisfying way, during this time in England, God provided a house for his wife and family through the kindness of a relative and his mother. Highland Road eventually became the base for the organisation he was to found in 1913. CT travelled throughout the UK 'preaching, informing, cajoling and challenging in his own inimitable way.'[41] This time he did not have the same quantity of responses he had received with the Cambridge Seven. Many young people would listen to him, but not many were willing to go. A young Cambridge graduate, Alfred B Buxton, who had intended to go on to study medicine, felt deeply challenged that God wanted him to join the veteran Christian.

## Off to the Congo

Up till the last day Studd had a very unhappy wife who, along with his children, family members and many of his friends in the Christian community, was critical of the step he was taking. But with his small group, he left on 13 January 1913, absolutely confident this venture was of God. What a time to launch out! Only months later World War I would start. When it broke out, Studd only saw another obstacle to be overcome by faith and said, 'The War is just one more trial of faith, but we laugh at the idea of it hindering us ... Always advance. No retrenchment.'[42] The Congo had just been taken over as a Belgian colony after the awful excesses and cruelty of the reign of King Leopold II of Belgium, who had controlled it as his personal fiefdom. It is claimed that upwards of ten million had died to satisfy Leopold's insatiable desire for personal wealth and power. Only brave people, pioneers in human rights, would fight to see justice prevail.[43] Some of the scars were still visible as the new workers undertook their task.[44] Cruelty and instability were the norm in the Congo. The country still knew the horrors of cannibalism, and life was certainly not secure for its own inhabitants or for those foreigners brave or foolish enough to enter.[45]

## The start of a new society

Because of Studd's approach, his relationship with AIM did not last long.[46] The three recruits for AIM moved on to join members of AIM who were already established in other areas. Soon CT and Buxton arrived at a market town in the Belgian Congo called Kilo where, unavoidably delayed and stricken by sickness, he declared the start of a new association, entitled 'Christ's Etceteras' and 'Heart of Africa Mission' (HAM) and wrote a booklet enshrining his views of what the organisation should be like, setting up an outline of the principles which eventually became the basis for WEC.[47]

CT's philosophy was to aim for the evangelisation of the remaining unevangelised areas of the world in the shortest possible time. Though cooperating with other organizations, he intended to target the places where nobody else was working and recruit people who would be willing to live sacrificially, entirely dependent on God for their support, committed to no appeals for finance, and with a simple faith in the orthodox doctrines of the Christian faith.

Writing about starting a new society, Studd said 'I have no ambition to start another water-logged craft in the huge stream of Central Africa, but to evangelize the world and have Christ back.'[48] His ideas were simple in the extreme.

> *God is the head of WEC, the government is on His shoulders and we have given Him our word to walk in His paths. Before I left England God made me declare on many platforms that we went trusting neither in man, nor in committee, except in that of the Eternal Three.*[49]

He enshrined the theological basis in a simple set of beliefs which he called The Five Smooth Stones, after the equipment David took with him to fight the giant Goliath (1 Sam 17:40).

1  Absolute faith in the deity of each member of the Trinity.
2  Absolute belief in the full inspiration of the Old and New Testament Scriptures.
3  Vow to know and preach none other than Jesus Christ and Him crucified.
4  Obedience to Christ's command to love all who love the Lord Jesus sincerely, without respect of persons, and to love all men.
5  Absolute faith in the will, power and providence of God to meet our every need in His service.

These, with slight editorial modifications in point four, have remained a basic feature of the various editions of WEC's constitutional *Principles and Practice*, but are now supplemented by a more formal statement of theological beliefs similar to those adopted by the World Evangelical Fellowship. Studd was very much committed to an evangelical view of biblical authority and inspiration and bluntly stated,

1   *We have vowed to run this mission according to the Bible and not according to human reason or tradition.*
2   *Whatever the Scriptures say we will do.*
3   *Whatever the Scriptures forbid we shall forbid.*
4   *Whatever the Scriptures do not forbid we shall not forbid.*
5   *We will at once alter any method that can be shown contrary to the Bible.*
6   *We allow no other authority than the Bible and never will do so.*[50]

## The work commenced

*Google map ~ 400 mi apart*

Studd and Buxton pushed on to Niangara and then Nala in the north-east Congo, where they were given concessions by the local chiefs with Belgian government official,s and set up operations. They subsequently explored to the west and south to the towns of Bambili, Poko, Deti and Wamba. Studd returned to England in 1914 when news came that a group of seven was on its way.[51] For Buxton and the new workers 1915 and 1916 were years of fruit and expansion. New converts at Niangara and Nala were baptised, scriptures translated, a hymn book compiled, schools commenced, industrial programmes initiated, church buildings erected, new centres opened, local believers involved in leadership and the main base moved to Nala.

During 1915 and half of 1916 Studd remained in Britain. This was to be his last visit home and he concentrated on recruitment and assisting in the development of the new society. In his absence his wife Priscilla, in spite of extreme weakness, had chosen to identify fully with him by setting up the main sending base in their home, putting together publicity, processing applications and becoming the face of HAM in England. CT spoke passionately to a wartime Britain pleading for recruits for God's war. He thundered, 'The "Let's-save-Britain-first-brigade" is in the succession of the "I-pray-have-me-excused" apostles ... Christ wants not nibblers of the possible but grabbers of the impossible.'[52]

With a party of eight new workers, Studd sailed for the Congo in July 1916. Priscilla always found it difficult to let him go. His letters to her during their times of separation were full of expressions of love for her, and yet overflowing with the burden for evangelisation and his visions for the future. Many have criticised Studd for going to the Congo when his wife was unwell. However his former leader in China, Hudson Taylor, similarly experienced painful separations from his wife and children for long periods of time, but said in an article to CIM friends that costly sacrifice was God's chosen way.[53] Studd, naturally ascetic, embraced this culture and Taylor's example formed part of the background to his willingness to be separated from his wife while in the Congo. When challenged by a young man as he left for the Congo in 1913 without his wife and children, CT uttered the famous and oft-quoted words which became the motto of the mission and the most memorable words he ever uttered, 'If Jesus Christ be God and died for me, then no sacrifice can be too great for me to make for Him.'[54] This was not the statement of a wild extremist but of an individual earnestly committed to the kind of life-style which Jesus had exemplified — compassion for the needy, love to all people irrespective of their background, and a willingness to share the gospel of God's grace with the marginalised of this world. Towards his wife he was in no way unfeeling, for his letters display a passion and tenderness that an unfeeling man would never have expressed. He and Priscilla were passionately committed to each other, but their joint devotion to Christ overrode everything.

The journey to the Congo was preceded by the public launch of HAM on 14 July 1916 in Westminster Chapel in London. The new group of workers included CT's daughter Edith on her way to marry Alfred Buxton.[55] Crowds welcomed them at Nala, and Studd was impressed at the growth of the work in his absence. By the end of the year there were 22 workers in fourteen centres with women taking crucial front-line roles. This advance continued unceasingly each year and many places were touched by the gospel, clinics were opened, schools for adults were being held, vocational training centres and courses were underway, girls were receiving education, and, above all, people were continuing to trust in God and being baptised.

With the necessity for some workers to have a time of home leave,

1919 was a year of extra pressure. Several of those remaining on the field, including Studd himself, faced serious illness. But at the same time there were wonderful stories of God at work in healing local people. The work continued to develop with more baptisms and increased training of new believers. At the home base, a strong team worked with Mrs Studd to recruit and process new workers. The day after CT returned to the Congo, Priscilla testified to have been healed by God, and from then on she became the powerhouse of the new mission, travelling all over the world, speaking at innumerable meetings, and being the strong hand on the tiller at the sending base. They were very much a team in the work. Mrs Studd's hesitancy was gone, and she was committed to back all that was taking place on the field. The name Worldwide Evangelization Crusade (WEC) was adopted by Mrs Studd and her son-in-law Rev Gilbert Barclay, who had become chairperson of the home committee, with the active encouragement of Alfred and Edith Buxton during their period of home leave in 1919.

In the group which arrived in the Congo at the end of that year were Norman Grubb and his wife Pauline, another of CT's daughters. They were destined to play a crucial role in the days to come and to carry the torch of International Leadership after the death of the founder. Although there was no obvious intention to discriminate, among the members of the executive committee in 1924 were three of Studd's daughters and their husbands, the Buxtons, Barclays and Grubbs. No other members of the field were represented; it was still a family dominated organisation.[56]

Turmoil characterised 1920. Not only was there outright opposition from the local witch doctors, but also undercurrents among some members of the field who were unhappy with Studd's ways and his stand on holiness doctrines. CT also had an intense correspondence with representatives of the home committee who wanted him to come back for a rest. This was a pattern which continued until the end of Studd's life.

## Growth and growing pains

When Alfred Buxton returned to the Congo in 1921, CT left him responsible for Nala and determined to turn his attention to the Ituri forest area to the south. In 1918 James Lowder had already started work in Wamba with impressive results. Now CT started fruitful work at Ibambi and this became his base and eventually the centre of the Congo work. Within ten years of the start of the work in 1913 there were over fifty foreign workers, in twelve centres in four provinces, among six unreached tribal groups. Medical, industrial and educational work was underway, translations of Bible portions had been made, books and hymn books published, elders and evangelists appointed, and there were an estimated 9,000 converts, of whom 4,000 had been baptised. Mrs Studd, in an address at Westminster Central Hall in London in 1922, spelled out what God had done. Provision of workers and money had been amazing. The work had seen representation established in North America, Australia, New Zealand and South Africa as well as the UK, booklets had been published, magazines were in circulation and a good group of people had signed up as members of WEC's home constituency.

It was said in 1920, 'Few of the recruits were experienced people, and most knew very little of church history or its variety in doctrine.'[57] Studd had said previously, 'Why seek higher education when what we need is a bricklayer who will talk of Christ – he doesn't need theology.'[58] However CT and Alfred Buxton became unhappy at the inadequate practical training of many of the new recruits. Alfred felt something needed to be done, especially since there were many huts going cheap after World War I, and the need was for something akin to the disciplined side of army training coupled with a good grasp of biblical theology. He and Gilbert Barclay were unanimous in a determination to push ahead, and were delighted when Alfred's younger brother Captain Godfrey Buxton, who had been recently wounded in the war, became available to take the lead.

The result was the commencement of the Missionary Training Colony in 1921. The curriculum focused on inductive Bible study, practical work, missionary principles, prayer and evangelism, and preparing people as much as possible for the conditions they would meet on the mission field. The students, all male, lived in simple quarters and had plenty of opportunity to informally learn principles of fellowship and conflict resolution. Each summer they took to the open road, sleeping where they could and sharing the gospel throughout the UK, becoming a model for similar training programmes. By the outbreak of World War II over 200 graduates had moved into ministries with various missions around the world. Only after Studd had died did a steady stream of recruits start arriving from other Bible colleges.

## Wider than the Congo

The HAM/WEC magazines for those years were full of accounts of people turning to Christ, centres opening and new workers arriving to help with the work. But there seemed to be an underlying message that God was urging consideration of other parts of the world. In 1921 the magazines contained several references to South America, with articles entitled 'The Amazon as a Challenge' and 'But when will the party for South America set out?'[59] The result was that in June 1923 a group of three landed in Brazil to work in the Amazon region under the name 'Heart of Amazonia Mission.' In the same year the 'Heart of Arabia Mission' was started and in 1925 a team of four commenced the 'Heart of Asia Mission.' The vision was the same, the aim being to preach the gospel to the remaining unevangelised peoples in the shortest possible time. CT's vision was being replicated around the world.

The new ventures had their share of challenge and danger. One of the graduates from the Colony and new recruit to the Amazon, Fenton Hall, died within a year of his arrival. His published story, written by Norman Grubb, was a powerful testimony of how a young British military officer, deeply touched by Studd's writings, felt God calling him to missionary work in South America. A sportsman, well accepted in society and a dedicated Christian, he showed by his robust way of life that following Christ was his priority. He was a worthy example of the kind of person called for and illustrated by CT. The work in the Amazon continued in outreach to the tribes, although eventually it was to secede from WEC and become part of a new mission, which grew strongly with some of those who had been part of HAM.[60]

The Heart of Arabia Mission team continued to serve until 1927 or 1929, and most of the workers eventually moved into independent ministries that bore fruit in the Middle East. [61]

Jock Purves, one of the pioneers in Central Asia and later deputy leader in UK to Norman Grubb, was called to missionary work through students at the Missionary Training Colony, and then trained there himself before going to Lesser Tibet. The years from 1926-30 on the borders of Afghanistan were opportunities for Jock, along with Rex Bavington, to serve and witness even in the face of extremely difficult conditions. This was the commencement of the Heart of Asia Mission, which eventually merged with the members of the Central Asia Mission and became the forerunner of the WEC Asian fields.

## Radical views and writings

A review of his booklets and letters shows that CT was an enthusiastic believer and promoter of those values that were close to his heart. He could be sarcastic with any who, in his opinion, watered down what he felt were high Christian standards. *The Chocolate Soldier* was an enthusiastic booklet full of Biblical examples of heroism but contemptuous of those 'chocolate soldiers' who refused to get involved in or stay in the battle to share Christ's gospel to the world.

> *Go where you will through Scriptures or history, you find that men who really knew God, and didn't merely say they did, were invariably Paragons of Pluck; Dare-Devil Desperadoes for Jesus; Gamblers for God. 'Fools and Madmen' shout the world and the Chocolates. 'Yes, for Christ's sake,' add the Angels.*[62]

He wrote poems about the fifty million sermons preached annually in Britain, and he lambasted highly educated theologians who 'teach our youths to know more than God.' He was scornful of the half empty churches, with more being built, multiple conventions held, yet the attention of Christians was on the people in the well-satisfied front seats, not on the masses of unevangelised in the world who had no opportunity to hear about Christ. There were several things that were central to Studd's thinking and way of life.

## Sacrifice

According to Studd the WEC organisation had to run on lines akin to the Salvation Army or the great armies (especially British) of the past. Sacrifice needed to be at the heart of the discipline Christian soldiers were to embrace. Alfred Buxton, his colleague in that early journey to the Congo and an astute observer of him over several years, said, 'From him I learned that God's ideal of a saint is not a man primarily concerned with his own sanctification: God's saint is 50 per cent a soldier.'[63] The soldier analogy was particularly appropriate, for large portions of the world were convulsed in the throes of World War I. Repeatedly Studd came back in his poems and small booklets to references to that conflict, to those throughout history who fought in various battles on many continents, and to the heroism of the Crusaders, as illustrations of the kind of courage Christ's followers should emulate.[64] The use of the word 'Crusade' in the title of the fledgling mission was intentional. 'The name "Crusade" preserves that fighting, daring, self-dedicating attitude to the calling which was so essentially CT's, and comes out of those little booklets which he wrote soon after arriving in the heart of Africa.'[65] However as noted in the Introduction, the name was eventually changed in 1982 to 'WEC International' with the initials WEC standing for 'Worldwide Evangelisation for Christ' realising that the word 'Crusade' had serious historical overtones that did not reflect a truly Christian attitude of love to all people.

Studd was committed to a highly disciplined lifestyle; to many it was extreme. He took no days off, holidays or times for recreation. Food was to be the plainest and accommodation was to be similar to that in which the local people lived. One key feature was his plan to rise very early in the morning for Bible reading and prayer. He relished this opportunity. From his time in China to his later years in the Congo he kept up this practice. It appears his father also had survived with very little sleep. CT was often occupied with a great deal of administration and personal correspondence and so at weekends chose to visit villages, travelling overnight carried by porters through the forest. He then preached and taught at length during the day, moving to other villages and then back to the main centre for weekdays. His ruthless adherence to this tough pattern of living, and expectation that others would do the same, caused great difficulty within the missionary team and led to several resignations.

For CT sacrifice and faith went together. Those who lived sacrificially could trust that God would meet all their needs, just as Paul had taught in Philippians chapter 4:10-20. When a person was contented in God through plenty or little, God could be expected to look after any needs he or she had. This was far removed from the emphases which affected the 20th century church that 'Christians should have the best' and the so-called 'prosperity doctrine.' Studd was keen to stress that Jesus had called his disciples to carry their cross and that they should do this with joy, even hilarity.

*Oh, it's good to belong to Jesus, it's the only life to live, it's glorious fun, it's heaven begun, when you've no more to give.*[66]

## Faith

Grounded in the teachings of Hudson Taylor of the CIM and strongly encouraged by the writings and example of George Muller of Bristol, CT was convinced that WEC should avoid any dependence on people for financial provision. He felt God wanted WEC to be an organisation which sought God's guidance first of all, then trusted him to supply every need. No collections would be taken at meetings, no fund-raising activities and no appeals for finance would go on. This was not confined to money, but was to embrace faith for doors to be opened, new workers recruited, spiritual breakthroughs in lives and districts, development of the church and its leadership, growth in holiness among the believers, provision of property or anything else that was required to further God's activities through members of WEC. Studd was blunt in his expectation of what God would do and what his people should expect.

*If a man joins our mission, he comes out on God. God is his Father, to God he looks for supplies whether in money or kind. If God sends much, he is rather cast down thinking God is afraid to trust him to suffer in patience. If God sends little, he thanks God and takes courage that after all he may be in the apostolic succession. If he has nothing, then he shouts hallelujah, for he knows he has come to the very entrance of the heavenly Kingdom where there is neither eating or drinking, but righteousness peace and joy, and loving service for ever and ever.*[67]

Money that came into the mission would be divided among the workers and sent out without deduction of any administration costs. CT and his wife took no allowance from mission finances but trusted God for their own needs. In a remarkable way God supplied through WEC during CT's lifetime nearly five times the amount of the fortune he had inherited and given away in China.[68]

## People relationships

Life was not straightforward when CT Studd was around. For some, like Jim Grainger who arrived in 1927 as a 20-year-old but eventually was to become the fourth field leader for the Congo field, CT was a gentle, very loving and caring man.[69] Others found him tough, autocratic, living a life of sacrifice and expecting others also to do the same, committed to a position of trust in God for all financial and daily needs, intolerant of those who disagreed, given to unusual decisions, often hostile to the home committee and determined to maintain his holiness position. Notably in the years 1921 to 1931, 87 workers joined the mission but only 35 stayed.[70] Even Alfred Buxton and Norman Grubb felt frustrated by his difficult attitude, and CT's wife, separated by long distances, sometimes could not cope with his fiery letters. Stewart Dinnen, later to become International Director of WEC, said,

*Studd's white hot zeal and extreme sacrifice were a challenge and blessing to many of the new missionaries, but others could not identify with his methods or views and left the mission. The home*

*council, too, became disenchanted with his leadership style and reached the decision to remove him from office.*[71]

In addition there was the problem of his taking morphine to counter what were constant and serious health difficulties. Prescribed morphine by a Belgian Red Cross doctor, CT continued to take it after consultation with a long-term physician friend in England who approved of the treatment. Only on his deathbed did a doctor present diagnose him as having 'surgically unrelieved gallstones and their consequences.' Some felt he was addicted or unwise in the way he obtained further supplies from a medical specialist in Uganda, but to him it was the means whereby he could continue in the Congo serving his Lord in long working days of 18 hours.[72]

Quite a few early workers took the difficult decision to move out and left to start work elsewhere or to go home.[73] Alfred Buxton and his wife Edith, daughter of CT, had given a powerful example of loyalty and eager involvement in the missionary task, yet they had a determination to lovingly challenge Studd and become a bridge to the Home Committee. Eventually they came to a parting of the ways and went to serve in Ethiopia. On the other hand they were always deeply appreciative of his example, dedication to Jesus and discipline.[74] Through this most difficult time some predicted that the mission would not outlast Studd.

CT had a core team of co-workers in the Congo who stayed with him through times of stress and difficulty. Many of these like Esme Roupell, Lillian Dennis, Jack and Jesse Scholes, Hubert and Mrs English, Jim Grainger, Charlie and Lily Searle[75], Harold Williams[76] and Sam Staniford[77] went on to long years of service with WEC. Then there was Norman Grubb who was destined, together with his wife Pauline, to take on the leadership of the infant worldwide WEC and move it forward into the next major stage. They had not always approved of Studd's actions and at one stage felt resignation was the only way out, but God restrained them and called them to submit and follow through with the calling with which they had been entrusted. Most significantly Jack Harrison, Studd's shadow and successor as field leader in the Congo, played a powerful role in maintaining trust and stability among the missionary band and the

African church. His life story, *Successor to CT Studd* told by Grubb, showed the discipline and humility of this multi-gifted man from a humble background, who for nine years worked very closely with Studd through the last stressful period of the old man's journey. These workers were loyal and committed, and managed to work together with the fiery pioneer, yet none could say they were weak or lacked an independent streak. In later years, courage, boldness, conviction and perseverance were hallmarks of their lives.

Mrs Studd had one visit with her husband, only one year before her death. She had implored him to come home and on one occasion had planned to go to him in the Congo but he had refused on account of his perception of her health needs. Eventually she made a trip to Egypt and he sent an invitation for her to come and see him. Priscilla joined CT in the Congo and they were reunited after thirteen years. The visit was a great success: her ministry to the African Christians and the missionaries was full of power and vision. CT was a shadow of the man she knew – illness and the tropics had taken their toll. She wanted to stay, he felt she should go home or she would succumb to sickness too easily in the Congo. She wanted him to come home but he felt God wanted him to stay in the Congo. The parting was tender yet sad. Priscilla left her mark on WEC. She laid the foundation of its international mobilisation ministry through her organising skills and her passionate advocacy for the unevangelised.

Studd's death came in 1931. Years of struggle with ill-health culminated in serious bouts of malaria, asthma, angina, dysentery, gallstones, nausea and breathlessness. His close friend and former physician in Manchester, Dr AT Wilkinson, had been aware of his condition for 25 years and said, 'He was a museum of diseases when he left China, and was afterwards hardly ever free ... He was one of the finest Christians, and the most heroic and loveable man I ever met.'[78] Jack Harrison was with CT to the end and heard his last faint 'Hallelujah.' A crowd of 2,000 attended his funeral, full of praise at what God had done in the life of this courageous man. They were testimonies to the way God had worked to transform their lives and to make them part of living churches. The vision of Studd was being realised, the remaining unevangelised peoples were being evangelised, and the church of God was growing in the most unlikely soil.

## Studd's passion

The existence of WEC grew out of Studd's determination to achieve his missionary mandate. To him the heart of everything was a passionate resolve to see people, who were living in the most inaccessible parts of the world, come to faith in Christ and he would not rest until this was achieved. He would not be deflected from the directive he was sure God had entrusted to him. The facts obtained by him or other authorities concerning the state of the unevangelised were to be accepted and followed up enthusiastically. He said, 'If I am going to have a short life, all the more reason for me to live fast and do more.'[79]

The Bible and its message were given priority. His evangelical convictions were held simply and boldly. Neither his ill-health nor that of his wife turned him aside. The opinions of doctors were to be considered but were not in the final analysis to stop him if God had called him. Criticisms from religious leaders were to be dismissed, if they did not come from those who were willing to make similar steps of bold obedience to God's will. In the context of the days in which he lived, his contribution was extremely relevant. Studd was passionate in his commitment to God and this breathes through his writings – letters, poems, articles and booklets. A quotation of a few verses from his poem *The Men for the Job* illustrates it clearly.

> *Oh, for a thousand men to do*
> *My Saviour's last command,*
> *To take the Gospel of our God*
> *To every heathen land.*
>
> *Lord, send the blessed Holy Ghost*
> *To make us play the man,*
> *To fill us with a fiery zeal*
> *To execute Thy plan. ...*
>
> *Gamblers for God are what we need,*
> *Like David's worthies each,*
> *Who never dreamt of counting odds,*
> *But raced to storm the breach. ...*

*Lord, send us lion-hearted men*
*With good courageous habits,*
*Who ne'er will run from the devil's gun*
*Like hares and bunny rabbits ...*[80]

Studd's example had, and continues to have, a strong influence on WEC. Even though he was radical and would probably not be accepted into WEC today, due to health factors and his demanding personality, yet his clear-cut convictions have formed the basis for WEC's foundation and initiatives.

## Potential negative influences

Studd's reputation has been a continuing bone of contention among the Christian public in western countries. Harold Fuller, journalist and author with SIM International, has declared that 'while Studd's intrepid missionary work captured the imagination of the Christian public, to many it seemed wild and irresponsible at times.'[81] Ruth Tucker, missionary historian, was critical in her assessment of Studd, describing him as a gambler for God who failed.[82] Norman Grubb contended, 'But my difficulty was the sharp sword with which CT seemed to write rather than with the pen.' Studd had the unfortunate ability to couch necessary truth in troublesome language.[83] The years of separation from his wife have been scorned by many as unloving or worse.

Assessments like these have continued to colour public perception of the mission, and it has taken many years of patient relationship-building to show that those who came later or were his co-workers were not all tarred with the same brush and personality. But the stories of CT Studd stand as reminders that pioneers do have their significant weaknesses and require, if at all possible, sufficient accountability structures, humility and effective communication skills. New fields of operation need co-workers who are adequately prepared for the rigours of missionary life and the development of issues in the life of a growing church. Theological doctrines and cultural practices held by pioneers have to be taught in balance.[84]

Within WEC the memory of Studd has been held uncritically by a few who have almost beatified him. Distance in time has made some forget his capacity for extreme behaviour, which bred severe criticism among some of his associates and similarly would not be easily tolerated in significant sections of today's Christian world. However, if his unusual conduct is acknowledged and countered, then his continuing contribution of passion and vision can be drawn upon to give impetus and value in the future.

## Studd's legacy

CT, and Grubb after him, were capable exponents of the principles Studd prized. He wrote down what he wanted to say and as a result has left a clear record of his values and the reasons for them. His championing of sacrifice, faith and holiness in their essential elements continues to contribute towards the vitality of WEC. Members of WEC today greatly respect the way Studd treated his wife and women as equals, and that people on the field were to make their own policy decisions without tolerating interference by those at the sending base.[85] What really stands out is that Studd was not an armchair strategist but a general who led the charge from the front. He believed absolutely that, unless there was a definite attempt to evangelise the remaining unevangelised world, the task could not be done. Imperfections he had in profusion, but he was honest and fully committed to what he believed were the divine orders laid upon every Christian. His real legacy is WEC's key objective, which is to concentrate on the evangelisation of the remaining unevangelised peoples of the world in the shortest possible time. As he said,

> *I blush for shame at the thought of all this work commanded to be done, and think of the thousands of young men at home who say they love Christ, yet like Saul's army run and hide when Goliath appears. If we don't do this work we are disobedient to God ... We have Christ's command and we shall have His blessing and His support also. NOW THEN LET US DO IT.*[86]

# CHAPTER THREE
## NORMAN GRUBB AND THE SHAPING OF WEC (1931–65)

### What would WEC do without Studd?

The over-arching purpose behind the creation of WEC was to evangelise the remaining unevangelised peoples on earth in the shortest possible time. This was in keeping with the missionary burden of the church down the centuries, and a fulfilment of the statements in Matthew 24:14 and 28:18-20, Mark 16:15-16, Luke 24:45-49, John 10:16 and 20:21-23, and Acts 1:8. The spirit of missionary enterprise runs through Acts and the Epistles. The magnificent scenes in Revelation 5:1-14 and 7:9-17 reveal a vast assembly of representatives of all ethnic groups and nations, in the ultimate future praising the glorified Christ. Stephen Neill has declared that the church of the first Christian generation was a genuinely missionary church.[87] Paul's ever-onward missionary passion, exemplified in Romans 15:15-21, was caught by the small team in the early days of WEC.

'Will WEC slowly fade away without CT Studd?' was the crucial question being asked about the mission in 1931. Looking at the catalogue of public relations disasters that had dogged the last few years of Studd's leadership, an affirmative reply seemed inevitable. For all of Studd's and early WEC's imperfections, God's promise to take the foolish things of the world to confound the wise (1 Corinthians 1:18-31) seemed to be the only formula for the mission. Studd had declared, 'All God wants is a heart, any turnip will do for a head!'[88] The prestigious supporters and wise leaders attached to home committees of the mission had distanced themselves from Studd and the DCD controversy. Nonetheless a deep missionary motivation burned in the hearts of the remnant of WEC members and galvanised them to greater efforts. At this juncture it fell on to the shoulders of Norman and Pauline Grubb, CT Studd's son-in-law and daughter, to take up the reins of International Leadership in the struggling organisation and to give a positive direction. Studd had sent them home to the UK to take on sending base responsibility when things turned sour with the Home Committee. To understand this next period in the history of WEC it is important to look at their lives alongside the many events, personalities and developments that took centre stage during these years.

## Norman Grubb

Born in 1895 of Irish background, Norman Grubb had caring parents, his father being a Church of England minister and his mother from aristocratic stock. In addition, his uncle, the Rev George C Grubb, exercised a profound evangelistic ministry around the world and had a beneficial and spiritual influence on Norman.[89] His parents gave their four children an excellent upbringing with the best of education at school and university. When he was eighteen he came to a personal faith in Christ which was to revolutionise his whole perspective on life. His new faith was soon tested by the start of World War I, and Grubb's involvement in the British Army for almost five years. Four times he escaped death and lived to tell the tale.[90]

Those were years of spiritual development and of learning how to share his faith with men who faced death on a regular basis. After being wounded in France, he was sent back to England to recover. While in hospital he was visited by an Anglican chaplain, who happened to be CT Studd's son-in-law and eventual chairperson of the WEC Home Committee, Gilbert Barclay. Norman was given by Barclay a copy of the HAM magazine, which so spoke to him that he felt God's call to the Congo and subsequently wrote to Mrs Studd telling her of it. Invited by Priscilla to pay her a visit, Grubb not only heard about WEC but met her youngest daughter Pauline, his future wife. Following his discharge from the army, he attended an abbreviated course at Cambridge University, married Pauline and, by the end of 1920, they were on their way to the Congo.

The Congo was a joy and a challenge. Norman and Pauline were delighted to be where God had called them and to see the Lord at work in the lives of many Africans. But coping with CT's personality, theological views and leadership style was another matter. As God revealed himself to Norman and his wife, they came to realise that only through a real appreciation of the life of the indwelling Christ could they cope with Studd, their own weaknesses and the many challenges they were to face throughout lives of Christian service. In 1928 CT asked Norman to return to the UK and be prepared to take on the leadership of WEC. Grubb wrestled over this until he accepted that simple obedience to God and CT gave him no option but to go home.

This was the midpoint of an era when missions were going through a major metamorphosis. The First and Second World Wars dislocated, disrupted and changed the world. West Africans fought in Europe, Indian troops fought in North Africa and Europeans, Americans and Australians gained an awareness of many different parts of the world. RV Pierard mentions that, as a result of the conflicts, German missions declined significantly, while traditional missions became embroiled in the politics of war. This led eventually to the founding of the World Council of Churches. According to Pierard, the centre of gravity shifted to the conservative, pietistic, evangelical groups who followed a more individualistic approach to missions.[91] During the colonial era mainly European denominational missions had grown strongly, as René Padilla has asserted many times, by bravely opposing their own governments in matters related to colonial policies.[92] (There is evidence that the colonial authorities inhibited missionary expansion.)[93]

With the demise of colonialism between and after the wars, a new period of development and dramatic growth of the American missionary movement took place. Eventually, 44 per cent of missionaries in North America came from conservative evangelical agencies.[94] K Fiedler has highlighted the way religious depression after World War I was countered by the religious revival which followed World War II. Eventually this led to a decline in ecumenical missions while evangelical missions significantly expanded.[95] Enormous changes took place in the world political scene and in due course resulted in a diminishing gulf between church and mission. Great opportunities arose for enlarged missionary outreach; as RD Winter pointed out, never before had so many new nations come into being so unexpectedly.[96]

WHATEVER HAPPENED TO CT STUDD'S MISSION?

## Advance in faith

After Studd died, the situation was devastating for the small mission. In graphic terms Norman Grubb explained how he saw it.

> *Our founders had been taken; not a single person remained on the staff of the mission whose name bore any weight with the Christian public; the home end of the work had just passed through a crisis; and as a last straw it was the time of the great financial depression through the country.*[97]

What were they to do? As a start Grubb had to issue a statement repudiating the use of the words 'Don't Care a Damn' and its specific vow, without abandoning the key commitment it entailed.[98] Then he set out his grand vision for the future.

As a practical step they changed the way the day operated at the London Headquarters. Previously a perfunctory 30 minute daily prayer time was held. Now they determined that all at Highland Road would spend as much time as needed each day to study the Bible, discuss together issues facing WEC and pray about God's direction, even if this took until lunchtime.[99] As they shared together in prayer and discussion, they came to the conclusion that God was asking them to trust him for 25 new workers in the next two years, ten in the first and 15 in the next, together with the money for passage and equipment, and all without making financial appeals. These new workers were to be a living memorial to CT Studd, as well as a faith investment in the future. They felt so strongly that God was going to provide this target, unlikely as it seemed to be, they first informed their own inner circle of friends what they expected to happen, then wrote to the Congo in order that the field members should prepare for the new workers soon to arrive, and finally published the statement of their expectations in the mission magazine. The first year turned out to be an adventure in faith as ten new recruits became available and God provided the exact sum of money needed by the due date. My parents, Rose and Ivor Davies, were numbers nine and ten respectively of 'The Memorial Ten.'[100]

In the Congo the church and field also trusted God for ten local African missionaries who would pioneer new areas for the gospel. The 20 new workers, black and white, formed a remarkable indication of God's faithfulness in spite of the obstacles, and an encouragement to trust for 15 more. Even so, when the Grubbs saw no new recruits in the first half of the next year, their faith was severely tested. Dr Helen Roseveare has written that it was a time of universal financial collapse and WEC itself was in desperate circumstances.[101] Yet, in time, God supplied the finances and 15 workers. With them came the realisation that 11 were for Colombia, Little Tibet, Arabia and Spanish Guinea.[102]

WEC had already been working in other parts of the world before CT's death. The Heart of Amazonia field had not stayed with WEC. The Heart of Arabia field continued for some time, and then because of misunderstandings the members left to work separately, only for the work to be recommenced later. The Heart of Asia field involving Jock Purves, in what was called 'Lesser Tibet' (now Kashmir) had continued to link with WEC. So the Studd memorial was to be not only for the Congo but also a significant push to other areas of the unevangelised world. In fact this international widening of the reorganised mission resulted in the centring of the work in London, rather than in the Congo as it had been in Studd's day.

Emboldened by the turn around in the mission's fortunes, Grubb and colleagues felt they should trust God for another 25 new workers by 16 July 1934. The growing fields needed workers and the optimistic goal was to advance to all the remaining unevangelised peoples of the world. Most of the new workers offered well in advance of the due date, for six different fields, and the money came through a series of big gifts. Challenged afresh to believe God for something more for the next year, they received the impression to trust for 50 recruits. A visitor, encouraged spiritually by contact with the WEC staff, felt God prompt him to give £6,000, enough to cover all the costs of the 50. God provided the money first of all and soon the personnel came. In 1936 the target was 75 taking the total number of people in WEC to 175; more than a 400% increase by the fifth anniversary of CT's death, certainly a significant change for the fledgling mission.

## Geographical expansion

Among these new workers were key people who would provide leadership for new fields, alongside others who were veteran workers from the Congo and other places. Studd and Grubb were both keen to locate places where there were unevangelised peoples. They had a heart for research and encouraged the same spirit in their followers. WEC developed a style as a mission which stressed local and regional leadership, and allowed diverse individuals who, carrying a passion for the unevangelised people of the world, were creative in the achievement of their objectives. Studd had embraced Hudson Taylor's and CIM's attitude that the people on the ground should make local policy decisions. This gave freedom for action, and bold leaders were therefore empowered to move ahead without needing to wait for permission from head office.

Colombia in the early 1930s was a country where evangelical Protestants were not well known, and the Roman Catholic Church had a profound political as well as religious influence. Local religion was a mixture of Catholicism and animism. Through the influence of his brother Kenneth, Norman Grubb was moved to send a team to Colombia.[103] To lead this venture Pat Symes, an Australian, appeared on the scene in London. He had worked in Amazonia and came to the conclusion that he had no alternative but to resign from WEC.[104] On the other hand he sensed God speaking to him challenging him to go to Colombia, and he decided to rejoin WEC with this in view. The narrative of this field includes stories of local opposition, often resulting in violent physical attacks on team members and early converts, but also of great faith. Pat believed God's promises and saw over 50 workers provided within ten years of his arrival. By 1945 there were 35 congregations meeting together.

Developments in West Africa moved ahead rapidly. Spanish (now Equatorial) Guinea, was identified by the Grubbs as a place with minimal mission activity and a need for new workers. Alec and Dora Thorne had been working without much success in Morocco, and on their return to UK attended a missionary conference, where they testified to God touching their lives and giving them a new commission to go to Spanish Guinea with WEC. In 1933 they arrived, but only after considerable difficulty were they able to stay and see churches established among the Okak tribe. By 1945 there were five Okak evangelists and growing congregations.

The Ivory Coast field was started in 1934 by Sam Staniford and his wife with Fred Chapman. Establishing the ministry was not without cost, for Lilian Staniford, who had been one of the earliest pioneers in the Congo with CT Studd, died of yellow fever within two years. On top of this, Sam Staniford developed serious eye problems and almost lost his life in a car accident. Work was begun initially among the Gouro people, then with other ethnic groups. Churches were formed, local languages studied and Bible passages translated.

Evangelisation of the Lobi people in the north part of Upper Volta (now Burkina Faso) began quite remarkably. Stanley Benington of the Qua Iboe Mission, discovered when he arrived among the Lobis in 1931, that God had spoken in a vision to a former witch doctor, telling him to give up his idols and wait for the white man who would tell about the true way. For ten years he and a friend had waited but now wanted to believe in Jesus. When Benington was asked by his mission to teach in a Bible School in Nigeria, Jack and Rose Robertson of WEC took over the work with the Lobis and were joined by others. Once more this new venture was not without cost, for new worker Albert Dean died within months of arriving on the field. Today there are thousands of Lobi believers and many others from groups in close proximity.[105]

Getting the work started in Guinea-Bissau took a courageous woman. Bessie Fricker was part of a group of four who took up the challenge in this Portuguese colony. From a disadvantaged home in London's East End, Bessie determinedly went to Guinea in 1940 and stayed, in spite of the other members of the initial party leaving the country and resigning from WEC.[106] Through various trials and challenges Bessie managed to hold on, and after her marriage to Leslie Brierley they built up the work together. By 1950 there were several churches, a Bible School project underway, a leprosy clinic started and other workers had joined them.

Leslie Brierley and Ted Gibbons began work in southern Senegal in 1936. It was temporarily halted when the French Vichy government ordered all British out of Senegal. Nevertheless the venture continued and spread to the Casamance, the Senegal River Valley and the centre of the country.[107] In 1938 a small team from Canada, Ireland and England commenced a new branch of WEC in Liberia called the Liberia Inland Mission, after receiving a strong petition from the leaders of the Bassa ethnic group to undertake missionary work among them. The ministry grew steadily and soon there were churches, Bible schools, medical work, outreaches to the Gio and Mano tribes, and translation projects.

In Asia a few women workers with a passion for Kashmir and the Nepal border and who had served there for some years joined WEC and became forerunners of growing teams witnessing in those remote places. These in turn led to the opening of India as a field in 1936 centred in Uttar Pradesh. Dr William Morris began this venture originally as an outreach to the Chamar people. In due course in the late 1970s India was to become WEC's largest centre of operations with four sub-divisions.

Meanwhile work in other fields continued. A letter in May 1936 from Keith Stevenson of the Arabia Mission based in Palmyra, Syria stated, 'It's about a month since my coming to live with the Bedouin, to see the Lord really give us His ground right in their lives ... We eat and drink from dirty old cracked pots ...'[108]

Even the outbreak of World War II was not seen as an insurmountable barrier; for members felt WEC was in a spiritual war and should not be deflected from the commission it had received from God through CT Studd. When confronted with the climate of war, Norman Grubb wrote to his former Cambridge friends in 1945,

> We have regarded these times of crisis as a special opportunity for proving the promises of God, and launched out in faith for advance and supply for existing needs ... We were led deliberately to trust God for increases from the day the war broke out, and the answer has been abundant. 140 have been added to staff in all branches, two new fields have been opened in the West Indies and Gold Coast, and the income increased from £12,500 in 1939 to £38,000 this year.[109]

## Research for future expansion

Right from the beginning Studd had been enthused with research, and acted on the results of facts and figures which showed that there were nations and people groups untouched by the Christian message. Norman Grubb had a similar mindset and acted deliberately to follow up any opening that presented itself to him and the growing WEC. 'He (Grubb) loved adventures with God.'[110] With the help of Leslie Brierley, WEC became a centre for research and demonstrated a continued willingness to brave the challenge of unreached places.

Always on the lookout for ways to expand the work and fulfil the long-range goals of the mission, Norman was encouraged to see that Leslie Brierley had developed gifts of research through an enforced stay in Sierra Leone. Compelled to leave first Senegal and then Guinea-Bissau in 1941, Leslie had been given a job in Freetown with the British Political and Economic Research Office (PERO), an intelligence operation to forestall German activity during World War II. He shared his survey of Sierra Leone with Norman Grubb which brought unexpected consequences for him. Following his resignation from PERO in late 1942 Brierley was asked by Grubb to undertake a world survey showing the areas of greatest missionary need.[111] *The Black Spot Survey,* as it became known, was a careful review of existing materials to show the locations of the unevangelised peoples around the world. Brierley put together his findings under a series of headings specifying the needs in the major continents and bringing the summary of results together in the booklet *Thy Kingdom Come.* Norman Grubb wrote to the Cambridge University Missionary Band (CUMB) in October 1945, 'Our post-war programme, after careful survey work, is the occupation of 26 of the remaining unevangelised fields with populations totalling 250,000,000.'[112] This became the heart of WEC recruitment and development for the immediate period ahead.

Over the next few years Leslie Brierley was asked by WEC to undertake significant research and eventually set up the WEC International Research Office. Stanley Davies, former General Secretary of UK Evangelical Missionary Alliance (EMA), has said,

'Leslie was the brains behind the research of WEC that enabled it to understand the trends of the world situation as well as trends in the world church and world mission.'[113]

A decision was made to hold an international WEC conference in 1961. David Bachelor, founder of the mission's recruiting centres throughout Europe, sparked off the conference by writing,

> *I cannot conceive of us coming up to the Fiftieth Anniversary [1963] of the Mission without our having some clear-cut word from the Lord, about the next stretch of the road ahead after we have rounded the bend. I have always felt that it was part of the warp and woof of the WEC, to break down the vast commission God gave us through our founder into manageable proportions ... and to go at it accordingly.*[114]

In preparation for the conference, Leslie Brierley was asked to do specific research and come up with a series of recommendations for future extension and advance. At the newly acquired WEC conference centre at Kilcreggan in western Scotland, fifty-four leaders attended the three intense weeks sharing inspirational thoughts from the Bible, praying, conducting serious discussions about policy and looking at the challenges Leslie brought to them about the world scene. A desire not to rush to conclusions, but to earnestly try to discern God's directions, pervaded all the consultations. The focus was on unanimity if at all possible. The conference confronted difficult issues for an interdenominational organisation, such as whether divorcees or Pentecostals should be accepted as members of WEC. At that time many inter-denominational organisations would not consider either for membership! When a stalemate occurred, discussions were postponed to allow for prayer and further reflection and dialogue, so that a joint opinion could be achieved. The final decision was that both matters had to be studied further. Eventually in 1978 and 1984 deeply satisfying agreements were reached. This pattern was to be a model for later conferences. Every morning began with a leisurely time of devotional ministry, given by a different member of the conference, before business was taken up. Reports of existing work around the world were given. By far the biggest item was discussing Leslie Brierley's analysis of the world situation and deciding which areas were to be targeted by WEC.

In the end, what became known as the *19 Point Programme* was adopted. This list included decisions to start work in 19 new areas of South America, West, Central, South and North Africa, Europe, the Middle East, and South-East Asia. Consultations were wide-ranging with decisions being made on numerous issues including the role of the Leaders' Council, the place of faith, development of a Co-ordinating Council, denominational emphases, inter-racial marriage, and the type of recruits needed. However the major significance of the conference was that now, with WEC's coming of age, it was seen there was a worldwide consensus of leadership recognised which could agree to move forward, rather than the former dependence on one leader. Decision-making was shared by all. As the report of the conference expressed it,

> From being school-boys of faith we are called to be adults of faith, and to see an enlargement which will dwarf the first 50 years: and it is to be based on a new dedication to corporate action, corporate sharing and corporate believing. On this corporate basis, then, as one Crusade, we affirm the following: the total rededication of the Crusade to the principles upon which it was founded 48 years ago – sacrifice, faith, holiness, fellowship, — as the basis for a new worldwide advance in Gospel witness which will eclipse anything in the past.[115]

## Growth at the Sending Base

The WEC philosophy that 'the person with the vision gets the job' spawned new ministries over the years of Grubb's leadership. As cross-cultural work in different countries developed, a new emphasis on sending base ministries grew. Youth work commenced under the name *Young Warriors*, a missionary children's home started in Scotland, Missionary Training Colleges opened in both Scotland and Tasmania, WEC Presses and Radio Worldwide began production of ministry materials. On the fields new ministries were also being launched. In the Congo a burden for sufferers with leprosy saw Edith Moules found the Leper and Medical Crusade as an inter-field ministry. As a unique venture to involve both field and sending countries, *Bientot* and *SOON* were launched to send Gospel broadsheets by mail to new readers of French and English, and eventually to millions of people in a variety of languages. This ministry involved interested Christians in the sending countries who banded together into Sending Units to pray for the readers, send the newssheets out, and pay the cost of the postage.

The largest movement was the development of a literature ministry in 1941 under the name Evangelical Publishing House as the publishing department of WEC, but eventually called Christian Literature Crusade (CLC). Ken and Bessie Adams headed up this new venture, initially in the UK, where in 1944 five bookshops were opened to make Christian literature available to a wider market. The vision, besides setting up 'spiritual supermarkets', was to take Christian literature around the world, as an evangelistic tool and a means of teaching and encouragement to believers who had no access to such helpful literature. Staff members were part of WEC and for some time undertook the same orientation as WEC provided. By their 20th year (1961) CLC had 225 workers and a decision was taken for it to separate from WEC. Today CLC International has continued to grow and exercises a needed literature ministry round the world. According to CLC Living Print, January/February 2007 there are more than 600 workers operating in nearly 60 countries.

In the UK by 1943 twelve WEC regional centres were staffed by full-time personnel who trusted God for their support. This gave great impetus to representation. The London base was extended through a significant step of faith in God's ability to supply all that was needed by way of money, permissions, personnel and physical resources. A team of 26 volunteers, under the direction of a committed Christian contractor, completed a three-storey building in eighteen months with all bills paid on time.

Sending bases proliferated in Canada, the USA, continental Europe, Australia and New Zealand. Alfred Ruscoe had been a co-worker of CT Studd in Congo, but was one of those who left due to disagreement with Studd's way of handling people. However Ruscoe was challenged to reconsider and eventually felt he should apologise to Studd and rejoin WEC. He was asked to speak on behalf of WEC in North America and South Africa. Later he felt a strong burden to move to North America and recommence a WEC base there. South Africa, Australia and New Zealand representation were originally started by Constance Brandon and Priscilla Studd, who had established local committees.[116] Arthur and Lilian Davidson, having been forced to leave Colombia due to ill-health, were led to start a full-time base in Sydney.[117]

## Organisation

Norman Grubb had a special gifting in the way he showed confidence in others. This had become the means by which he would encourage people to start new fields and ministries, and to trust them to carry the responsibility. Ken Adams speaking at the 1961 International Conference said, 'Why do we all go to him and respect him? Because of his unbounding belief in us. When any of us crashes, he doesn't say, "I told you so," but picks up the pieces and says, "Well let's start again".'[118] Michael Tarrant, one time field leader in Portuguese Guinea said 'Rubi (Norman) was a great encourager – he sent books and carried out doctrinal discussions by post.'[119]

In *After CT Studd*, Grubb explained the structure by which WEC operated. The mission developed along democratic paths, with policy decisions being made by all the full-time workers in unity. On matters of local significance mission fields could make their own independent policies. Field leaders were to serve terms for three years, and had to be approved by their own fields before taking up or continuing in office. The international leader could only intervene in field matters on issues of emergency or disunity. This was a far cry from Studd's autocratic leadership style. Grubb refused the title of President, but rather chose to be known as General Secretary.

The mission's approach was experimental, with a determination to follow the leading of the Holy Spirit and not be tied to current practice. In a wide-ranging letter to all field leaders in 1953, Grubb addressed the issues of the integration of the foreign mission into the national church, development of Bible Schools, methods of conducting services in the churches, practice of the Lord's Supper, role of full-time pastors and evangelists, and payment of full-time workers. The letter was available to all members of WEC for their information and also soliciting their input. As WEC's *Principles and Practice* put forward the need of corporate and preferably unanimous decision-making, it was wise strategy to make radical concepts widely known and appreciated. These were significant concerns for a mission, which had not regarded itself as a denomination, but now was faced with growing churches in many countries. In the same letter Grubb wrote the following,

> *After all, a foreign mission, as such, has no final Scriptural authority for its existence. It is merely a convenience for spreading the Gospel in certain areas of the church's history ... I believe our danger spot is in allowing our meetings to become 'one man shows', where the pastor does all, and the people sit and share in nothing but the hymns ... We would think that the idea of one selected person 'administering the sacrament' quite unscriptural ... It is plain from the Scriptures (1 Cor 9: 11-14) that there are full-time ministers of the Gospel, but it is not plain that they are necessarily in charge of local churches ...*

In the years to come there was constant discussion at regional and international conferences on these and other issues.[120] People from all denominational backgrounds and from many nationalities needed to agree on policy and spiritual structures for the churches they were planting and the relationship of the mission to them. There was no agreed procedure on church policy. Brian Woodford in his book *Master Plan* (2007) and unpublished thesis *One Church, Many Churches* (1997) revealed years later that, although different in origin and location, there were common features in the WEC-founded churches he studied.

## Fruitfulness and revival in the Congo

Whatever happened in the Congo continued to have an impact on the rest of WEC. The size of the missionary team rose from thirty-five in 1931 to sixty in 1949. Both Jack Harrison and Norman Grubb played a part in maintaining balance and stability after Studd's days. God worked in the lives of the African believers, so that they threw themselves into the advances of the work without grumbling and with significant sacrificial commitment. Norman Grubb wrote a life story of Jack Harrison and described him as a remarkable character endowed with great skills, who lived an exemplary life of discipline, gentle where Studd was tough, and well able to provide the leadership style the field required.[121] By the time of his early death at the age of 45, the WEC work covered 1,600 square miles incorporating seventeen tribes.

On several occasions the field in the Congo experienced a touch of spiritual renewal and revival. In 1935 God moved at the mission centre at Imbai to affect the lives of many of the African Christians and the resident missionaries. At the end of 1934 siblings Jack, Lily and Ivy Roberts had felt the church members were lacking in spiritual fervour, so prayed that God would move among them. They cancelled the scheduled Christmas services and held a concentrated session of prayer. Within three days widespread repentance and confession began during public meetings.[122] This continued for many days and involved young and old, making a strong impression on the church and its public testimony.

On his return visit after 18 years at the WEC sending base, Grubb's exposure to a movement of revival in the Congo in 1949 was a breath of fresh air to him and evidence of the great work God had done in the Congolese church.[123] A short time later the revival in Rwanda, which took place mainly among Anglican churches during the 1930s and 1940s, had a substantial influence on WEC leaders and members in the Congo. Various WEC personnel paid visits to Rwanda and they were also touched through a tour of meetings in the UK by William Nagenda.[124] Grubb wrote a booklet, *Continuous Revival*, which expressed the essential message of renewal for a wider WEC constituency.

Again the Congo was touched through a widespread move of revival in 1953 and 1954. A time of profound significance for the Congo Church, the missionaries and also the wider WEC constituency, it was a remarkable visitation of God upon almost all the mission centres and churches. One of the missionaries wrote,

> That evening I was called out to the workmen's quarters. I shall never be able to describe all I saw. There was a strong sense of heaven and hell. Some were in ecstasies of joy, jumping about like wild men. Others were in fear of hell, lying around, the nearest thing to 'wailing and gnashing of teeth' I have ever witnessed. Those who were through came rushing to tell me of their wonderful relief, now that the burden of sin was off their shoulders. Others came asking for forgiveness for deceit, hypocrisy, laziness and disobedience. When most of the folk got through, there was a scene of hectic joy. I have never seen anything like it.[125]

Helen Roseveare wrote years later, 'And the revival swept on, village by village, over the whole region, through the ensuing months, the ensuing years. The church doubled in numbers – and then trebled.'[126] Many people around the world were deeply affected by the stories and preaching of those who had been personally touched by the revival.[127]

This series of events continued to strengthen the holiness emphasis in WEC, and led to an earnest desire to see similar things happen in other places where its members worked.

## Books, teaching and spiritual impact

Norman Grubb's teaching and books had, and continue to have, a widespread influence. He was a prolific writer and was responsible for over 35 titles. His books, pamphlets and articles played a significant role in the development, popularisation and impact of WEC. For instance his biography of CT Studd sold about a million copies and he also went on to write six other biographies. Parallel with his historic publications about the growth of WEC, he undertook to write a range of books explaining the secret of the inner life of 'Union with Christ.'[128]

According to Grubb, following a spiritual revelation which his wife Pauline experienced in the Congo and then he some two years later, he spent almost a year studying and thinking about the issues of personal maturity and spiritual progress. It seemed to be something akin to a breakdown or 'dark night of the soul' experience. His deputy, Jock Purves, had at short notice to take over the mission's leadership. Grubb became intrigued with the whole question of Christian spirituality. Through reading William Law, Jacob Boehme and many of the mystics he developed his own understanding of the kind of life God expected of a Christian. As a result he came to the conclusion that God had given him a double commission 'to COMBINE the getting of the gospel to peoples with, not just objective church-planting (highly dangerous to me), but Paul's *travail again* till Christ is formed in them.'[129] This double objective rubbed off on the mission because of the way Norman Grubb's devotional sessions spoke to many missionaries about their need to grow in an awareness of their relationship with Christ and understand the implications for their ministry. Helen Roseveare recalled that he once stated, '"God gave Moses the vision to take the people to the Promised Land but he never told Moses there were going to be ten plagues." I can remember him saying that in prayers, and he gave us the vision to stick to what God had given through thick and thin.'[130]

Eric Smith recollected that Norman 'shared quite a lot in morning prayers. He knew where he was going and got us involved with him.'[131] John Lewis, founder of SOON Ministries was deeply affected.[132] Jack Aitken, formerly of the UK HQ staff and later at the base in Canada, remembered,

> As a candidate in London headquarters in 1947, when Rubi [Norman] spoke in the daily morning prayers he flipped back and forward through the Bible as he talked on the lives of Abraham, Jacob, Moses, Joshua, etc ... This was dynamic training! When Peggy and I came to Canada in 1980 we were always thrilled to have the visits of Rubi to the Canadian headquarters in Hamilton, Ontario. He opened the Scriptures in his inimitable way and shared the early days of WEC when he and Pauline served with CT in Congo. It was always inspiring.[133]

Grubb came to be known in many quarters for his teachings on the life of the Christian and a deeper relationship with God. On speaking engagements he spent much of his time talking about the Christian's walk with God instead of solely promoting the work of the mission.

These doctrines ('Union with Christ', walking in the light, continuous revival, approaching God through the prayer of faith and acknowledging the presence of God in us and others) played a large part in giving spiritual momentum to the mission and its supporters. The regular flow of books Grubb wrote explained these themes and widened the appeal of WEC and its message. Patrick Johnstone said, 'It was his writings which met my deep heart hunger for reality and pointed me to the Spirit-filled life ... He was a spiritual giant through whom so much of eternal value came into being.'[134] His worldwide travels and public speaking made them known. WEC centres sponsored conventions for deeper life teaching and ran regular monthly conferences and camps. The spiritual message promoted by WEC workers developed spiritual growth among people, and this gave a foundation in their allegiance to God rather than just an adherence to an organisation.

After completing his term in International Leadership of WEC in 1965, teaching and writing on the Christian's spiritual life became his full-time ministry. He had spent 1950-51 and 1958-60 in the USA as interim leader of WEC USA, as well as continuing to carry the role of International Secretary. This opened to him a large door of ministry in the USA which continued until the end of his life. Although widely appreciated for his 'elder statesman' role in WEC, his later opinions on sanctification diverged somewhat from generally accepted views and led to a distance between Grubb and some in WEC.[135]

As a result of the International Conference in 1961 it was decided that there should be a continuing group who would consult on matters of international importance and help the International Secretary to make decisions. The Co-ordinating Council comprised the Sending Base Leaders of UK, Australia, North America, New Zealand and Europe and had an advisory, rather than executive, function. Their first meeting took place in 1964 at Fort Washington,

Pennsylvania where WEC USA has its national centre.

## Reflections on the contribution made by Norman Grubb

### Leadership qualities

Norman Grubb's style was to trust people with leadership and his personality loomed over the work of the mission in both spiritual and administrative ways. Alastair Kennedy, a later leader in WEC, said that Norman was able to discern the abilities of those he worked with and gave them freedom to develop their ministry and gifts. He allowed people to move forward when they had a big vision and backed them.[136] Klaus Fiedler has said, 'Why was WEC able to expand during the depression? One reason was the readiness for sacrifice which was part of "WEC philosophy" and the other was Norman Grubb's fascinating personality.'[137] His style, teaching, way of handling workers, vision and organisational skills influenced all areas of the work. The fact that he trusted leaders and workers to make their own decisions, while at the same time backed their vision for development of the work, gave a sense of freedom and local responsibility. This unique blend of gifts possessed by Grubb clearly showed that he was the overall leader of the mission, although Jack Harrison had been appointed as leader in the Congo.

The harmonious way that Harrison and Grubb connected, Grubb's excellent public relations and the remarkable supply of new workers, significantly reversed the climate of mistrust which had dogged the mission in the later days of CT Studd.[138] Under Jack Harrison's leadership in the Congo, unity and close fellowship prevailed and there were minimal resignations for any reason. The years to come showed that, among the new wave of recruits to the Congo, a generation of leaders was born who brought their own significant contributions to the life of the mission.

### Vision and values

The main value that comes, through all the many developments within WEC during this period, is resolute adherence to the primary objective in WEC's *Principles and Practice* 'To evangelise the remaining unevangelised peoples in the shortest possible time.' This goal drove expansion into new fields, daring initiatives into new ministries, targets of faith for workers and properties, and led to the expectation that, irrespective of world events, God expected Christians, and specifically members of WEC, to continue expanding their work and fulfilling the commission they had received. Together with this was a desire to spread the message of the resources available through union with the living Christ and the indwelling Holy Spirit. This message was shared with the new churches being developed on the mission fields, WEC missionaries at home and abroad as well as to the individuals to whom WEC ministered in the home constituencies. Norman Grubb's ministry on the themes expressed in his booklet *Continuous Revival* (1952) was appreciated and made a deep impact on many. His articulation of the *Four Pillars of WEC* (1973) gave an insight into the central principles that were dear to WEC—sacrifice, faith, holiness and fellowship which have continued to be embraced as a definite legacy of his ministry and teaching.

## Organisation

In many ways Grubb was the main architect of the structure under which WEC would operate. The *Principles and Practice* of the mission, as set out by him, were a significant distance from the AIM-based constitution Studd had worked with.[139] In fact the original document *Christ's Etceteras* (1915) Studd wrote as the 'call to arms' of WEC was not included as part or foundation to the Constitution, although the sentiments were basic. With each field making its own policy decisions, and no central international committee or leader to direct matters, responsibility rested on the people doing the work within a specific cultural location. This took note of the need to share the load and not be dependent on the founders and central leadership—it was 'leadership-in-fellowship.' Fellowship decision-making strengthened trust and dependence on the Holy Spirit to guide individuals, so they could also be an active part of a team who were listening to God. The system of triennial elections for all leadership positions required a serious commitment to accountability among all leaders. International Leadership in the future was not by appointment, or from the Studd or Grubb families, but by an international election following nominations made by WEC members.

## Quality and development of leaders

Additional factors that contributed to the survival and growth of WEC International in this period included a group of capable leaders, who were able to embody the heart principles of WEC and lead pioneer teams, usually in most isolated situations. People like Pat Symes, Jack Staniford, Harold Williams, Bessie Brierley, Wilf Overgaard, Len Moules, David Batchelor, their partners and many others were not only able to keep teams together but train others of a similar mindset to take on leadership. In addition, the 1961 conference played a part in strengthening the vision of the mission and presenting great new challenges. The contribution of Leslie Brierley and his research department played no small part in this.

# Potentially negative developments

## Lack of strong ties to local sending churches

Grubb tended to ignore close relationships with churches in his home country, often choosing not to attend a local congregation. He preached regularly at different churches, but affirmed that all days were holy days and therefore Sunday was not of special significance to him.[140] His non-attendance at church was infectious in some quarters, with a few WEC members choosing also not to attend.[141] This confirmed to those who wished to believe it that WEC was a 'law unto itself' choosing to go its own separate way, and could have led to an estrangement from church leaders and members. Grubb however maintained excellent relations with various church leaders of diverse denominations. Over the following years, strong links have been fostered and maintained by WEC with many churches, and a great deal of trust built up.[142]

## Excessive trust in individual action

Freedom to make individualistic decisions could have ultimately led to a casual attitude of freely permitting new ventures if discipline had not been exercised. Autocracy is one error to avoid but anarchy is another. Permission granted to fields to make their own policy decisions fortunately curtailed any runaway guidance, because the field fellowship applied corporate wisdom under the direction of the Holy Spirit. In addition, the development of the Coordinating Council became a means for international consultation on matters affecting basic principles.

## Development of institutions

In this period the extensive expansion of various ministries at the sending bases, and the development of Bible colleges, schools and medical work on the fields brought new challenges. Grubb had allowed fields and sending bases to make their own policy decisions about institutions without conducting any analysis of the wisdom of this course of action for the future development of the churches. A consistent supply of personnel, competent leadership, regular funding and careful monitoring was needed, to see that professional and spiritual standards were maintained. Although all the goals included evangelisation as the ultimate aim and the growth of biblically based churches, the progress of other institutions could well end up deflecting the resources and attention of the mission. Also it raised the question of these institutions jeopardising the ability of newly founded churches to cope economically.[143] Would they be able to develop structures which would allow them to maintain evangelistic initiatives, or establish churches that were able to self-multiply, without outside funds?

## A particular theological mindset which would be regarded as mandatory for all members or adherents of WEC

Norman Grubb's views were strong and his teaching was all-pervasive in this period of WEC's history. His many books from 1933 to 1965 were widely circulated among WEC members and supporters, and included several of a theological and didactic nature. A set formula of secondary beliefs could have become the accepted code within the mission. Grubb's style was provocative rather than autocratic, and his teachings were challenges to promote spiritual growth and faith-filled expectations. Stewart Dinnen told me on many occasions of the way that Grubb, in his morning open Bible Studies or in conference discussion times, would deliberately state a challenging thesis to which he expected people to react. This would then lead to a joint (sometimes heated) discussion but with normally irenic conclusions. Grubb was not threatened by opposing views but expected the proponents to justify their conclusions. Of course immature people could and did accept the '*shibboleths*' (Judges 12:5-6), and had to learn through experience that personal development was as important as the godly example and proclamations of their elders.

## Principles that emerge from an analysis of this period

### God speaks through the community of faith

It was seen, from the way that WEC was managed in this period, that people should not be afraid of the Holy Spirit's ability to manage his work. The mission ran by principles which showed that it was possible to live by trusting the Spirit to give guidance to the most unlikely and disparate group of people.[144] When there was heart unity on spiritual essentials, adequate time to sort through issues that needed to be resolved, time for prayer and trusted leadership, then the Holy Spirit could be expected to bring clear guidance. 'Christ in you' was a necessary premise of field unity. 'We are all part of the same Person, as the body is of the head.'[145]

### Personal and corporate spiritual development was important

Analysis of this period of WEC's history reveals that Grubb's emphasis on personal and corporate spiritual progress was important for the mission's development. Helen Roseveare said, 'He was always moving one on spiritually. There was always a push to be striving for the top, to keep your vision clear, not to get bogged down in details. This would come over again and again.'[146] Grubb wrote, 'WEC has always maintained that the spiritual equipment is supreme.'[147] Wise decisions about field and mission policy, choice of leaders and future initiatives to be taken in the ministry, all depended on the spirituality of team members. Time for spiritual understanding, growth and experience should be factored into the daily and annual timetable. The community at sending base or field needed to learn together and appreciate each other's personalities, skills and way of responding, as these were all important for ease of operation and trust. This was as important as the mechanics of missionary work.

## Policy decisions should be made by those who do the work

Grubb strongly supported the idea that home committees should not be given oversight of the work on the fields, and the same is true in reverse.[148] Nevertheless due to the need to create a workable form of government following Studd's autocratic pioneering style, it fell to Grubb to formulate a practical system. In WEC, responsibility was vested in the committed membership, comprising each particular sending country or field, to handle the matters of policy they alone were in the position to understand.

> *Mutual faith in each other was the necessary foundation of the new relationship, for while we at home must trust them to direct the fields wisely and well, they must trust us in the very important points of the distribution of finances and the selection of candidates.*[149]

Appraisals and judgements of international matters were delegated to the leaders of all fields and sending bases together, with day to day matters handed to the Coordinating Council and International Leadership.

## Keep the end in view from the beginning – a holy and self-supporting, self-governing, self-propagating church

The outcomes of missionary work needed to be worked through as early as possible. God glorifying, biblically obedient and spiritually dynamic Christian communities as well as self-governing, self-multiplying and self-propagating churches were crucial goals of missionary work. Not only individuals needed to be fully Christianised, but also the companies they were part of. Planning for a prospect, independent of missionaries, was essential for the well-being of the church of the future.

## A manageable and understandable constitution

Keeping the constitutional document *Principles and Practice* manageable and up-to-date was a wise way to make sure core issues were embraced by the whole mission. The members needed to agree on this document and re-sign them every three years. A weighty detailed document could become a tool for discouragement and disenchantment. God blessed WEC through Grubb's visionary administrative structure and his wisdom to enshrine it in a simple format. This was a happy recipe for continued revision and progress.

# CHAPTER FOUR
## WEC'S COMING OF AGE (1965-1983)

Now the question to be faced was, 'Would WEC survive without the strong personalities of CT Studd and Norman Grubb in leadership?' The answer came in the provision of an experienced WEC missionary who had spent fifteen years in India and most of World War II as an officer in an Indian unit of the British Army. With the appointment of Len Moules as International Secretary in 1965, for the first time in 52 years there were no relatives of the founder in the leadership of WEC.

### Len Moules

Brought to faith by the witness of a fellow workman, Len embarked on a life in which mission featured prominently and the needs of Tibet became a personal challenge.[150] He had been brought up in a godly London home and trained as an electrical instrument maker. He attended a 'holiness' Bible college called Emmanuel[151] near Liverpool and the UK Missionary School of Medicine. In 1936 Len left for India and spent three years learning language and culture, until World War II broke out. Called up by the British Army he was sent with an Indian unit to North Africa, to fight through some of the fiercest battles there and later in Italy and the Middle East. In 1945 he returned to India as a major, and by the next year was freed from the army and able to return to his missionary task on the Tibetan border. In the years up to 1956 he made scary journeys mainly on foot among the Himalayan peaks, visiting villages and towns, making friends, giving medical treatment and above all sharing the gospel with those who would listen.

Ken Booth, Len's successor in field leadership in India and fellow-worker, said 'He was an outstanding leader: warm, vibrant, living, very human ... He had a commanding presence with a distinguished bearing, and could take his place without effort in any level of society.'[152] His extensive notes on leadership give an insight to principles that were dear to his heart and developed from his personal life experience.

Exhaustion and his children's education needs sent Len and his wife Iris and family back to the UK. Eventual recovery from weariness and depression coincided with Norman Grubb's relocation to the USA in 1957. To his great surprise Len was asked to take on responsibility as UK Leader of WEC. This brought him into contact with large numbers of WEC workers, and into a position where he had to deal with many issues of international consequence for the growing mission.

## Critical and tragic events

During the latter part of Norman Grubb's tenure and of Len Moules' British and International Leadership several events occurred which were influenced by the demise of colonialism. The British Prime Minister, Harold Macmillan, said of Africa, 'The wind of change is blowing through this continent.' The years 1960 to 1975 ushered in a major period of struggle for independence, great change and instability as well as 'indeed a time of growth and maturity for the church in Africa.'[153] This was not only an African phenomenon, but also took place in many parts of the world where the old colonial powers had ruled and were now replaced or forced to concede independence.

This affected WEC work in Africa, the Indian subcontinent, the Middle East and South-East Asia and led to major changes in the way missionary work was perceived and executed. Grubb stated that he felt these international political changes were to be the catalyst for an expansion of the gospel. 'For ourselves it means a basic re-orientation in our concept of being a missionary society.'[154] Interestingly Professor Lamin Sanneh has said 'The end of colonial rule inhibited the expansion of Islam in Africa, whereas the opposite has happened with Christianity.' [155] This was the 'big picture' background and affected the future of the churches, but, on a smaller scale, hugely emotional scenes were being played out because local events deeply affected the foreign and missionary community.

Reluctant expatriate Christian workers were often forced by threat of expulsion to hand over leadership of local churches. Others like WEC's Ron Davies, caught up in the swirl of events in Kashmir, paid the price of being in the wrong place at the wrong time—although to him, he was where Jesus wanted him and ready for any consequence. Ron had been a communist in his Welsh homeland, but, when he was found by Christ, life turned around and he volunteered for missionary service in Kashmir. Called up through World War II he too became a major in the British Army and for six years was in charge of an Indian unit. Returning to Kashmir in 1947 he was held up in the fighting during the division of Indian and Pakistan. As Field Leader he ensured the safety of all workers but, along with a Kashmiri widow he was protecting, was confronted by warring Pathans and asked to deny his Lord. Refusing, this gentle Christian giant and the lady were shot.[156]

Simultaneously thousands of local Christians suffered through these events but were not at the time given their due recognition by the international community or foreign Christian churches. Yet it was to come, for there were significant moves towards a closer appreciation of all Christians around the world through the ecumenical movement and evangelical associations. The World Council of Churches had developed from the daughter movements spawned by the 1910 Edinburgh Conference which had so affected CT Studd and many in the missionary world.[157]

In evangelical churches there were new developments destined to break Christians out of their denominational and nationalistic cocoons. Groups like Operation Mobilization (OM) developed from a small beginning in 1957 under the leadership of George Verwer and Dale Rhoton, and went on to mobilise hundreds of young people worldwide to serve for short or long terms around the world and on their growing fleet of ships. Youth with a Mission (YWAM) was started by Loren Cunningham in 1960 and became one of the largest multi-national Christian organisations in the world. Some of the most significant evangelical developments were more than 30 events hosted by Billy Graham, including the trans-denominational World Congresses of Evangelism held at Berlin in 1966, Lausanne in 1974, Pattaya in 1980 and Manila in 1989. These brought thousands of evangelical Christians together for serious consultations and opened many eyes to what had happened in the non-western world as a result of missionary work.[158] As Dr Ralph Winter has affirmed, Christianity was outgrowing other forms of religion and becoming truly international because of its transforming influence.[159]

## The Congo

The events in the Congo in the period 1960 to 1964 were devastating for the churches and Christian missions, creating worldwide publicity, negative and positive. The political situation surrounding the independence of the Congo and the appointment of Patrice Lumumba as Prime Minister, had violent and tragic outcomes in the north-east, the area where WEC worked. The *Simba* movement, which grew as a response to the assassination of Lumumba, brought a return to tribal religion mixed with elements of political opportunism. This challenged the role of the Roman Catholic Church, foreign business entities and international involvement in the Congo.[160] Unwelcome attention also fell on the churches and foreign missionaries of many different organisations.

The resultant tension deteriorated into inhumane treatment and massacres of local Christians and foreigners—business-people and missionaries alike. During months of uncertainty and public interest Len Moules was the international spokesperson for WEC. His simple and hastily written book *This is No Accident* told the graphic story of the deaths of five WEC workers, the mistreatment of several others, and described the large inter-mission memorial service held in London. Missionaries from many other societies including WEC's partner mission, Unevangelized Fields Mission, lost members and also some children. Later, news came of the murder of WEC missionary, Winnie Davies, who had been kept in captivity for two years. The church leaders and members suffered terribly through cruel persecution with many Christians having to flee into the forest for safety.

Dr Helen Roseveare, one of the WEC Congo team, writes and speaks widely of lessons learned through her own cruel experiences.[161] Eventually some of the missionaries returned to the

Congo, but things would never be the same. The church was now fully in charge and proved to be resolute and competent, in spite of the years of hardship ahead.[162]

## Vietnam

Since 1958 WEC had been working in Vietnam concentrating on the people in the Da Nang area and the hill tribes (Montagnards) especially the Hrey. The field was founded by Gordon and Laura Smith, formerly American missionaries with Christian and Missionary Alliance, and had developed quite strongly. Nonetheless the work was in a situation where the Vietnam War was increasing in intensity, and all life in the country was ultimately drawn into its web. Tragedy struck in 1964 when WEC workers Roy and Daphne Spraggett and their baby daughter barely escaped with their lives as their house was blown up. In 1966 a young British member, John Haywood, was killed during a roadside ambush. Eventually the WEC team was forced to withdraw from the country.

The 1960s were tough years in contrast to the revival years of the 1950s, and included a tragic event for the UK sending base in 1969, involving the deaths of Leslie Brierley's extrovert and pioneering missionary wife Bessie and Cuban missionary Quirino Baro, who were killed in a road accident in Scotland.

## Issues occupying the attention of International Leadership

From the beginning of 1966 Len Moules took over as International Secretary of WEC as well as British leader. This was an increasingly complex task, and Len faced many challenges both internationally and locally. A large personal correspondence was preserved by Leslie Brierley and gives an insight to the issues which occupied WEC's leadership during this period. For instance, Len was concerned how they would handle work in Mauritania, what would be the shape of the Coordinating Council after Norman Grubb moved out of the scene, and how the India field would continue as a result of the changes in the political situation there.[163] In the 1960s and 70s God was at work in Indonesia, and WEC workers involved with the Indonesian Missionary Fellowship enjoyed being part of a time of profound spiritual experiences and revival. There were also discussions about the need to encourage missionary interest in newly developing churches in Asia and how WEC would relate to them.[164] As well as dealing with the consultations and events that were dominating international correspondence, Len Moules made extensive trips to visit WEC workers around the world. He also had to supervise the location, purchase and transfer of WEC's UK and international headquarters from south-east London to a large property, Bulstrode, 24 miles outside the city. This had been the former home of the Dukes of Somerset. When a compulsory purchase order had been imposed on WEC's London properties, a search led WEC in 1967 to the large house in Gerrards Cross, Buckinghamshire, which was in a dilapidated state and would require several stages of renovation. The fascinating story is told in Mary Rowe's booklet *Why on earth a mansion?* Life was rather hectic for Len Moules and he faced continued health challenges.

## International Leaders' Conference 1969

In 1969 an international leaders' conference was held at Bulstrode and called by Norman Grubb 'the first full Leaders' Conference in our history.' Len Moules said that it had been 'born in the heart of Ivor Davies' who felt that there were several matters of grave importance which needed face-to-face consultation.

Business at the conference ranged widely, but most time was taken up with a revision of *Principles and Practice* and certain questions: What did 'international' really mean in the mission? What were WEC's ultimate objectives? What was involved in setting up an International Office? What did field autonomy and interdependence represent? What was 'interdenominational' to mean in a mission like WEC? How should relationships with WEC-founded churches and local missionary societies function? The value of having all WEC leaders in one location to talk and pray through such issues was invaluable.

During the conference Len and Iris raised with the delegates their own inability to continue with the dual roles of International and British leadership of WEC, and guidelines were laid down to protect Len from overwork. Ultimately the decision was taken to ask Robert and Isabel Mackey, former missionaries in Liberia and at that time exercising a pastoral role at the Welcome Hall in Belfast, to take on the British leadership.

From 1969 there was an acceptance of conferences of WEC's International Leadership and Coordinating Council on a more regular basis. These became very significant and necessary in the life of the widely spread mission. However, the question whether these became purely administrative gatherings or were contributing to the expansion of the mission should be raised. In 1981 Leslie Brierley said 'Conferences since 1961 have been called, not so much to solve problems but to promote growth ... (they) have apparently not appreciably enlarged our "frontiers" or even our "frontier–vision"...'[165] His passion was that new unreached areas of the world should be penetrated by WEC, but at the same time he was applauding the growth issues that were being addressed. For a developing mission with workers on all continents, face-to-face discussions were crucial to enable the organisation to keep functioning smoothly, but in spite of Leslie Brierley's fears they usually resulted in bold new ventures being adopted.

Norman Grubb had not disappeared from the scene.[166] Although released from active International Leadership at the end of 1965, he was treated with respect and asked to be an honorary member of the newly formed Consultative Council. His opinions were sought on various occasions, and he was never reluctant to express his views if he thought a spiritual or foundational issue was at stake.[167] For delegates at the International Conference of 1984 he produced a small booklet with the original title *Are we still on target?* His concern centred on the thought that the radical holiness standard of CT Studd was being lost in the pursuit of baptism and church planting, and that there was a need for revisiting what he called 'achieving faith.' However by the end of the conference he had hand-written a new title on all copies of the booklet: *We are still on target!* On the other hand, his tendency to radicalise his views and embrace what has been called *panentheism*, was a cause of concern to many in WEC especially in the USA where he lived and had his main itinerating and publishing impact.[168]

## What was to be the pattern of church-mission relationships in WEC?

Len Moules had other issues on his mind. Events in Africa and other places where colonialism came to an end resulted in much missiological heart-searching. What should be the pattern of church-mission relationships? A significant conference was held in Indonesia in 1968 which brought together a group of WEC missionaries, Asian Christian leaders and some other Christian representatives to discuss matters of common interest. In addition to this, within WEC the 1969 Leaders' Conference spent considerable time on the subjects of 'cooperation', 'partnership' and 'integration.' These mainly referred to the role of the missionary as co-worker with or under the local churches in the countries where WEC had planted the church. The Indonesian experience played a large part. It had involved a complete section of the Java field of WEC becoming a separate subdivision which was closely aligned to and integrated with the Indonesian Missionary Fellowship at Batu-Malang, East Java.[169] In South India a WEC team became incorporated as partners into the ministry of the Brethren-style Bakht Singh Assemblies but retained an organisational link with the overall WEC India field. In Japan integration took place by means of a fusion of the WEC field with the WEC-founded church. In Colombia a significant section of the WEC field merged with one of the WEC-founded denominations. In Congo and many other countries, the newly independent churches became the leaders in church matters, and the WEC teams worked in co-operation with them while retaining their own organisation and separate objectives. For some time within the organisation there was a strong feeling that 'integration' was the pattern that must take place around the world. In addition, some felt WEC should recruit non-western Christians to join the mission. An equally strong group held that this should not to be so. Len Moules said,

*I believe the thing coming out of your report which is intriguing me,*

63

*and I think possibly is the line which will have greater acceptance right through the Crusade is the fact that we should in our future programmes be looking for the Lord to raise up mature nationals from all our fields, but to see them going through the existing national missionary groups ... We do not want to redevelop a Western agency in other countries.*[170]

A concept was developed by Leslie Brierley and accepted by WEC's leadership to promote missionary consciousness in countries where newly developing churches were starting to grow in spiritual maturity. WEC's plan was named 'Fellowship Centres for Outreach Worldwide' and its aim was to foster a deeper spiritual awareness, challenge towards cross-cultural evangelism and church-planting, encourage training programmes to this end, foster the acceptance of local missionaries, cultivate the commencement of local sending agencies and offer the assistance of WEC to these new ministries. Originally centres were started in Taiwan, Brazil, Singapore and Hong Kong with this concept in mind, but eventually they became regular WEC sending bases.[171]

## Numerical expansion

Numbers in WEC had reached 820 workers by 1970, showing a significant jump from 357 in 1950.[172] It would seem the impact of the '*19 Point Programme*' adopted at the International Leaders' Conference in 1961 had been the catalyst for this. The years after 1961 had seen a steady forward move into Mozambique, North Africa, Chad, the Middle East, Western Asia, the Senegal River Valley, the Gambia, Sardinia, France, and a new concentration on recruitment in Brazil.[173]

## Major changes

The momentum from the 1969 conference raised issues that required a meeting of the Consultative Council in 1974. During this latter conference a decision was taken to recommend the selection of Robert and Isabel Mackey, Leaders of the British Sending Base of

WEC, on the Moules' retirement to the post of International Secretaries; the appointment of Alastair and Helen Kennedy as Deputy International Secretaries; the re-appointment of Leslie Brierley and his second wife Jill as Research Secretaries; and Stewart Dinnen as Resources Secretary. As an interim measure, the former Swiss leaders and Regional Advisers for Europe, Heini and Jo Schnyder, were appointed Acting International Secretaries for part of 1975. It would seem that Robert Mackey wanted to make sure that he had a successor in place in the British Sending Base and that certain international business was completed before he took over.

The 1974 conference included 15 delegates and four co-opted members who worked through a daunting series of 43 business points. The restructuring of international administration was proposed, with the change of name to Coordinating Council and the first appearance of the concept of regions and Regional Advisors. The regionalisation of WEC was a significant step. The election of leaders every three years resulted in many in leadership needing advice from those more experienced. Appointing Regional Advisors would allow experienced personnel to be helpful mobile advisors to the Field Leaders. It was intended that Regional Advisors would be chosen by the Co-ordinating Council but approved by the local fields with an 'emphasis on helping the fields rather than seeking to impose new methods or structures.'

During the 1974 conference there were several references to recruitment policies which affected different fields, upgrading of the *Principles and Practice*, a decision to encourage leadership training, apology for the failure to achieve a total of 1,000 new workers between 1963 and 1973, and discussions about training expatriate workers and local Christians in WEC-founded churches. Len and Iris Moules were farewelled with warm appreciation and deep regret, and moved into a fruitful ministry until the end of their lives based at Gold Hill Baptist Church, Gerrards Cross.

## Was Len Moules in the same pattern as CT Studd or Norman Grubb?

Len Moules was an administrator in the military mould, and in that he differed from Grubb who was a visionary, enthusiast and mystic. But as a man of vision, Len was a worthy successor and carried the flag high, never failing to keep the goals clear. In his passion he was a man of the Spirit believing in the need to press on spiritually and to enter into all the fullness the Holy Spirit had for him and WEC. His teaching and preaching was with depth and personal application just like his predecessors. Mady Vaillant, former Field Leader in Burkina Faso and Regional Director in Africa, wrote:

*The way Len was ready to recognise his shortcomings stands out clearly in my mind. For instance, once he had said something in public about his brother-in-law Eric Smith and realised it was not said in love. Later on in chapel hour he apologised to Eric before us all. To me that was the type of leader I wanted to follow.*[174]

Painting the broader picture, Norman Grubb in a diamond jubilee affirmation of God's work in the world, enthused,

*I have been awakened to find that a fantastic dream has become a glorious reality ... There are now vigorous churches of almost all nations, conscious of their status as part of the one Body of Christ ... Now in 1973, WEC, though greatly increased in numbers, still retains the flexibility in the leading of the Spirit to fulfil our worldwide commission by any means – 'all things to all men, that I might by all means save some' (1 Cor 9: 22).*[175]

## Robert Mackey

Robert Mackey was a different kind of leader. He was godly, prayerful, thorough, organised, but reticent to share too widely the issues he was dealing with. As a result there is a paucity of resources by and about him in comparison with those of his predecessors. From an undated profile held at the UK Sending Base we have the telling comment that 'Robert and Isabel set a standard of prayerfulness, quiet authority and loving tact in leadership that many still remember with thanksgiving.' Robert was from Northern Ireland, and with his Canadian wife Isabel had served in Liberia for twelve years, until they were forced to return home due to the severe illness of their oldest son Keith. Robert became the pastor of the Welcome Hall in Belfast for five years. Isabel was a woman gifted in music, loving in hospitality and passionate in prayer.[176] As already mentioned above, an invitation was given to Robert and Isabel to become British Sending Base Leaders following the 1969 International Conference and then to take on the International Secretaries' role at the 1974 Coordinating Council Conference. Renate Kuhl has indicated that Robert was a great listener and encourager and she had discovered recently that he had a profound influence on one couple who were faced by a difficult co-worker. 'I would say it is due to Robert's encouragement that (they) stayed and made it on the field.'[177] Alastair Kennedy worked very closely with him in International Leadership and in his opinion

> *Robert was pastoral ... [He] was a student of the Word. He respected confidences - this was very important to him, and he guarded them jealously. Some resented this [calling him 'secretive']. Robert prayed about these issues and didn't share because he didn't want people hurt.* [178]

Roland Muller's estimation was that Robert Mackey's contribution in promoting 'tent-making' was to allow flexibility to and trust in new workers which would facilitate entrance into some of the most difficult places in the world.

> *A watershed [in WEC] was the leadership of Robert Mackey ... Robert was a deep thinker and a very spiritual person who laid the foundations for tremendous change that would ripple through the mission for years afterwards. Robert thought and allowed change ...*[179]

Len, Leslie and Robert helped to steer WEC through initial discussions on the need to treat seriously outreach to 'closed countries.' Eventually a majority of WEC's field members would be ministering in these complex areas which have become known as 'Restricted Access Nations' or more positively titled 'The 10/40 Window' or 'Creative Access Nations' (CANs).

## The Charismatic Movement and its effect on WEC

From the International WEC Conference in 1961 right through until the International Leaders' Conference in 1978, as in the wider evangelical communties worldwide, one issue continued to raise its head — WEC's attitude to Pentecostalism and its outgrowth, the Charismatic Movement. For an interdenominational mission like WEC which had majored on holiness and the work of the Holy Spirit, there were two areas where strong differences of theological opinions and church practices could have caused havoc — disagreements among workers and the setting up of new churches. In the 1961 conference Donald Gee, a key British Pentecostal leader, came and spoke about his experience. Healthy discussion centred on the need for love and openness, and concluded with the requirement that within WEC the mission could not cope with those who stated that speaking in tongues of necessity had to be the sign of the initial evidence of the filling of the Spirit, due to its divisive outcomes. As the years went past, there was seen to be the need for a more specific series of guidelines. Len Moules stated that there was wide and deep concern through the whole fellowship as to where we were going doctrinally.

In the 1969 Conference, after discussion and consultation, a series of principles had been drawn up for the guidance of the WEC fellowship. The aim was not to be confrontational but to do all in a spirit of love and unity. However, matters still simmered and gave rise to further worldwide discussion and consultation. Alastair Kennedy affirmed that

> Robert [Mackey] was moderate. In Ivory Coast there was a problem over this issue ... and there was some trouble brewing ... Robert's guidelines were important and precious – they were fed into WEC at the next Intercon ... This was a Kairos moment – it prevented a split. [He] handled things carefully and prayerfully one step at a time.[180]

At the International Leaders' Conference in 1978 an improved Statement on Spiritual Gifts was carefully introduced by Robert

Mackey which, after an unhurried and harmonious discussion, was approved.[181] This subsequently proved to be successful, for the most part, in laying the matter to rest and forming a useful basis for harmony, within the membership of WEC and in its role in church planting and development.

Education as well as decision-making became an important part of this and subsequent conferences. Most subjects were introduced by preliminary papers which required prior study and response. The presence of eleven visitors, representing churches on fields where WEC was working, brought a realistic perspective to the debate. Discussions took place on the role of leadership in WEC, church-mission relationships, church growth on the fields, qualifications and training of local pastors and foreign workers, the involvement of non-westerners in mission and reaching the unreached.

This conference was to be crucial as well through the choice of Patrick and Jill Johnstone to replace Leslie and Jill Brierley in the International Research Office.[182] Patrick was well known around the world for his authorship of the prayer survey book *Operation World*.[183] He and Jill were members of the Dorothea Mission working in Southern Rhodesia (Zimbabwe) and South Africa. Up to that time it was not normal practice to invite people from outside WEC to take on leadership roles in the mission without moving through the normal lengthy orientation process.[184] Leslie Brierley was convinced that Patrick would make a worthy successor, and he proposed to Robert Mackey, the Coordinating Council and then to the International Conference in 1978 that Patrick should be invited to take his role. This was unanimously approved.

After a year gaining further worldwide insights and exposure on OM's ship *Logos*, Patrick and Jill moved quickly into their new role. They applied the benefits of their research to an understanding of what God was saying to them about world needs and WEC's future targets for advance.[185] Stanley Davies of EMA has said that 'Patrick built on Leslie (Brierley)'s work and both gave it visibility and also an even greater depth. He cooperated with other key global researchers such as David Barrett and enriched the missions' world but also benefited WEC.'[186] The ramifications of this appointment would only become fully apparent at the 1984 International Leaders' Conference and in the years to come.

The theme of internationalisation of WEC's membership continued to be raised. In both the 1969 and 1978 International Leaders' Conferences discussions were held exploring the involvement of people of all nationalities working within the ranks of WEC. The strength of the missionary-founded churches was becoming obvious and colonial attitudes to non-westerners were slowly diminishing. Pat Symes gave an excellent talk at the 1969 conference stressing the implications, and Ken Booth spoke at the 1978 conference where initial ground rules were drawn up encouraging the recruitment of non-westerners. The involvement of Bob and Bev Harvey as field leaders in Brazil in 1977, following Leslie Brierley's outward-looking ministry at the Brazil Bible Institute, led to the recruiting of Brazilians into WEC. Their boldness and strong faith-filled enthusiasm were a refreshing, although initially an uncomfortable, addition to WEC ranks. This became a distinctive catalyst in promoting truly worldwide membership of WEC.[187]

## Crucial emphases

Spiritual emphases were kept uppermost through people like Len Moules, Charlton Smith, Detmar Scheunemann, Ivor Davies, Stewart Dinnen, Phil Booth and many others in WEC who travelled worldwide speaking on issues of personal Christian development.[188] A God-closeness was cultivated within the mission through prominent times given for worship and devotional messages at international and field conferences and constant periods set aside for prayer. Devotional books such as *The Fifth Dimension* by Phil Booth and *Ascent of the Inner Everest* by Len Moules reached a wider audience. Special conferences for the deepening of Christian life and imparting of missionary information were arranged for the general public and were a long time WEC practice.[189] This was part of Norman Grubb's legacy. A WEC hymnbook, *The Crusade Hymns*, focusing on the kind of spiritual sentiments that tugged at the heart of WECers was produced and went through several editions. People became friends of WEC because of the personal spiritual blessing they received. Jean Barnicoat, who later joined WEC, has said,

*I was attracted to the WEC lifestyle — as in the Scriptures, real Christianity. The people had a baptism of love and all 'seemed tarred with the same brush'... They lived the life. There was simplicity and an uncluttered lifestyle. They were clearly directed and focused. [I] saw the lives of WECers as awesome — and wanted it, and for God to do it in [my] life. They were role models in NT living.*[190]

Faith for God's supply without any appeal for funds was a very obvious demonstration of God's faithfulness to WEC in this era. The purchase of Bulstrode, extensions at the Australian Missionary Training College, development of Kilcreggan Conference Centre, provision of WEC presses in Britain, USA, Brazil, Colombia and Australia, a Brazilian counselling centre and Bible School, visas for missionaries, finances for travel, were all evidences of God at work. As well there were stories of God's intervention in the lives of missionaries compiled by Len Moules in 1963 and Robert Mackey in 1973.

Patrick Johnstone has commented, 'There were challenges for Robert. His health was seriously impaired after 1980, and by his last year Alastair, and to a lesser extent, we were making up for his inabilities.'[191] In a tribute to the Mackeys, Alastair Kennedy wrote,

*His appetite for office did not grow with time ... As leader Robert never shirked the difficult challenges ... Robert found strength for responsibility in prayer ... In our strident, conceited world, the Mackeys' brand of leadership is scarcely understood, far less admired. But no one who has seen Christ ministering through their gentleness and care for others, can doubt that many lives have been enriched through these patient servants of His.*[192]

The proposal of Drs Dieter and Renate Kuhl as future International Secretaries was a godly bequest of the Mackeys. Nonetheless WEC was not just a story of conferences and leaders, for God was working through the lives of people who had never expected that they would be used to accomplish surprising things.

## The SOON story

Radio Worldwide, medical institutions, primary schools, Bible schools, youth work and prayer networks all had their stories of guidance, financial supply and provision of personnel. The development of *Bientôt, SOON* and what became known as Gospel Literature Worldwide were thrilling records of vision, patience and mass-media sowing of the gospel.

In December 1959 Fred and Lois Chapman, missionaries in Ivory Coast, felt challenged to produce a free gospel newssheet in French for the newly literate. It took years for their colleagues to give them permission to go ahead, but finally they succeeded and commenced direct mailing of *Bientôt* with the help of Christians in Europe who would personally send the sheets, pay for postage and pray for the recipients.[193] Subsequently *SOON*, an English version, was produced by John Lewis and then a Portuguese edition *CEDO* by Leslie Brierley. Bases were developed to handle the administration and coordinate follow-up.

The work continued to grow and for several years there was a successful South East Asian edition. 'Even today, with 750,000 copies [of *SOON*] printed per issue, a single broadsheet can often be read by as many as twenty people.'[194] Millions of lives around the world have been touched, like Josiah of Zimbabwe who wrote,

*After receiving a copy of SOON, I came to notice that I had sinned against God. I realised I needed a change of nature. From that day my life started to rebuild ... I know that God is there and he has forgiven me and he is now heading my life.* [195]

Compiling, financing and organising these ventures involved remarkable faith steps for properties, regular printing and mailing costs and keeping a series of teams efficiently working together. Many different individuals and organisations have combined to make this possible. Significantly Christian Publicity Organisation

(CPO) in the UK has printed millions of the broadsheets at very economical rates. In 1996 a *SOON* evangelistic website was launched and has attracted thousands of hits daily.[196] Fred and Lois Chapman's vision for 'literature, easily available, culturally relevant and evangelistic' has born abundant fruit in the lives of millions.[197]

## Radio Worldwide

Another media ministry, Radio Worldwide, was born in the heart of Phil Booth, who had served with Christian Literature Crusade for seventeen years and became well-known for his devotional ministry through preaching and writing. He became aware that there was a need to provide programmes of a special evangelistic nature for the many international Christian radio stations that were in operation, and also for government and commercial stations looking for creative programmes.

Encouragement was received from a well-known authority in radio who believed WEC's worldwide network could help with the provision of suitable resources for such a project.[198] The administrative and residential base started in southern England and eventually moved to the Leeds area, where a suitable facility was obtained and remodelled. From the beginning lives were impacted worldwide through innovative programming from Radio Worldwide's studios.[199]

One of the integral components of the ministry was the training unit which provided specialist courses in radio to international students both in the UK and many countries around the world. The provision of various properties is a chronicle of God at work in giving finance and people power to help. As Dick and Flora Davies, previous leaders of Radio Worldwide, have said, 'We recognise the need for Radio Worldwide to move forward with an open mind, ready for God to reveal his ongoing purposes.'[200]

Training has become the core focus of several Radio Worldwide staff, who now travel extensively to equip people in skills necessary for programming and running local radio stations. Radio Worldwide sees itself as a partner in media with other like-minded organisations.[201]

## Reflections

In this period there was significant evidence that WEC was not dependent on Studd or Grubb for life and continued existence. New leaders, new initiatives, the ability to handle potentially explosive issues, increasing organizational structures, a widening network of new fields and international centres were all undertaken without the mission stumbling or moving into decline. WEC had a life of its own.

### The faith principle

WEC's faith principle continued to be demonstrated in practice in many ways through purchase of buildings, provision for large ministries and the general running costs of mission branches and workers. The manner of operation was commended by some — Godfrey Osei-Mensah, Executive Secretary of the Lausanne Committee, was amazed that in all Intercon 1978 discussions there was no mention of finance — and yet this was disparaged by others who felt the mission's planning without budgeting was irresponsible. Alastair Kennedy at the same time felt the way finance was taught to the WEC-related churches did not give the correct perspective, especially when it came to their desire to send out missionaries. 'We have to handle finance differently from the church.'[202] The churches needed to be taught stewardship and corporate responsibility.

### Alastair and Helen Kennedy

Alastair and Helen Kennedy played a crucial role. From years of service in Senegal trying to get a church started at Diembering, followed by a move to university work in Abidjan, Côte d'Ivoire, then to a new role in the International Office as deputies to Robert Mackey, and finally in their strategic position as Regional Directors for Africa, they were respected and appreciated. Alastair had brilliant French, excellent insights on how the church could function in a non-Christian community, and a gentle godly manner coupled with a twinkle in his eye. Jean Barnicoat states 'Alastair had a great under-standing of West African fields.'[203] His 1992 booklet on *Ecclesiology* was relevant, practical and deeply insightful. In many conferences his and Helen's contributions were appreciated and timely. They were a team who expressed lucidity, wisdom, stability and balance into countless situations in Africa and around the world. Patrick Johnstone wrote that Alastair was a man of God ... with his humility, self-effacing ministry, quiet dignity and his consideration of others.

### Detmar Scheunemann
Detmar Scheunemann was known within worldwide WEC, but also in Germany and Indonesia, for his spirituality and wisdom. His involvement in the Indonesian revival gave him authority. His harmonious relationships with Asians made him an illustration that internationalisation could work well. He preached with passion and conviction. During the International Leadership ministries of the Moules and Mackeys, his involvement at WEC business conferences was appreciated and respected.

### Handling the topic of spiritual gifts
The decision on how to handle Spiritual Gifts which was arrived at over three international conferences in 1961, 1969 and 1978, was critical for WEC's stability. Klaus Fiedler has commented, 'Some missions, for example WEC, consciously attempted to straddle the charismatic divide.'[204] The final statement in 1978 was a remarkable document at an opportune time, for the issue had the potential to cause unhappy division. Robert Mackey persisted until a deeply satisfying conclusion was reached.

### The choice of Patrick and Jill Johnstone
The decision to choose Patrick and Jill Johnstone to succeed Leslie Brierley released WEC into a new stage of outward expansion. The role of the International Research Office continued to feed into the WEC consciousness the areas of need and potential opportunities for involvement. This became very apparent in the 1984 International Leaders' Conference.[205]

### Creative Access Nations
This period in WEC's history (1965-78) was not known for the start of many long-term new fields. Yet it was a time for experimenting with entry into countries that were not normally tackled because of

their difficulty. By initiating new work and with their burden for the wider Middle East scene and South-East Asia, Len Moules and Robert Mackey set the stage for the later strong developments into what became known as Creative Access Nations (CANs).[206]

### Appointment of Regional Directors
The Role of Regional Director appears on the scene in this period and became one of the significant factors in WEC to strengthen leadership and give cohesion to the fields in a way that was practical without adding a heavy administrative structure. Renate Kuhl expressed that this was a most significant watershed in WEC's development.[207]

### Mass media developments
The arrival of the mass media departments, SOON Ministries and Radio Worldwide, were creative and bold initiatives that impacted millions through literature, radio and later the internet.

### Role of the United Kingdom sending base
The United Kingdom was a fortuitous base of operations as it provided founders and leaders of calibre. Their leaders seemed to wield a noteworthy amount of influence at early conferences and in international affairs. WEC UK had also spawned dynamic ministries and a strong supportive community which could provide a steady band of workers and committed and articulate prayer teams. But the very success of WEC UK seemed to have a challenging, example-setting but restrictive effect on the other sending bases. Some sending bases seem potentially capable of showing more radical initiatives. As new sending bases start to show exciting development and rapid numerical growth, creative Korean and Brazilian ideas, for example, may soon influence the whole mission.

### Spiritual basis
A spiritual underpinning in all that was done through the membership and leadership of WEC continued. People who depended on God to supply all their daily needs, and to confirm every step they were to take, and who had to review their leadership

every three years, needed to maintain a close relationship with God. Norman Grubb's books, and the clear expositions given by diverse WEC speakers, helped members and a wider supportive community to value spirituality and the 'Christ in us' emphasis. As Grubb said, 'Every battle of life is fought and won within ourselves, not without. Gain the inner spiritual victory and the outer follows as sure as the day the night.'[208]

In addition to the personal spiritual development that was emphasised, there was a corporate dependence on God. Len Moules said,

*In WEC business meetings we bathe the agenda in prayer. When discussions terminate in a 'lock-up', we force no issue, but drop the matter for prayer and later take it up again. We always move nearer on each occasion. Eventually the one mind is attained. It may not be within the compass of the conference, a postponement to the next gathering has occasionally been essential, but unanimity is usually attained.*[209]

This way of handling business remains a valuable example for future Christian workers as they grapple with issues arising in the real world.

### Prayer networks

In addition to the people who adopted individual workers as 'their missionary', WEC had by the 1980s developed networks of hundreds of prayer partners around the world, meeting weekly or monthly for specific prayer for missionaries or praying daily as individuals. This was the engine that kept WEC running, predominantly in Australia, New Zealand, the UK and Germany.[210] These people were fully committed to obtaining information and maintaining contact about situations worldwide, making sacrificial time available and warmly welcoming into their homes others with a like mind or those overseas and sending base workers who were able to visit. Often these people were more in touch than the mission office about specific people or situations. They were passionate, like the lady in UK who indicated she had only missed one or two prayer meetings in 36 years![211] Tom Scotland mentioned Daphne Flynn from Wollongong in Australia. She led a team of women who prayed for WEC members in crisis situations, handled a SOON dispatch and prayer group, helped the Scotlands in practical ways as they set up the WEC base in Perth, and involved her church in her outreach ministry.[212] Without this core of praying friends, many struggles — permission and finance to enter countries, learning languages and cultures, overcoming spiritual opposition and seeing the birth of the church — could not have been easily faced. As workers retired from the fields, in many cases they were delighted to join this prayer force and give personal expert input and assistance.[213] WEC public meetings, magazines, books and prayer news networks were all significant parts of the information flow. The prayer backing of the mission was seen and remains crucial to its success.[214]

## Community living
Bases and ministry centres on fields and sending bases often became communities of the participating workers. People lived on site and shared the workload. There was a timetable of Bible study and prayer, meals, work and free time. All shared in common duties. As has been seen in the Israeli *kibbutz* or *moshav* settlements there were economic benefits to all, more were able to participate in the common objectives, and encouragement and comradeship became the norm. Many WECers look back with affection to great experiences in spiritual dimensions, lifelong friendships made, fun and fellowship enjoyed, and the corporate opportunity to pray, trust and do God's will together in these communities.[215] This style of living continues in many of the sending bases, missionary training colleges and other educational establishments. Some nonetheless have found the experience negative. One says 'The disadvantage is not being able to make decisions alone and lack of privacy from some individuals.'[216] There are the difficult aspects of this lifestyle, such as restrictions of personal freedoms, public perceptions of being an odd group or sect, insensitivity of some leaders, and breakdowns in fellowship. As Andrew Bowker has said echoing some current perspectives,

*I think — financial considerations apart — there is little to commend community living in WEC for its own sake. It may be beneficial for a time of training, but as a long-term option I think we can generally do better with a closer involvement in the local community.*

On the other hand others have claimed that the benefits have outweighed the disadvantages. 'It forces us to resolve issues that can easily be swept under the carpet in church situations. Also working so closely together towards a common goal has led to many deep and lasting friendships.'[217]

In many ways the 1970s and early 80s marked the end of the era of the veteran WEC leaders. CT Studd had moved into the realm of ancient heroes, Norman Grubb's shadow was no longer looming when decisions were made, and slowly and significantly the old 'warrior' leaders were handing over and phasing out of the worldwide scene. Was WEC running out of steam? Were the newer leaders able to carry the mission forward? Did WEC have a dynamic role to play in the future?

# CHAPTER FIVE
## WINDS OF CHANGE (1983-1998)

The eighties and nineties were critical times of major change politically, socially, technologically and demographically: the era of Chernobyl, mobile phones, fax machines, the 'Three Tenors', Live Aid, Stephen Hawking, the Ayatollah Khomeini and a change of power in a multi-racial South Africa. The Soviet Union collapsed in 1991 and opened the whole of Eastern Europe and Central Asia to international influences. By means of 'ping pong diplomacy' in 1971 China had commenced dialogue with the United States, and the results of this were seen beyond the 1980s through increasing trade, relaxation of boundaries and openness to international influence. The developments in many of the former colonies had demonstrated that the so-called western 'powers' could not hold on to an appearance of global control and the United Nations would not be easily dominated by the few. Oil was now becoming a weighty financial and political tool also held by Middle Eastern, African and Latin countries. Yet economically the west continued to maintain a 'neo-colonial' hold on many less developed nations.

The world of missions was also facing change. Patrick Johnstone stated that by 1990 Evangelicals had reached a 9% annual increase in the non-western world against a global population growth of 1.7%.[218] Missiologist Ralph Winter explained in 1991 that new research and realistic understanding of the actual size of the church worldwide was enabling Christians to grasp the dimensions of its considerable missionary success and also the nature of the remaining task. Urban mission, people groups, the attitudes of world religions, the myth of closed countries, new ideas of ministerial training, working among ethnic minorities, and concepts of closure and countdown were issues preoccupying mission leaders.

As Christianity had gained a foothold in almost all countries, there had developed the perception that the day of missions was over and all that was needed was to develop partnerships with the local

church. Ralph Winter, Leslie Brierley, Patrick Johnstone, David
Barrett and others drew attention to the hundreds of people groups
and millions of people who still had no contact with or
understanding of the Christian gospel. Winter called the needed
group effort 'frontier mission' and aimed to clarify areas of
missionary neglect, amid semantic confusion within the worldwide
church community.

## New leaders in WEC

WEC did not originally intend that Stewart and Marie Dinnen were
to assume International Leadership after the Mackeys; for Robert
Mackey had come to the clear conclusion that Drs Dietrich (Dieter)
and Renate Kuhl were to be their successors. 'He made the dramatic
proposal that the Kuhls succeed him in 1982. Hardly anyone in WEC
outside Germany and Indonesia knew them. It took courage,
inspiration and much discussion.'[219] As husband and wife had
thought and talked over the succession, Robert asked Isabel to pray
about this for a specific period of time and then share with him what
God had said to her. When they brought up the subject again they
were greatly blessed that the names they felt God had given to both
of them simultaneously were those of the Kuhls.[220] They shared this
leading at the Coordinating Council Conference in 1982 in Germany.
Dieter and Renate said, 'We were shaken to the depths when asked
... and thought it was a joke ... We prayed that the WEC leaders in
Germany would not be able to agree to our nomination and would be
led to nominate somebody else.'[221] There were seven couples whose
names had been proposed for the position of International Secretary.
As the conference discussed the options, 'the Lord quickly brought
them to the conclusion that the couple recommended by the
Mackeys should be approached.'[222] There was a major obstacle, for
Dieter and Renate were deeply involved in the work of the
Indonesian Missionary Fellowship (IMF) in Java, where Dieter was
the vice-principal of the Indonesian Bible Institute and was on the
point of commencing a new IMF 'School of Missions.' They could
not be released until successors were found. Eventually Stewart and
Marie Dinnen were asked to take on interim leadership of WEC

initially for 15 to 18 months, but this stretched to more than three years.[223] Alastair and Helen Kennedy were requested to continue temporarily as Deputy International Secretaries.[224]

Apart from this significant decision, the Coordinating Council Conference in 1982 changed the name Worldwide Evangelization Crusade to 'WEC International' with the initials standing for 'Worldwide Evangelization for Christ.' The term 'crusade' was and is seriously offensive in the Muslim world (and is difficult to translate into German).

## Stewart and Marie Dinnen

Stewart Dinnen was to steer the mission through a period of remarkable change. Under Robert Mackey's leadership the process of advance had seemed to slow in favour of consolidation.[225] Coming from a non-Christian home, Stewart had been led to faith in Christ in his native Scotland by the witness of John Meikeljohn of the Scripture Union. Called up to the British Army Signals Corps during World War II, he was promoted to captain and gained experience in India and Malaysia. He was an accomplished pianist and seriously thought of entering music as a career, but eventually trained as a maths teacher. Norman Grubb said that Stewart's story is 'of a man who himself first went through God's mill ... and took the grinding, until Christ and the world's need of Him became his meat and drink in place of self-interest.'[226]

Stewart originally felt God calling him to serve in India but at the end of training at WEC's newly developing Missionary Training College in Glasgow, he and his new wife Marie had been redirected to join the staff team there.[227] They were convinced this was God's way for them, and so they embarked on what was to be a clearly focused ministry in Scotland, then the USA and eventually Tasmania, Australia. The development of a series of missionary training colleges which offered a hands-on and biblically centred training was due to the initial desire of Fran and Elsie Rowbotham before being taken forward by the Dinnens. Marie Dinnen explained, 'We could see the priceless advantage of a practical missionary training where the academic, though by no means disparaged, did not have more than its rightful place in a course that was spiritual and vitally practical.'[228]

As Fiedler has said, the role of Bible Colleges was originally to train people for the work of faith missions.[229] WEC's intention was missionary and today there are colleges in Australia, Brazil, New Zealand, Holland, Canada and Mexico similar to the one begun in Glasgow.[230] For eighteen years the Dinnens led the college in Tasmania, Australia, and stories of lives touched and steps of faith taken, as the college grew, are told in Stewart's autobiography *When I say move!* The long-term impact of this ministry on WEC was seen in the 2002 International Conference held at Rehe in Germany, where it was estimated that 30 Tasmania-trained WEC leaders were in attendance.[231]

As well as his teaching role in Glasgow and Tasmania, Stewart had a very fruitful and widespread ministry on the themes associated with the subject of 'Union with Christ' — the Christian is united with Christ in his death, burial, resurrection and ascension.

> *The fact of Christ's death to sin is the ground of the Christian's freedom. He paid the penalty for sin and satisfied the demand that sin made totally and completely in one act of dying. Now he lives for God. The Christian is to count it as a fact that he too has died to the demand of sin and has come alive through Christ. Hence he has no need to go on living in sin.*[232]

Greatly influenced by Norman Grubb and his own study of the Bible, Stewart was able to present profound truths in concise and memorable forms, part of his rich legacy to WEC. He was a man of action, discipline and decisive opinions. Stewart also developed a strategic ministry passing on management skills through seminars and helpful letters primarily written for leaders in WEC but also shared with many others and summarised in his book *You can learn to lead.*[233] His sharp mind and ability to explain concepts in simple terms made his time in office memorable and remarkably effective. Alastair Kennedy stated that 'Stewart had this gift of being able to make concise, succinct, telling statements.'[234]

## A New Forward Push

The International Leaders' Conference, called Intercon 1984, was a WEC watershed and similar in outcome to the significant 1961 leaders' meeting. Patrick Johnstone later said it was part of a Holy-Spirit-directed movement that year, among 28 missions, to initiate bold new advances for the gospel. Major extensions to fields and numbers of workers were envisaged. Wide-ranging and careful discussions were held on the thorny question of the status of divorcees in WEC, handling cases of moral failure, candidate training, the role of single workers, sending church interaction, education of missionary children and in-service training. Patrick Johnstone had communicated possible areas for further involvement ahead of time to all the delegates, to enable suitable discussions to be held among field members.

When the conference started, Patrick introduced the subject and then arranged for delegates to meet in regional groups and come up with their own proposals. When these were compiled it became apparent that a combined target – called the STEP program [235] – of 700-800 new workers, entry to two new countries and 44 new people groups, with a focus on 39 new cities, had been agreed on. It was a time of special guidance and unity. Stewart Dinnen expressed the mood of the delegates when he said 'the result was cataclysmic.'[236]

In addition, the conference boldly tackled contemporary issues and came up with impressive resolutions on divorce, processing applications into WEC, contextualisation, interpersonal relationships, contact with the House Church movement, church planting, cooperation with Third World missions, education of missionary children, security guidelines and in-service training.[237] Alastair Kennedy wrote,

*All who were [there] felt that they were making history, though none of us could say exactly how this would be worked out in the coming days. We felt that the Master was revealing to us part of His purpose, and we know that the purpose was linked to the vision of a redeemed multitude.*[238]

From this point on, a series of new ventures were adopted embracing expanding areas called Creative Access Nations or CAN fields. There had been times when WEC's caution and preoccupation with countries that allowed free entrance to missionaries caused the mission to hold back from embracing challenges seen as not WEC's business. Brother Andrew, well known for the ministry of Open Doors delivering Bibles and literature resources into what was then known as behind the Iron and Bamboo Curtains and later into the Muslim world, had been trained at WEC's Missionary Training College in Glasgow, Scotland. He became aware that Christians in the Soviet Bloc needed supporting and no-one was involved in this kind of work. 'Much as I loved WEC and its training college, it had never once sent a man behind the Iron Curtain.'[239]

Not until the early 1980s did it become obvious that God was speaking to WEC through several people including Roy Spraggett, former missionary in Vietnam and member of Scottish WEC. Various individuals had contacted Roy with an interest in outreach to Central Asia, which was at that time dominated by the Soviet Union.[240] Roy started doing research and finding out more about the countries and other mission groups interested in them. The 1984 conference took the lid off WEC's cautious approach and opened the door to many new CAN ministries. Within a year of the conference new workers were on their way to restricted countries in Asia. Remarkably God had prepared a team for action prior to the collapse of the Soviet Union, and this dovetailed with CT Studd's long-term vision for a ministry which he had originally called the Heart of Asia Mission.

Following on from the 1984 international conference and its many strategic decisions, helpful guidelines were soon put into place with flexible criteria regarding the acceptance of new workers, in-service training of missionaries in ecclesiology, the development of a system for funding International Office basic expenses and the proposal of a voluntary structure of supplementing emergency financial needs for field workers. A review by Patrick Johnstone of the STEP program, which had been launched at Intercon 1984, showed noteworthy progress, and in some cases an expanded list of goals had been attached to the 1984 targets. The mission was dealing with increasingly complex issues and needed a thinker who had the experience and gifts to provide the kind of leadership required.

## A new hand on the helm

Surgeon, theologian, missiologist, writer and teacher, Dietrich (Dieter) Kuhl's leadership was crucial to WEC at a time when numbers were increasing and difficult subjects required careful thought and courageous handling. He showed breadth and depth. He was a scholar, administrator and interpreter of the vast issues of change that were affecting the world and impacting WEC. His wife Renate, also a doctor, was an enthusiast for God and missions.

Their stories were explained in Dieter's account 'Strange twists on a desert road.' God had clearly and unexpectedly called him to become a missionary doctor when he was still at school. 'During my second year at university I came to know Jesus as my personal Saviour and Lord.'[241] Eventually he and Renate moved towards the belief that they were to serve with WEC in Indonesia. Initially they had expected to do front-line medical work in South Sumatra but due to a government restriction when they arrived in 1972, it became obvious that God wanted them to be involved in the Indonesian Bible Institute (IBI) in Java, training rural pastors in practical subjects. Eventually Dieter became Vice-Principal of the IBI and along with Renate served in Indonesia for fourteen years. They loved this ministry, even intending to take out Indonesian citizenship so they could stay permanently. They were very reluctant to leave when invited by WEC to become International Directors.

Patrick Johnstone, who worked very closely with Dieter for quite a time as Deputy International Director, has written

> *[It was] his dedication, courage, relaxed relational manner ... which actually made the changes from 1984+ to work. He also made our present internationalisation happen ... He probably took consultative decision making to its absolute limit, but he certainly made everyone feel involved.* [242]

During his time in the International Office Dieter Kuhl completed a Master's degree in missiology in 1996 writing a dissertation on the subject of internationalisation. When coming into the role of International Secretary he shared his conviction that a greater influx of Third World missionaries would strengthen WEC. His thoughtful and practical emphases were significant factors in helping WEC integrate many different nationalities and move from approximately 70 non-western members in 1985 to 249 in 1998.[243] In his teaching role in the mission, Dieter emphasised that humility and openness were essential for good relationships. He stressed that there was a need to choose the right time and have the right mind-set if confrontation was necessary. Affirmation was important in relating to Asians first of all, and faith, patience and prayer were all fundamental ingredients in wise interaction. In addition he showed there was a need to pay the price to achieve good outcomes, a willingness to acknowledge attitudes of superiority where that was a national attribute and over all a passion for personal and corporate holiness.[244]

Similarly Dieter took time to offer an administrative framework for workers who were involved in ministry in CAN countries. For a mission like WEC the challenge was how to make its rules, which were originally planned for Free Access Nations where members held visas openly stating they were Christian workers, apply to those in restricted situations where they could only serve through business, agricultural, educational, medical or NGO channels. This subject was reviewed at the International Leaders' Conference in 1990 and the Coordinating Council Conference in 1992, and resulted in guidelines being drawn up to help those who were often part of what became known as Trans-National Fields. Difficulties in obtaining long-term visas with the resulting insecurity led to a focus being placed by a WEC team or 'field' on the people group involved rather than always a single country. If workers were forced to move from a country, they sought to work with people of the same ethnic and language group in an adjoining country. In the initial stages of moving into this kind of insecure ministry, a field could be composed of members who were living and working in different culturally-related adjoining countries until each local team of workers was strong enough to be an independent group. This adjustment afforded special flexibility, that enabled WEC workers to adapt more easily to political uncertainties and gave birth to strong new fields. By 2008 there were over 200 in CAN situations out of a total of 1141 cross-cultural workers.

Dieter was in the office of International Secretary for twelve years, the longest since Norman Grubb. His role in WEC was to steer the mission through the expansion and upheaval which arose both from the historic 1984 Intercon, and from completely unexpected events.

## Spiritual renewal and resourcefulness

When assessing the hectic business and educational agendas of each conference, whether on the international scene or a field or sending base, it is not right to overlook the spiritual environment. A pattern had been developed and strongly emphasised that Bible ministry and prayer were to have primary space. Holiness was one of WEC's guiding principles but it was also to be a way of life in all its activities. Dieter Kuhl gave a memorable address at Intercon 1990 in which he said that he believed a continued emphasis on holiness was important in dealing with the significant problems he had encountered on many fields. Outside devotional speakers were freely invited, but in most cases the delegates themselves were asked to take the stage and share from their hearts what God was saying.[245] This formed a powerful illustration of the spiritual resources within the WEC fellowship and showed a strong commitment to the founding principles.

However what was happening in the conferences was only the curtain raiser for the main events that were occuring around the world. A remarkable event was taking place in Spain that was to have worldwide implications.

## A remarkable encounter with far-reaching results

Europe has been a continent in recent years inured to the gospel, having a history of 'Christianity' that was often at odds with the kind of life taught and demonstrated by Jesus Christ. Spain was no different and WEC workers found it difficult to see much headway there. An incident in 1986 occurred which was to have far-reaching consequences for church planting and drug rehabilitation, in Europe and in other parts of the world. Faced with a court appearance in Madrid and wanting to get off drugs, a young addict named Raul asked Australian WECer Lindsay McKenzie to help him. Lindsay hesitantly invited Raul to move into his apartment. This meant caring for Raul around the clock and being his 24-hour shadow. Amazingly it worked and not only did Raul break free from drugs, but also came to faith in Christ and enthusiastically suggested they invite others into the apartment.[246]

For some time Lindsay, along with colleagues Elliott and Mary Tepper and field leader Billy Glover, had been praying for a way to reach people on the streets in Madrid. The individuals God seemed to be pointing them towards were drug addicts, but how could they cope with them? In addition to this, the people they were meeting were those that drug centres were finding too difficult to handle. Lindsay's experience with Raul was the key. As time went by a pattern emerged: drug addicts needed centres where there were people resident who had already been delivered and converted to faith in Christ; these would then partner the newcomers and stay with them until they in turn became committed disciples. Work programmes were developed, enabling the ministry to become almost self-sufficient.

The number of those entering Lindsay's apartment embarrassed the neighbours and meant he had to move to a bigger place. Eventually centres for both men and women were opened. Of course there were many disappointments. There were those who freely chose to leave because they could not take the restrictions and style of the centres. There were also many who had contracted AIDS as an outcome of their previous way of life and, when at their most fruitful, key leaders like Raul died. Nevertheless Elliott Tepper, who became the overall leader of what became known as Betel, states that the percentages of those who recovered from drugs through the centres were exceptionally high.[247]

Through the whole process a church came into being in Madrid, and the liberated drug addicts became members and leaders, and eventually were able to pioneer further centres. First of all these were in Spain, then in Portugal, Ceuta (North Africa), France, Germany, Italy, Greece, Mexico, England, the USA, Russia, Czech Republic, Bulgaria, Australia, India, and Argentina. Today Betel keeps growing, with embryonic churches as a definite outcome. WEC workers continue to be involved, as do some from other Christian groups, but the strength of the structure is that the rescued people have become the catalysts for leading the work and starting new projects. Yet it was not just through Betel that God was at work.

## Progress worldwide

As has been stated previously, WEC began work in many countries in the pre- and immediate post-war years. Often the work was difficult and the people unresponsive. The true picture of fruitfulness in many countries was only seen in the 1990s, when the churches had become strong and the expatriate contribution was greatly reduced. In the country of Burkina Faso some former workers wrote, 'We visited Kodjo, where we used to go faithfully for services and reading classes but did not see much fruit. Now there is a church of 47 baptised believers and an attendance of 150 plus. Guess it was worth it after all.'[248] From a start in 1939, God used WEC and Qua Iboe Fellowship workers in an effort that now touches six ethnic groups and through the Eglise Protestante Evangelique, reaches out to several others.[249] Brian Woodford has expressed that the supreme delight of being a church planter among the Birifor people in Burkina Faso is in seeing the church today standing on its own feet with its own leadership, outreach and vision.[250]

Churches in Liberia, Ivory Coast, Gambia, Ghana, Guinea-Bissau, Senegal and the Congo also came into positions of independence and maturity. The field in Liberia started in January 1938 under the name Liberia Inland Mission. A team of eight moved inland and commenced work in three centres.[251] In spite of war conditions and uncertain communications with home (Canada and UK), many new workers joined them and developed the centres. The focus was on evangelism among the Mano, Gio and Bassa tribes, leading to discipling, Bible training for potential leaders, translating Scripture and establishing of the church. God touched many lives giving release from sin and sickness, and setting people free from occultic bondages; schools and medical centres were established; leadership was officially transferred to Liberians in 1970, and by 1988 the church had grown to over twelve thousand believers.[252]

In 1940 Leslie and Edna Seamans started the WEC ministry in central and northern Ghana, previously called Gold Coast. They were welcomed warmly by the officials and before long established their first base at Tuna. Soon they were joined by Don Theobald, and together they moved out to evangelise villages in the Gonja and Wala areas. They received friendly responses from the animistic people and discovered many who wanted to follow God's way.

> *When the chiefs tell us that they only want One Master (teaching) in Gonja district and they believe that we are telling them the true way and they will not allow anybody else to come in with any other doctrine, then how great is our responsibility to see they get adequate teaching that will lead them to the feet of the One Master who alone is worthy.*[253]

Over the years the work grew, many new workers joined, and other centres went ahead. A large leprosarium, clinics and Bible schools were founded.[254] The Evangelical Church of Ghana (ECG) was birthed and leadership transferred to local leaders. Years later in 1993 God sent a Brazilian couple, Ronaldo and Rossana Lidorio, to Ghana with a burden to continue the church planting outreach to the Konkomba tribe. God gave them remarkable insights into cultural links with the people and as a result many turned to faith in Christ. Today the ECG has over 6,000 members, 130 congregations, 60 pastors and a small team of missionaries.[255]

Ivory Coast had been pioneered by Jack Staniford and Fred Chapman in 1934. Through the years God had worked in the mainly animistic central section of the country.[256] John and Grace Rieder were involved in the hard effort of consistent evangelism. Travel over a significant area had resulted in opportunities to preach and share the gospel, and see many people becoming Christians. They were also part of one translation project which brought the Bible to the Gourou people in 1977.[257] In 1996 somewhere around 60 pastors were ministering to 235 congregations and a total constituency of over 20,000 believers.[258]

In Colombia, by 1996 there were '220 congregations with 300 national workers and 30,000 members.' After the horrific persecution and traumas of the early days, the church had found a spiritual momentum and abundant fruit.[259]

The churches planted by WEC in three northern provinces of Thailand celebrated fifty years of life on 2 May 1998 and 'fifteen hundred lovers of Jesus' were present. 'When Wilfred Overgaard and his tiny team broke into this area in 1948 there was not one known Christian.'[260] More than 62 churches have been developed among the Thai and Karen, and new centres for outreach have been established in Bangkok to reach the middle-class professionals.[261] A recent letter tells of regular baptisms, newly appointed church committees, new church planting ventures, and the challenges of many needing follow-up and discipleship.[262]

## A cataract of conferences

International consultations continued over these years, with Coordinating Council (CC) conferences every two years and Intercons every six. Each played their part in the overall development and strengthening of WEC.

A well-structured review of the STEP program took place in 1988. Patrick Johnstone's careful presentation highlighted the way the whole mission was grasping the 1984 challenges, target areas were being occupied, research was being treated seriously and recruitment numbers continued to inch upwards.[263] Evidence of Dieter Kuhl's wide interests and skilful attention to detail lay in the scope of subjects that were handled at that time – establishing new sending bases in Hong Kong, Singapore and Korea, making interna-tionalisation work, developing trans-national fields, composing guidelines for property investment and establishing an internal

International Fellowship Fund to provide help for low supported workers. This latter fund was a response from WEC serving members to make voluntary contributions to help colleagues who needed specific financial help. Regular reports detail a continuing record of tens of thousands of pounds donated and widely appreciated.

In 1990 a conference of the International Leaders' Council (Intercon) was held in Scotland. This represented a meeting of WEC's highest executive body, comprising all leaders of fields and sending bases and those appointed to specialist roles. These conferences now contained educational sessions for leadership development. This one included sessions by Dr Bruce Thompson of YWAM, and by Stewart Dinnen on 'Pastoral Care' and 'The Leader and his Team.' Intercon 1990's slogan was 'Advancing Together Beyond the Bridgeheads', as there had been remarkable areas of unity and success since the 1984 project launch which included 763 new recruits, 59 people groups entered, 38 cities in which WEC workers were newly located and a good measure of cooperation with other agencies. 120 new goals were adopted. However, in contrast with these glowing achievements, the number of members who had resigned was higher than expected and there was a determination to adopt better member care strategies.

The conference reflected the changes which were happening worldwide and the need for missions to review their practices. Intercon 1990 was a conference which was a work-in-progress rather than a major initiator of new directions. For the delegates the key areas were the opportunity to get an overview of WEC, the daily devotional sessions and 'the call to prayerfulness and holiness.'

At the 1992 CC conference at the WEC training centre in Australia, administrative procedures in the election of international and field leaders were firmed up. There was a review of financial policies, pastoral care of missionaries, development of leadership training, structure of immigrant teams within WEC, acceptance of national workers for work in their own country, and the orientation and training process. Other issues included the start of work in Bulgaria and the South-West Balkans, and an analysis of worldwide trends, which led Dieter to state,

*Our organisational flexibility and grass-roots decision-making, together with openness to all the gifts of the Spirit, are important strengths ... We need to recognise the possibility of being over-stretched; moving into many new areas has made it difficult to find adequate leadership. Our individualism sometimes threatens our 'flowing together' in cooperation. Our aim for unanimity in decision-making sometimes hinders the introduction of change.*[264]

Two years later the CC again met in Fort Washington, Pennsylvania. While wrestling with possible new thrusts for WEC, the conference also was preoccupied with subjects of major concern to sending bases and international administration. Development of new missionary training colleges in Asia, Canada and New Zealand was affirmed.[265] Issues of crisis management, spiritual warfare, setting up leadership training seminars, and the future of sending bases in Korea, Taiwan and Hong Kong were among the matters discussed.

Intercon 1996 was held in Rehe Germany demonstrating the independence of international WEC from its UK roots. The theme for the conference was: 'Sharpening our vision; strengthening our teams; reaffirming our Core Values.' From the introductory message on 'Worship' by Dieter Kuhl and through the individuals who gave the daily ministry messages, the conference highlighted a strong message of devotion to Jesus. A significant change was the alteration of the leadership title 'secretary' to 'director', eg. International Director instead of International Secretary. It was stressed that this was not to reflect any change in 'servant leadership' roles but purely to make the titles more recognisable in modern society. Within WEC, servant leadership meant that this office was by election every three years, accountable to the team and with appropriate authority. However the leader was not regarded as being a cut above the others on their field, but one who showed a humble commitment to practical responsibilities and who walked in step with their team. Against the backdrop of the 'Toronto Blessing movement' the 1978 statement on Spiritual Gifts was reaffirmed. The guidelines drawn up on acceptance into WEC of divorcees and their permitted remarriage were revised to include those who had been divorced as Christians because of their partner's adultery or who had been permanently deserted by an unconverted partner because of their faith in Christ.

A new advance project called *Reaching the Unevangelised Now (RUN)*, was launched in 1996 targeting the ten major blocs with the fewest committed Christians, cities with large numbers of non-Christian peoples, and also unevangelised ethnic groups. A survey within the conference suggested that to attain the personnel required for the new thrust would mean 1639 new workers and would lead to most sending bases recruiting double their present numbers of workers. Additional to this was a stirring challenge about the needs of children abused and ignored in so many countries. This came from well-known author Phyllis Kilbourn, an experienced Liberia field worker from the USA, with expertise in Christian education and in active touch with the needs of children around the world. As a result WEC agreed to launch Rainbows of Hope, a new ministry to the world's underprivileged children.[266]

One of the key issues at the conference was the formulation of and agreement on a list of WEC's Core Values, to give members a summary of WEC heart concerns which would be useful for new workers and interested people.[267] Significant pre-conference discussion and enthusiastic debate produced a unified declaration.[268] Included was a commitment 'to demonstrate the compassion of Christ to a needy world' which arose from those who served in holistic ministries, and a 'conviction that the gospel is for the whole person.' Subsequently there was a strong reaction to this statement from some fields, and its addition to the WEC Objectives was not incorporated into the next edition of *Principles & Practice*. The strength of opposition came from a conviction that for WEC the evangelistic mandate overshadowed holistic ministry.[269]

Prayer was a special emphasis with an on-site prayer team in residence, longer periods of prayer and fasting, regular stoppages in the programme for specific intercession, and the circulation throughout WEC worldwide of a daily prayer book with emailed updates from the conference. The 158 delegates represented many fields and nationalities, and were responsible to pay for their own travel and accommodation. Fascinatingly additional gifts had been sent to the International Office in excess of UK£20,000 to cover any shortfall. Most of these gifts had come voluntarily from WEC members who wanted to share in the costs of those who had to attend.

Although weighty matters were occupying international leaders during these conferences, yet hard work was continuing in the fields where WEC missionaries were getting to know cultures, learn languages, cope with religious opposition and live through the day-by-day uncertainties of life in cross-cultural situations.

## Life out of the public eye

Many workers followed their vocations with devotion and persistence, even though they lived and worked well out of the public eye. The following are a small sample.

Among the Karen hill people in Thailand, God worked miracles where spirit powers had ruled for many years. Maw Dta, a Christian Karen, had moved from Burma with his backslidden wife and waited forty years for another Christian to join him and help to reach his family, his village and the area around. God sent two young women, American Nancy Ashcraft and Mary Lewin from Britain, to serve in extreme conditions in a totally strange culture and to endure, until spirit powers were broken, hearts were opened and the church was born. When she saw the fruit in lives changed by the gospel, and Karen elders taking responsibility in their village and others, Nancy Ashcraft marvelled,

> We were a church of miracles. But we were also a church of mistakes. We had made so many mistakes and would doubtless make many more in the days and years to follow. But the meaning of salvation is that God has stepped into history, into flesh and blood, into our situation of sin and mistakes.[270]

Joan Eley was a most unlikely missionary candidate. Called a 'jillaroo' (farm-girl) back home in her native Australia, she was an experienced but not well-educated recruit from outback Queensland. When God called her to train at Bible College she willingly gave up a life she loved. Called to Venezuela, she embraced the harsh life in a remote desert region to plant several churches. Her story is full of remarkable events such as the time when, riding home alone on her motorbike, evil men planned to attack but were restrained when they saw a 'figure dressed in white' riding pillion behind her. The story came back to Joan from villagers, and to her it could only have been an angel.[271] Since 1959 she has continued in Venezuela, but has moved into a deliverance ministry through meetings held in a wide circle of churches.[272]

A story that cannot be easily told for security reasons describes the way one CAN team came into being. Called to reach what was one of the most restricted parts of the world, two New Zealanders pushed against the doors and found a way to get through the windows. Opportunities to teach English, run businesses and set up effective NGOs have all provided ways for 'tentmakers' to have valuable contributions to the countries involved. A 'CAN Consultancy' has been set up to give technical advice to team members. As a matter of policy all of the members have spent initial time learning language and culture, to give them an effective edge in their Christian vocation. A steady stream of workers joined in the 1980s and 1990s and eventually the field divided into five strong sections, with remarkable fruit in growing churches and changed lives. In spite of restrictions, dangers and not knowing how long team members might be able to stay in the area, this has become the largest concentration of workers with WEC. Normal WEC team structures have been followed, but ways of operating have had to be creatively designed to cope with local conditions. Over these years a similar process to this was taking place in many other parts of the world with varying degrees of success.

## Expansion among the sending bases

Sending bases were also expanding worldwide as Christians from newly emerging churches were waking to the world of missions. Leslie Brierley's slogan 'The whole church taking the whole gospel to the whole world' was bearing fruit. By 1993 forty-seven Brazilians were serving God in places like Portugal, Guinea-Bissau, Senegal,

Italy, South Africa and Cambodia. God had used Bob Harvey and Leslie Brierley to encourage the Brazilian mission movement into action. This produced a flow of enthusiastic Brazilians into aggressive evangelism. A new sending base was emerging in Korea under the leadership of ByungKook and BoIn Yoo, who had together served ten years in Gambia with WEC. By the end of 1993, 14 South Koreans had joined WEC. There was a growing interest in their country to give back to the Lord in service something of what the early missionary pioneers had sacrificed when they brought the gospel to Korea. In a survey conducted in 2006, Steve Sang-Cheol Moon estimated that 14,905 Koreans were serving with 174 mission agencies in 168 countries. Three agencies, of which WEC was one, were evaluated by the respondents in the survey as 'the most excellent and respected international mission agencies.'[273] As with all non-English speakers, all Koreans joining WEC were required to learn English and they were also expected to attend a candidate orientation course in another country. In spite of this, the excellent people skills, tireless energies and enthusiastic recruitment strategies used by the Yoos resulted in a steady stream of highly qualified Koreans from different denominations into WEC.

## Reassess and reorganize

For its 1998 meeting the CC chose to meet at a recently acquired Betel property *Betania* at Ciudad Real in Spain. Seminars tackled the subjects 'Is WEC losing its cutting edge?', 'The internationalisation of WEC', 'Making the most of our pioneers' and 'The teachings of Norman Grubb.' These were complemented by a thought-provoking paper by Traugott Böker on the theme 'What will happen to those who have never heard the gospel?' presenting the historical conservative view against suggestions being promoted by some prominent evangelicals. Patrick Johnstone gave an assessment of the 547 *RUN* goals adopted in 1996; 53 had been completed, others had been abandoned or adjusted, 357 were unchanged and 132 new ones had been added. However recruitment for the new goals and current needs had not come up to standard: half of the sending bases had not embraced any target figures, with the result that work had slowed down in several places.

Major attention was given to administrative details about information technology, strategies for reaching nomads, cultural implications of financial policies, English competency for non-English applicants, training and recruitment. A detailed revision of *Principles and Practice* had been underway for four years and time was taken during the conference to finalise this. As their retirement from International Leadership was imminent, Dieter and Renate Kuhl were given a well-deserved farewell by the conference delegates on behalf of wider WEC. Their ministry had been timely and exceptional in the way they had led and inspired the mission.

## Crucial factors that catalysed WEC during this period

### The STEP program for advance
The structure of Intercon 1984 was exceptional in the way that Patrick Johnstone's vision and experience, coupled with Stewart Dinnen's gifts and the unified assessment of specific goals, meshed with remarkable timing. There was a combined sense in the mission that God was pushing it forward to significant new ventures.

### Values
The delineation and affirmation of WEC's Core Values was an important step that took place at Intercon 1996. The Report stated 'We ... want to express clearly both to ourselves and our constituency what it is that makes us WEC.' The effort to clarify the current composition of the Core Values exercised many people in the lead-up to the conference.[274] Acceptance at that time and beyond showed that rank and file membership had a good understanding of the Core Values and gave strong support to the key principles.

### The development of Betel
Betel became a force for reaching the drug and alcohol world, but was also guided to embrace a strategy which has resulted in a unique church planting movement in many countries. Its commencement was more than just the start of a specific ministry, but was a

powerful illustration that a social ministry did not need to be in competition with church planting but could partner with it.

## Personalities who contributed to WEC's survival

Patrick Johnstone's arrival and contribution served as a catalyst for action and vision. Similarly Stewart Dinnen's availability and gifted personality, at the crucial stage when the Kuhls were not ready to move into office, were critical in implementing the major changes proposed in 1984.

Dieter Kuhl possessed the kinds of gifts WEC needed in those vital 12 years while he was in the International Office (IO). Pauline Nicholas said, 'Dieter saw the overall needs and began to delegate. It was a time of tremendous change in WEC. Mission grew, IO grew and Dieter saw it and delegated appropriately.'[275]

Bob Harvey and ByungKook Yoo were timely tools for a major move of Brazilians and South Koreans into WEC missionary service. Their personalities and energies made them eminently suitable to win the confidence of leaders and pastors, and to bridge the gap for those wishing to move into missions.[276]

Illustrative of hundreds of rank and file WEC workers who have made WEC what it is, Canadian Helen Krueger spanned a long period in active field ministry (1944 to 1997) and accomplished a variety of tasks, as evangelist and church planter in Ivory Coast and Burkina Faso. Starting with a 300-mile walk from the ship in Liberia to her place of ministry in Ivory Coast, Helen served in many different towns, preaching wherever possible, pulling teeth, facing incredible physical and spiritual obstacles and seeing God protect and heal. She was able to observe the church grow from nothing to committed groups being led by their own trained pastoral leadership. Reluctant to leave the field, health difficulties finally made it mandatory. Her story is a fascinating account of what God can do through a willing servant, and was similar to what was happening on numbers of fields through 'ordinary' WEC workers.[277]

## Significant structures

### WEC colleges

WEC Missionary Training College (MTC) graduates were having an impact on fields and sending bases, as they supplied a steady stream of needed workers. Additionally, those arriving on the fields from MTCs came with knowledge of WEC's principles and worldwide work. They often provided potential leadership candidates. In this era a significant proportion of MTC graduates were joining WEC.[278]

### Geared for Growth Bible Study movement[279]

Word Worldwide was another ministry which made a profound impact in many parts of the world. Started by Marie Dinnen in Tasmania, as the result of helping a woman whose personal situation required an evangelistic Bible study, it soon mushroomed into a system whereby groups were formed around the idea of sharing the results of their daily Bible study. The *Geared for Growth* studies were written with non-Christians and new believers in mind. From its Australian beginnings Word Worldwide was embraced in different countries around the world, the studies translated into several languages, many people helped and good incentive to outreach given. By 2008 groups continued in Germany, the UK, Holland, Pakistan, Hong Kong, Slovenia and South Africa. Through Christian Focus Publications the studies in English were available worldwide.

### Useful organisation

The regular international conferences kept the mission together in its focus, and enabled all field leaders to have personal knowledge of other aspects and personalities in WEC life. For a mission that relied on unanimity in decision-making, this enhanced the worldwide process and dealt more smoothly with any areas of misunderstanding. Dieter Kuhl's transparency and hard work ensured that the structure of WEC was professionally handled and altered to cope with the changing situations facing the mission. Production of a series of useful manuals carried on a tradition commenced by Stewart Dinnen, and ensured corporate wisdom and experience would be preserved and disseminated.

Leadership Training and Development Seminars were very important in keeping leaders in touch with developments in management, pastoral care and spiritual equipment for their tasks. Thoughtful spiritual input was enhanced by the quality of theological offerings at conferences and through the writings of key leaders. Dieter Kuhl's scholarly approach encouraged others who had abilities to address theological issues in a biblical way.

## A growing central administrative structure

The development of excessive bureaucratic structures was a risk that flowed from strengthening the International Office in this period. A growing organisation and more full-time administrators had the likelihood to create superfluous procedures with extra funding requirements. More offices were acquired, correspondence tripled, further consultants and advisors were appointed, and additional visits overseas were made by the combined team. On the other hand a common comment received from Coordinating Council members was that International Office expenses were well below what they were expecting.[280]

## An attitude of continuing advance

The inability of sending bases to reach recruitment goals had the potential to hinder WEC's progress. The mission in the past remained healthy as it tackled new goals and brought in recruits to meet these and to supply existing opportunities. As could be seen from the 1996 and 1998 conferences, many of the sending bases did not set national goals, although they had been involved in the discussion which clarified the required number of new workers to achieve the RUN targets. The sense of openness to advance needed to be continually fostered to keep true to the founding charter. Essential to this was the International Research Office which had a crucial and continuing role. As Patrick Johnstone kept up to date with the production of *Operation World*, he also did specific research for WEC and made surveys of areas under consideration. Awareness of what was happening in the global scene kept WEC in touch. The initial and over-riding objective speaks strongly about the 'remaining unevangelised peoples' which denotes a finishable task, and also its mention of 'as quickly as possible' speaks to the necessity to remain alert to the briefness of time. Consolidation is valuable but could not become the guiding principle.

## Making multi-cultural teams effective
In a mission with over 40 nationalities, internationalisation remained a crucial area of concern and called for vigilance and discipline. Dieter Kuhl's thesis (1996) and the production of helpful manuals needed to be taken seriously. A multi-cultural organisation which has a public face in a multi-cultural world must work together in an obviously interconnected manner.[281]

## Handover to Evan and Jenny Davies
One of the surprising features of the development of WEC was that the mission did not have many adult children of former missionaries joining as members. This was increasing but not in significant numbers. Interestingly, when looking for successors as International Directors, the Coordinating Council unanimously nominated my wife and me to be presented to the Leaders' Council for election. My parents were Ivor and Rose Davies, who had been numbers ten and nine in the 'Memorial Ten' sent out to the Congo following the death of CT Studd. Both Jenny and I were linked to a network of relatives who served with WEC. We had been serving as Deputy Directors to the Kuhls, and at the 1996 International Leaders' Conference were elected as International Directors designate to take effect from 1999.

For us, moving into International Leadership of an organisation which was addressing so many issues and contained such an army of gifted leaders and dedicated multi-national workers, was a daunting assignment.

# CHAPTER SIX
## REVIEW AND REFOCUS
## (1999-2010)

By 1999 Christianity had emerged as a worldwide phenomenon, against the background of a globalised world and a globalised church.[282] The dramatic events of 11 September 2001 seemed to drastically affect the balance of the USA on the world stage and, as a result, its subsequent invasion of Iraq and unilateral actions to counter terrorism caused large outlays in finance, personnel and respect. Russia was striving to redress the imbalances that occurred after the collapse of the Soviet Union, whereas the European Union and NATO were endeavouring to extend their membership and influence. However Jeffrey D Sachs reported that European dominance in politics and economics seemed to have been overturned by the end of the 20th century and, according to current trends, this present era will see American control replaced by that of China, India and Brazil.[283]

Worldwide events in science, education, media, sociology, trade, religion and politics were full of change, insecurity and challenge. Information technology had come into worldwide prominence and, through the invention of the microchip computers, had become the possession of millions of people, with communications systems transformed and information freely available through the internet. Environmental concerns were increasingly occupying a dominant position. Globalisation affected humankind everywhere and any activities in one part of the planet could drastically affect many other places within a short time.

For the Christian church the ramifications of globalisation incorporated human rights, economic equality, health, youth cultures, security, the environment, gender issues, contextualisation, organisational dominance, contact with a range of conflicting influences, grassroots involvement and overwhelming exposure to trends which made it more difficult to live and think Christianly.[284]

These have become the concerns of the whole church. Issues affecting the western church have traditionally dominated missiological thinking but the greater numbers now in the non-western scene mean the position is in process of reversal. As John Taylor prophesied, there would eventually be recognition among all Christians that we can no longer say 'we and they' but 'us' as the definition of world Christians.[285]

Christianity was demonstrating immense changes in shape and growth. Patrick Johnstone and Jason Mandryk stated that in 2000 the percentage of non-western Christians was 59.5%. They have also declared it is now a truly global faith – a status it had lost 12 centuries ago.[286]

David Barrett, who has kept abreast of trends and statistics since the mid-1980s and produced an annual 'Status of Global Mission' in the *International Bulletin of Missionary Research*, affirmed that by January 2008 Christians of all shades represented 33.3% of the world's population and Christians were increasing at the rate of 79,000 every 24 hours. However he claims there still remain 86% of all Hindus, Buddhist and Muslims who do not know a Christian, there are 1,192 unevangelised ethno-linguistic peoples who have never ever been targeted by Christian agencies, and the population of unevangelised peoples is estimated to be 1,787 million.[287] As a result of these statements, Christian disciples who seek to pursue Christ's commands to be witnesses of the Gospel (Acts 1:8) can be both encouraged and overwhelmed; encouraged at the remarkable success of the missionary movement, and over-whelmed at the enormity of the challenge and issues still facing the church.

The worldwide growth of evangelical and charismatic Christians has resulted in immense new missionary resources. Brazil has an evangelical populace larger than that of Europe with a rapidly expanding missionary force, and Singapore has for some time been the country with the highest proportion of missionaries to Christian population.[288] Johnstone and Mandryk affirm that South Korea has attained more than 30% of Christians among all its inhabitants, and is producing a Christian missionary total of upwards of 10,000 who are working outside of Korea, while India remains the country with the largest missionary force of over 44,000 in 440-plus agencies.[289] The way these figures were affecting WEC can be seen by contrasting the numbers of members from non-western nations with those from the western countries. By 2008, out of 50 nationalities in WEC there were 342 Koreans, 139 Brazilians, 37 South Africans, 36 Singaporeans, 21 from Hong Kong, 17 Indonesians and 16 Malaysians in comparison to 414 from the UK, 262 from the USA, 191 Australians, 154 Germans, 123 Canadians, 117 Swiss, 106 New Zealanders and 74 from the Netherlands.[290]

WEC started this period under review being confronted by worldwide concerns and internal needs, facing questions such as 'Are we respecting rightly our church planters and evangelists? Is our commitment to our faith principle only a historical and token position? Should we stress evangelism and discipling as a clear component of our compassion ministries? Are our training programmes producing the best kind of workers? How can we make newer and younger members feel more at home? How can we network more effectively with other organisations to get the work done? In what practical ways can we embrace a servant lifestyle and be passionate for spiritual progress? Is there a way to revitalise our prayer ministry? What sort of changes do we need to concentrate on, if we are to become more effective?'[291] These were issues that had to be faced at the commencement of the 21st century and especially at the 2002 International Conference.

As Dieter and Renate Kuhl came to the end of their time in office, WEC elected a different kind of leader to be involved in the review process, one who knew WEC well from personal experience and had trained under respected wise leadership, but who would be a bridge towards the change and renewal that seemed necessary.

## Home-grown leaders Evan and Jenny Davies

Born in the Congo in 1940, I had the benefit of being part of WEC's origins. My parents, Ivor and Rose Davies, after a first term of 13 years were able to return to the UK in 1945. When it came time for them to go back to Africa in 1947, along with my older brother and sister, I moved into WEC's Missionary Children's Home in Arbroath,

Scotland, and remained there for eleven years to take advantage of adequate schooling which was not available in the Congo.[292] Living in the children's home was a valuable training ground, being part of a life of faith evidenced by visible answers to prayer and living in a community where Bible study, prayer for missionaries, daily disciplined life and fun were normal. This was all in the context of UK WEC which brought us into contact with international leaders and missionaries.[293] Eventually I relocated to New Zealand where my parents had been appointed WEC Sending Base Leaders. After working as a salesman, I felt challenged to move into Christian work, specifically through missionary training. On completion of the course at the WEC Missionary Training College in Tasmania, Australia, the staff invited me to join them.[294] At that same time Jenny came into my life.

Jenny, of German Australian background, was brought to personal faith through the encouragement of her uncle Murray Wilkes, the local WEC representative and youth worker. After nursing training and experience, she felt God's call to missionary work and enrolled at the same college. Her strong intention was to serve God overseas and she was surprised when invited to stay at the college, but after our marriage we remained on the staff team for 27 years.[295] Much of that time was spent under the godly leadership of Stewart and Marie Dinnen. Lessons of faith were experienced, team relationships were fostered, lasting friendships were made, further studies were undertaken, student lives were impacted and opportunities were taken to visit many countries where WEC workers and graduates of the college were serving. Those years formed a kaleidoscope of memorable events. The college grew in size and influence and in 1978 we were appointed Principals, as the Dinnens moved into a wider WEC ministry. We were blessed as God supplied resources for building extensions through remarkable timing, and the student and staff body continued to develop numerically.

Because of our role as Principals we were invited to attend Intercon 1990. Arising from this, a request came from Dieter and Renate Kuhl, who had been advised to find a full-time deputy to join the International Office as Deputy International Directors. Disengaging from the college in Tasmania was a big wrench and took time, but eventually in 1992 we moved to WEC's UK centre at Bulstrode, Gerrards Cross, where the International Office was located. For six valuable experiential and educational years we were Deputy International Directors and then became International Directors from 1999 to 2004. Richard Hibbert described me as a diplomat and pastor.[296] Jonathan Chamberlain, former Deputy International Director, reinforced this view by saying, 'Evan Davies fostered the family and pastoral emphasis in WEC.'[297] Jean Barnicoat, former MK Educational Advisor, said, 'Evan Davies was a man of pastoral gifts. He had a clear mind and was in touch with what was happening around him.'[298] Noel Gibson, who had held many roles in WEC from serving in India, leader of the Radio Worldwide ministry and then UK Treasurer, said that 'Evan Davies held steady under increasing workloads, handled the absorption of a growing number of Korean workers, and strove to remind members of WEC's core values.'[299]

## A turn in the road

The Coordinating Council conference in 2000 was held in the USA and majored on the future role of the International Research Office (IRO), facilitating growth in WEC and the primacy of evangelism and church planting in the life of WEC. Three new Asian fields were agreed upon. However it became evident subsequently that this conference marked something of a sea-change. The role of the IRO altered, evangelism and church planting were re-emphasized and structural changes were envisaged. Drs Richard and Evelyn Hibbert were invited by the conference to succeed Patrick and Robyn Johnstone as International Research Directors but in a restructured ministry which would focus more closely on strategy, evangelism and church planting. They had come with experience in Turkey and Bulgaria and with a growing interest and burden for a strengthened church planting ministry in WEC. The new ministry proposed by the Hibberts was to change the concept of the International Research Office, from research gathering and transmission, to becoming a supportive and educational department within WEC specifically to assist and advise church planters. The new section was to be named

the International Department for Equipping and Advance (IDEA).
Meanwhile what else was happening in WEC?

## Significant milestones – more jubilee celebrations

To be in the International Office in the 1990s and early 2000s was a
privilege, for we had the joy of seeing the fruit of long years of
missionary work in many places. In 2000 and 2001 the WEC-planted
churches in Japan and Uruguay celebrated fifty years of life; in Japan
we joined with 500 believers for special meetings and celebrations.
From a start in 1950 when General MacArthur had invited missions
to send 1,000 workers to Japan, WEC missionaries majored on
evangelism and church planning in the Kyoto and Lake Biwa area.
Japanese pastors were trained and fifteen congregations established.
Over the years the work has been a tough challenge and still looks
for a significant breakthrough for the gospel in that strongly
Buddhist-Shinto society.

WEC members had moved out from Uruguay in 1975 and the
work was left in the hands of local leadership. A couple from the
WEC-related church in Colombia went there in 1979 to be of
assistance and, along with their son, stayed on commencing work in
the capital Montevideo. Several churches in towns near Melo are
functioning well and reaching out to other districts and countries.
Former missionary in Uruguay Peter Murray attended the jubilee
celebrations in 2000 and reported, 'It was thrilling to see progress of
the work after the early years when it had been really hard.'

## People of significance

WEC continued to have a range of missionaries of all backgrounds
living and serving Jesus. These were of crucial significance in
enabling the mission to achieve its sense of divine mandate. For
several years, French WEC workers Luc and Beatrice Greiner had
been living for God and trying to share the Good News with
Senegalese people in a Soninke village. This seemed impossible, for
the people claimed that to be Soninke one has to be a Muslim and no
change is allowed. The language was difficult and the people were

not interested in any change. How long would they have to wait before there would be any transformation?[300]

Then there were those who served in Guinea-Bissau and were a microcosm of what was taking place around the WEC world. It was a field started in 1939 where the church continues to grow and the Bible School has a good number of students. Anna Clarke from Taiwan had sensed God's call to work there, in spite of family obstacles and the challenge of major cultural and language change. She testified that God had guided and strengthened her to serve in the ministry of evangelism in an African country where 85% are non-Christian. Married to an Australian, she and Kevin became field leaders of the Guinea-Bissau team which included Brazilians, Indonesians, Nigerians, Brits and Americans.

Margarida Virgilio had been brought up in the *favelas* of Rio de Janeiro, and knew what it was to suffer physical and emotional abuse and see her family wrecked by drugs, spiritism and poverty. By the mercy of God she had been introduced to the gospel of Jesus and knew a total transformation. Her family ultimately knew a similar liberation. For Margarida it led to a journey through university, Bible College, English language school, cross-cultural orientation and into service with WEC in Guinea-Bissau. Miracles small and great have followed her trail, as God has used her to see people delivered from the power of evil spirits, and healed of sin and physical complaints. Before long the girl from the *favelas* was lecturing in the field Bible school and being used by God to touch many lives, who themselves would have influence far and wide.[301]

Lily Gaynor had worked with the Papel tribe in Guinea-Bissau from 1975 to 1993, translating the New Testament and seeing the church come into being. In 2005 she was invited to return and help in the project of dubbing the *JESUS* film into Papel. In spite of the years away she found the language came back fluently, and happily the whole work was completed in three weeks. It was then that she realised that the vision which Leslie and Bessie Brierley had embraced in the early 1940s to see the main four language groups contacted with the gospel had been achieved! There were now churches among them all, with many believers, some even numbering thousands.

As well as naming many field workers, it would be unwise to ignore the continuing influence of retired workers in WEC in the 1990s and early 21st century. They are not people that have 'dropped out' but remain active in prayer, maintain contact with their previous places of service, and bolster the work of God in their country of residence. Retiree Beth Allinger, Canadian pioneer of Nepal outreach ministries in India with the late Elaine Crane, continues in contact with the burgeoning church in Nepal. David Davies, Welsh author and missionary statesman after years of service in the Congo, was still supporting Congo pastors with his gifts and prayers into his 90s. Canadian Gerhard Bargen, torpedoed during World War II on the way to the field and interned with his bride-to-be for years in Japan, returned to commence a flourishing regional centre for WEC in Brisbane, Australia, and remains enthusiastic for God in his golden years. Ken and Betty Roundhill, after many years in Japan, returned to New Zealand to retire, but in 1991 helped to set up a Japanese church in Christchurch. It has been written about WEC retirees worldwide,

> *Their passion is unabated. They are involved in active service in their local churches, enjoy running mission prayer meetings, love getting the latest news of the field and encourage WEC leaders. They may have grown old but have lost none of their fire.*[302]

## The place of women in WEC

From the days of Priscilla Studd, women continued to play a major role in WEC's leadership structure very appropriate because the majority of WEC missionaries were women, as in fact was the situation in many other missionary organisations.[303] Intercon 1990 agreed that 'We reaffirm that women in WEC can and should serve according to their gifts and that fields have the right to elect them to leadership.' Liz Hentschel, after service in Spain and Holland's Cornerstone training centre, had been appointed as Australia's Sending Base Leader in 2004. Flora Gibson was on the lecturing staff at WEC's college in Glasgow, participated in over twenty years' service in the Middle East and then became one of WEC's Deputy

International Directors. Deanne O'Donnell has said of Flora, 'Her example has always been one of caring servanthood. Her leadership came out of her obedience and love for the Lord.'[304] Anne Kelland and Pauline Wager were WEC's Regional Directors for half of the Africa region after many years' involvement in the Gambia and Chad respectively. Eileen Summerville from New Zealand was Feld Leader in Burkina Faso. This meant being involved with the WEC-related church in discussions about church planting among Muslim people, weddings in the church, when tribal dancing is acceptable, and Christian involvement in politics. These all took place alongside the normal responsibilities of a field leader and coping with the consequences of living in one of the world's poorest countries.[305] These ladies were well respected and, as with all WEC leaders, had been unanimously elected into leadership by their male and female co-workers.

## Holding together

By now the organisation was continuing to grow, obviously international in membership and worldwide in influence. Although this demanded competent leaders, WEC had developed a well-proven structure which demonstrated the organisation had a life of its own not dependent on figureheads or charismatic personalities. However, at the same time the mission was growing older and had to regularly re-evaluate its progress and future directions. The customary international conferences were essential in enabling the different parts of the mission to keep in touch, and to establish strong personal links between leaders.

Frank sharing and spiritual ministry set the tone of Intercon 2002 in Germany. The conference commenced with an address on 'The state of WEC' and focused on 'Where we are'; 'Where we want to go'; 'What we must do to get there.' Three visiting speakers (Peter Ozodo, Dr Detlef Bloecher and Dr Allan Adams) gave relevant ministry, as did many individual leaders who focused on the theme 'Renewed to run for Jesus.' Their thoughtful contributions were collated in a study booklet for the use of WEC members and interested friends.[306]

The conference agreed that WEC would have a corporate faith aim to trust for 150 viable church planting teams in place by 2008 and 50 prayer advocates for the most resistant peoples. A recruitment coordinator was to be appointed; a radical review of candidate orientation decided; a sample church planting seminar was greatly appreciated; and sessions were held on understanding CAN issues and generational differences. Later I wrote,

> A challenge to be passionate for Jesus came through loud and clear ... We were challenged to concentrate again on our main emphases — evangelism and church planting ... It was a wonderful time of fellowship ... The evaluations from the delegates were overwhelmingly positive.[307]

An interesting component of Intercon 2002 was that a clear cut decision needed to be reached on the choice of a new International Director (ID) for the 2005-2007 triennium.[308] When a couple who had already been nominated by the Coordinating Council and were due for election at the conference felt they should decline, I shared my belief that God could guide the conference to a right solution even though time to make the appointment was limited. Two couples serving as Regional Directors, Mike and Wilma Dwight and Trevor and Jen Kallmier, were willing for their names to be considered. After public interviews before the approximately 100 Leaders' Council delegates from all round the world, and through skilful chairing by USA Sending Base Leader Dr Louis Sutton, the question was 'Who were the right candidates?' as both couples were acceptable. After times of prayer and further discussion, clear unity emerged and Trevor and Jen Kallmier were unanimously elected. 'Many people commented that the selection of the new IDs by the Leaders' Council was a highlight of the conference', not just the fact that it took place but the way it was done.[309]

## Was WEC still on track?

In an effort to evaluate ongoing mission effectivenesss during this period of the early 21st century, the IO conducted a study in March 2004 of what was happening in WEC. Were people coming to faith in Christ through the evangelistic outreach of WEC workers and was church planting resulting in actual numbers of Christian congregations developing? From figures collected in the IO by the staff team and collated by Jonathan Chamberlain, Deputy International Director, the estimate from letters, magazine articles and field reports was that 50,901 had heard the gospel for the first time, and that between October 2002 and July 2003 2,652 people had come to faith or been baptised and 126 Christian fellowships commenced. In addition, through the work of Gospel Literature Worldwide, 360 people had come to faith in Christ. Hundreds of thousands had read the gospel message and Christian stories through broadsheets, internet contact and Radio Worldwide programmes.

These were not conclusive figures as they were not taken from every field and international team member, but were an indication that headway was being made in many of the most difficult places of the world. As Jonathan said, 'We are conscious that this is only a fraction of what is happening.'

In addition to the enormous challenges around the world, traditionally Christian Europe was presenting a stark reality. As Stewart Moulds, UK Sending Base Leader said,

*Remnants of spirituality, whether New Age or formal religion, have no power to change lives or to deal with the sin that is deeply rooted in each person. Since World War II, WEC has recognised Europe's spiritual needs and has been committed to making Christ known in France, Spain, Portugal, Italy, Belgium, Greece, Albania, Macedonia and Russia.*[310]

## Decisions in Korea

In view of the rapid growth of Korean membership in WEC, it was fitting that the 2004 conference of the Coordinating Council should be held in Seoul.[311] The conference was held in one of the large theological seminaries, and delegates had opportunity to visit and speak in various churches. WEC's current goals were reassessed; recruiting was reviewed; a new Spanish-speaking sending base for connecting with Latin American agencies was envisaged; a Mexican cross-cultural training programme was mooted; a fully integrated training review was commissioned; steps were taken to investigate any possibilities of recruiting from Eastern Europe and of connecting with the 'Back To Jerusalem' movement of Chinese Christians.[312]

This conference was most distinctive for its alteration of the length of the candidate orientation process. From what had been stipulated as a 'period of time' which initially could be of any length, then recently settled on four months, the length was changed to a minimum of eight weeks.[313] This move was connected to a radical reappraisal of requirements for new workers, which was specifically aimed at more short-term applicants and the expectation of larger numbers of recruits. Also included was the stipulation that all applicants must achieve Bible school training within their first five years of arriving on the field and they, with all members of WEC, were to be committed to life-long learning.

## Structures for effectiveness

All of these events took place against the background of the ongoing work of the mission. Arising out of the successful leadership seminars conducted by Stewart Dinnen in previous conferences, steps had been taken by the International Office to set up Leadership Training and Development Seminars, and most of the current leadership in the 1990s and early 21st century had attended one or more of these seminars held in different parts of the world. Brian Woodford, International Director for Training (1989-1999) and Jonathan Chamberlain, Deputy International Director (1999-2005) played key roles in their development.

These seminars were vital because of the nature of the WEC leadership selection process. As was normal practice, all leaders were elected by their field members for a period of three years, after which they had to either be re-elected or replaced. This process resulted in the distinct possibility of people with little experience of leadership assuming field leadership unprepared. Additionally the field leader's role carried with it the duty of being a member of the Leaders' Council, WEC's international executive body, and speaking to matters of worldwide concern.[314] Leaders needed all the help they could get and the seminars were very much appreciated. The International Office (IO) also invited WECers, on approval of their field or sending base, to join the staff of the IO for two or three weeks as 'Global Interns' to understudy the international leaders on the internal workings of the agency.

A series of manuals were prepared, dealing with internationalisation, crisis management, leadership, candidate orientation, the task of Regional Directors, the implications of being field workers or sending base workers, and useful guidelines for those relating to members' children. These provided specific and valuable help in a simple format and were useful tools for those in a coaching or mentoring role.[315] Other resources were regularly produced and updated, in print or on the internet, by the International Director for Training or the other consultants. Increasingly encouragement was given to WEC members to undertake further studies in their chosen fields. This was a significant philosophical shift from the early days when CT Studd stated, 'all God wants is a heart, and any old turnip will do for a head',[316] or as Grubb had declared 'men die by degrees.'[317]

As the years passed, there was a growing awareness in WEC of a need to give more careful input to workers. 'Member care' became needed as an essential component of missionary support structures.[318] The whole subject of missionary attrition raised the spectre of more of the younger generation resigning or leaving missionary organisations because of pressures on the field, increasing dangers in the modern world, relationship issues and the intention of putting more workers in unstable areas.[319] Within WEC, member care facilitator roles on fields or sending bases were being developed to support workers and leaders. Dr Tom Marks, qualified counsellor and former worker in the Middle East and later the USA Sending Base Leader, provided a counselling service and training resource.

By 2007 WEC's organisational structure had developed considerably. There were International Specialist Directors: the

International Directors for Training and those in the International Department for Equipping and Advance. As well there were many other international appointments: Candidate Directors' Coordinator, Recruitment Consultants, IT Security Service Consultant, Medical Advisor, Member Care Consultant, MK Education Advisor, Rainbows of Hope Coordinator, Word Worldwide Coordinator and Consultant-at-large. These were all precise roles which had arisen out of a specific need at a unique time in the mission's history. They were not static appointments, but could be discontinued as in the cases of the International Director for Research, International Media Consultant and International Director for Prayer. Specialists were directly responsible to the International Director who bore responsibility to sense the fluid requirements of the mission and be willing to suggest a change.

Thus the changeover of International Directors (IDs) at the end of 2004 was crucial in many ways. The new IDs were to supervise the above roles as well as imparting vision, chairing the Leaders' and Coordinating Councils, encouraging and evaluating WEC initiatives, managing the International Office, safeguarding the policies of WEC International, and acting in an executive role if an emergency required it.

## Trevor and Jen Kallmier

The new International Directors of WEC, Trevor and Jen Kallmier, brought with them a wealth of experience about life, ministry and WEC involvement. Trevor came from Australia, had worked in a legal office of a government department, and then felt the call of God into theological training and pastoral work. Jen had been involved in outreach to inner city children. They met on a beach mission when Trevor was the team leader. Both were touched by the ministry of the Holy Spirit in those years, leading to a deeper love for Jesus and a desire to serve him in mission. After a couple of years in pastoral ministry with the Australian Churches of Christ they responded to the challenge of serving in Indonesia with WEC.

Arriving in Java in 1976, they were involved for eight years in theological and leadership training and also church planting ministry. While holding the role of Field Leaders they faced a crisis when their third child, Andrew aged 4, was taken ill with leukaemia. Returning to Australia they experienced several uncertain years while he underwent treatment. During that time they fulfilled the role of Candidate Directors, Australian Sending Base Leaders and Regional Directors for East and South-East Asia, before moving to the UK as International Directors in November 2004.

Trevor and Jen had read and were influenced by the writings of Watchman Nee, Gordon McDonald, Philip Yancey, Francis Schaeffer and Norman Grubb. They had also been impacted by the teaching of Stewart Dinnen on 'union life.' It was an ideal preparation for the tough assignment they faced in the International Office. On being asked where they would like to see WEC in five years, they said,

1 *Greater synergy in internationalisation;*
2 *Many more GenXers in leadership throughout the mission, who are passionate about our Core Values and our vision to reach the unreached;*
3 *Increased strategic input and impact in self-multiplying church planting around the world;*
4 *Increased (deepened) networking with international and indigenous missions that have a church planting perspective;*
5 *WEC worldwide expressing a deeper level of dynamic faith and fervent prayer that catches the hearts of the young generation for mission.*

Trevor and Jen chose as their Deputy International Directors, Young Choon and Elaine Lee, and Traugott and Hanni Böker. A major development was the mix of nationalities in this international team. The cultural blend was full of variety: Australian, Irish, Korean, American, German and Swiss. In view of this change Dieter Kuhl commented, as a reflection from his period as International Director, 'We all together as an international team found the synergy was more than we could achieve alone. So when I was appointed ID I wanted to choose multicultural DIDs. At that time it was not possible, but it is a joy to see it now.'[320]

The role of International Director had much history behind it and could be regarded as rather daunting to those new in the task. I sometimes described it as being at the helm of an ocean-going liner, for making and seeing the effect of a change of course took a long time. The geographical diffusion of the membership, differing denominational affiliations and cross-cultural implications in communication required care and tact. The advantage of working with WECers was their genuine sacrificial commitment to the task in hand and openness to share honestly.[321]

## Lives of influence

There have been many who played a significant role in contributing to the overall ministry and who were supportive with advice and example to those in leadership.

Helen Roseveare's worldwide speaking and writing ministry has spiritually challenged many, especially young people. She has made WEC known and explained truths learned on the anvil of suffering in a form that would bless thousands. Beeson and Hunsicker have said she was able to learn through her traumatic experiences because of the way her Christianity was authentic and very personal.[322] She has been a living treasure in WEC and a wise counsellor to many.

Neil Rowe, who served on the staff of WEC's Missionary Training College in Scotland, was at different times founder of the WEC Press in the UK, UK Sending Base Leader and Regional Director for Africa and the Middle East. He died in 2005. At the time of his death I wrote,

*From the beginning I sensed he was an activist, enthusiastic for Jesus and passionate about WEC. International WEC benefited enormously from his keen brain, analysing our finances and faith position, proposing and setting up our highly successful International Fellowship Fund. We have been blessed by his passion for Jesus that did not fade the older he got.* [323]

He loved talking and writing about union with Christ. Stewart

Moulds said Neil trusted God's sovereignty and those leaders who
followed him, and he was willing for the new things God was doing,
even when they seemed different from the way he did things in the
past. Stewart emphasised, 'I believe Neil was able to be who he was
because he had discovered the secret of union life with Jesus.'[324] He
helped facilitate the smooth running of the international structure by
sharing his wide experience and a constant willingness to advise and
assist.

Gentle, godly and gifted leader, Ken Booth was the kind of person
who was good to have around. He left his native Australia soon after
his 21st birthday to join WEC's Himalayan field. Many years of
service in India took a toll on his health and required a period of
convalescence back home. Subsequently, instead of returning to the
field with his wife Cecily, he was invited to succeed Arthur and
Lillian Davidson as Australian Sending Base Directors, a task they
carried out with distinction. 'They had much to give from their years
in India where Cecily had been born. Cecily had the wonderful gift
of leading us into the presence of God as she prayed. Ken was an
intense person, who proved to be a capable leader, at times fun loving
and entertaining … Ken emphasised vision.'[325] Following two terms
in that office the Booths were willing to return to Asia as Regional
Directors, and walked through testing times which at one stage
resulted in their carrying the leadership of the Pakistan field. As
leaders they exhibited wisdom but not dogmatism, interest in others
but not intrusion, sacrifice but not pride. Ken was sorely missed
when he died in 2006. He had been a wise counsellor to leader and
follower alike.

It is impossible to ignore those who were doing 'front-line'
evangelism for they were examples of the heartbeat of the work.
Among these are Matt and Margaret Paton, UK workers in France
since 1964, who have been church planters *par excellence* and have
left their mark in five places in France where today there are ongoing
churches resulting from their pioneer efforts. Gannat, Le Puy,
Peronne, Dunkerque and Boulogne are centres where they have
worked hard, shared the love of Jesus and seen people respond. They
have wonderful stories, among these was the way God provided a
house to act as the base for the church in Gannat and led them to a

woman who had been a previous contact.[326] They have asserted, as they continue in ministry, 'God is on his throne and wants to build his church wherever ordinary people will plant themselves down in enemy territory, and trust for grace not to move until a witnessing active church has come into being.'[327]

Ronaldo Lidorio, scholar and anthropologist from Brazil, was used by God to touch many lives in Ghana. He tells the story of Meba, a powerful witch doctor who, after hearing the story of Christ's love and life from Ronaldo, dramatically came to a sudden conversion and, even though severely persecuted and ostracised in his community, continued in wholehearted commitment with his family along Jesus' way. Eventually a significant sub-section of the tribe was impacted by the gospel.[328] Since then Ronaldo and Rossana returned to Brazil and are leading a new team in the Amazon.

On another level, Australian Ian Case has played a significant role in WEC as he helped the mission to adjust to the internet age. From 1984 when he and his wife Chris joined the mission, Ian's training in electronics and familiarity with what was going on in the IT world was invaluable to WEC. Service in Ghana gave them the feel of a field, involvement with the International Research Office (and an informal link with the International Office) made them part of a department in WEC and, eventually when they were appointed to the role of WEC's Computer Consultant, Ian was enabled to speak to the mission from a position of broad experience. His vision of a facility tailor-made for WEC's needs has resulted in a working service that has been invaluable, assisting communication with the most restricted field situations. His performance has shown that missions need competent and professional people who can handle technology in a sympathetic manner.

## Old principles in updated attire

For the Kallmiers as new leaders, hosting Intercon 2006 in Germany was a quick turnaround after their assumption of leadership at the end of 2004. However they managed to find time to plan the programme, choose presenters, combine the research, collate answers and get adequate feedback from delegates before the conference.

Against the background of the theme '*On fire for the King with a passion for the lost*', there was a spiritual and devotional emphasis throughout the conference as various delegates and the visiting speaker, Dr Sang Bok Kim from South Korea, shared daily thoughts from biblical perspectives coupled with personal experiences. Illustrative of the style of ministry given were the following: Young Choon Lee, Korean Deputy International Director and former Field Leader in Mongolia, expounded in his session, 'We are born-again to be radical. WEC was founded on bold, radical leadership ... Jesus was bold and radical ... Boldness results in suffering and sacrifice. Boldness is in the obedience to God's will for each one of us.' Susan Sutton, former missionary to Chad and with her husband in leadership of the USA base, contended, 'We don't sacrifice because it is a WEC pillar: we do it because He (Jesus) is worth the sacrifice.' Eliki Drodrolagi, Fijian leader of the Chad field, pointed to Joshua as one who passed on a message of courage and passion. He asserted that 'In WEC passion and courage need to be there from one generation to the next.' Ronaldo Lidorio affirmed that 'Our relationship to Jesus will define our ministry.'

As the aim was on reaching unanimity it was vital to provide adequate time for participants to get to know each other, have a full understanding of the issues under consideration, and take ample opportunity for prayer. Prayer information issued during the conference illustrated something of the atmosphere.

> *Patrick Johnstone and Jason Mandryk took us through a two-hour whirlwind presentation of the victories and challenges in today's world, drawing out some of the implications for WEC. We have had glorious unity within the allotted time on such weighty matters as the composition of the CC, regionalisation, new worker status, and training, praise the Lord!* [329]

Decisions of the conference majored on re-emphasising the church-planting goals of 2002. There were now 110 WEC church-planting teams, and 61 of them were 'viable' (having five or more members). The Coordinating Council was restructured to include all Regional Directors rather than a preponderance of

Sending Base Leaders. Training in WEC was to be interlinked with a common goal, specifically focused and incorporating in-service training. Each WEC team was to develop 'accountability as a lifestyle' to help each person to clearly articulate their ministry and goals, and all team leaders were to encourage 'initiatives for spiritual, relational and moral accountability and growth.' A plan was made to incorporate suitable and existing full-time tentmakers into WEC, rather than the previous strategy that full-time workers only would train as tentmakers for the purpose of finding entry to difficult countries.

Tim Paton, French worker in Cambodia and one of the delegates said, 'Intercon 2006 will stay as a landmark in my life and ministry ... I was more refreshed at the end of the conference than when I arrived.'

## Sudden losses

The conference was not long over when a well-known leader died suddenly while on a visit to the WEC team in Portugal. Colin Nicholas (1939-2006) was highly esteemed within WEC and by the various communities he had influenced by his life and leadership. Converted at the age of 15, he felt God's call to missionary service in the Congo. Pastor Kibuka acknowledged that the majority of the present leaders in the WEC-founded church (CECCA-16) in the Congo regarded Colin as the formative influence in their lives. Due to his wife's health and family considerations, he returned to the UK where he became WEC's Treasurer, subsequently UK Director, and finally Regional Director for Europe, as well as carrying a range of responsibilities in and outside of WEC. It was said of him that he 'gained respect as a servant leader whose honesty, integrity, pastoral care, theological astuteness and preaching/teaching abilities endeared him to many.'

Hard on the heels of this came deeply affecting news from Western Asia. A father of three was killed alongside two local Christians in 2007. At the funerals the wives of two of the men stunned many by expressing forgiveness to the perpetrators. One widow elected to stay on in the town where her husband had died. It was a reminder that from earliest times suffering and danger had been part of the challenge of living for Christ. Through deaths in the unstable years of conflict in the Congo and Vietnam, troubles in Colombia, misrepresentations in Asia, rapes, political instability and evacuations, kidnappings and other brutal attacks, Christian workers have to be alert to the unpredictable situations that are part of today's volatile world.

## Urgent concerns impact conferences

Because delegates felt there was a need to meet more regularly due to constant change in world events, the timings of international conferences were altered: that of the CC to take place annually and Intercons every four years. In the official report of the CC conference in 2007 the greater proportion of time was spent looking at the progress of WEC's Faith Goals, the role of Specialist Directors and tentmaking from the 'Priscillan perspective' as it could affect WEC.[330] Training was reappraised; church planting effectiveness revisited; conflict resolution discussed and strategies were formulated to facilitate new advances and help small fields.

Later conferences and international discussions were centred on the rapid advances that were taking place around the world and the challenges the new fields were facing. The Intercon held in Thailand in 2010 set the stage for a new era of change and challenge. Ministry was fresh and relevant, prayer featured prominently and decisions were made to increase church-planting and recruitment goals, develop a series of 2013 centennial objectives, strengthen in-house training, improve conflict management awareness, make progress in church-planting skills, and build on communication facilities that were appropriate and effective. Trevor Kallmier stressed that WEC needed to be a flotilla of sailboats rather than a supertanker, with a dependence on the wind of the Spirit and having a higher level of trust in the Lord and each other. As a decision had been made to move the international base to Singapore and appoint Louis and Susan Sutton as incoming International Directors, the mission faces change and opportunity to prove God anew.

However, opposition is intensifying from those who do not believe that all people everywhere have the right to hear about Jesus, or that people can freely choose to leave the religion in which they were brought up. New believers face severe persecution, and churches have a struggle for survival in hostile communities.

Yet God is building his church, and there is ample evidence of a deep desire in many hearts for the truth which Christ can give. The task to share the love of Christ with all people is not finished, for as Louis Sutton, USA Sending Base Leader explained,

> My wife Susan visited an elderly lady in our village one day and told her about Jesus Christ and what an amazing difference He had made in her life. At the conclusion of the story the woman perked up and said 'This Jesus sounds like a really nice man. Next time he comes to town would you bring him by? I'd like to meet him.' In all her sixty-plus years this Chadian woman had never heard the name of Jesus Christ. And she might never have heard unless someone cared enough to enter her culture, learn her language, 'touch her skin' and give her opportunity for cure. Spiritual depravity still ruins lives. And there are almost 7,000 identified groups of people in our world today who ... have no way to know the diagnosis or treatment for their souls unless someone goes to give them opportunity for cure.[331]

## Encouragement and refocus

As a backdrop to the continued strategies and proposals an event was being played out that showed the vitality of the work which had been undertaken in Africa. In consequence of the civil war in Ivory Coast almost all of the WEC field members had left, and the well-constructed buildings and lovely property of the Vavoua International School had been handed over to the WEC-founded (AEECI) church. During Easter 2008 a retreat was held at the school with approximately 1,000 in attendance, which commenced with a time of repentance and confession for misunderstandings between church leaders and church members, and between churches and mission. The singing and worship was enthusiastic and the challenge was to take possession of the opportunities for service ahead. One of the pastors said, 'It began with three missionaries and look, here is the fruit.'[332]

WEC's International Leadership retained the keen desire to chart a new way forward for the mission. Although the IDEA structure had been dismantled, a continued emphasis on evangelism, discipling and church planting was being vigorously pursued. Strong initiatives were taking place in the Amazon, Central Asia, and CAN countries in Asia and the Middle East. New fields continued to be opened almost every year although details cannot be shared publicly for security reasons. Patrick Johnstone and Jason Mandryk have estimated that over 60 per cent of WEC's cross-cultural or overseas members are in ministry in the Muslim world. To preserve the cardinal values of the mission and its effectiveness on fields and sending bases Trevor Kallmier has said, 'We must take advantage of the opportunities for the sake of the nations, knowing our frailties and weaknesses but living in the power of the Almighty One.'

# CHAPTER SEVEN
## LEARNING FROM THE PAST AND THINKING ABOUT THE FUTURE

God seems to delight in difficulties. The early church, the Reformation and the modern missionary movement all started in dark times. As has been seen, WEC began in 1913 just before the dark days of World War I. Early pioneers went to places where Jesus was not known during times of financial depression, and local and world conflicts. In the strength of God they faced sickness, demonic opposition, visa restrictions, shortages and human weakness. As a result hundreds of churches have been planted worldwide and millions of people are contacted annually. Today there are thousands of believers in 70 countries, many trained leaders, medical facilities, schools, rehabilitation centres and radio programs. These are all testimonies to the power of God released through those who have been partners in the vision the Lord gave to WEC.

Yet the task is not finished. The spiritual forces standing against the church are clever and ruthless. The places still to be evangelised are the most difficult and inaccessible. As WEC presses on, along with other like-minded groups, we know that the assignment will call for ongoing costly commitment. It will demand a new level of holiness and discipleship, for this assignment is for the glory of God and the extension of his kingdom. It will lead to enormous steps of faith because the obstacles and the potential opposition are awesome. Now is not just a good time, it is the right time. There can be no turning back!

So the question that must be asked is — can WEC do it?

## What are the factors that have contributed to the survival and development of WEC International?

**There has always been a clear focus**
The primary objective of taking the gospel to the remaining

unevangelised people in the shortest possible time has remained the desire and objective of WEC from the beginning to this day. This underlies all its activity worldwide, with evangelism and church planting being the 'leading partner' over any kind of holistic ministries.[333] This commitment has preserved a clear unifying focus among a diverse membership engaged in a multiplicity of roles in dissimilar fields of service. Just as Jesus gave clear and repetitive instructions to his followers to take seriously the commitment to make disciples among all nations, so WEC has made this charge central to its objectives. The ardent re-dedication to the original mandate in the 21st century has shown an underlying historical continuity from the days of CT Studd and to the command of Jesus himself. New fields have frequently been opened up to the date of writing, and the work of evangelising and church planting are being pursued vigorously.

## Theological views are consistent

The theological views held within WEC were significant factors in its ability to work harmoniously and maintain momentum, especially after 1931. WEC was very much in the evangelical stream, theologically conservative and traditionally orthodox. From the earliest Statements of Belief and CT Studd's 'Five Smooth Stones' in the *Principles and Practice*, there has been an unswerving adherence to the same views.[334] Any theological conflicts have come from those who were afraid of any issue which might have taken WEC from a strong biblically conservative position. The charismatic debates of the 1960s and 70s, the divorce discussions in 1984, the search for an adequate ecclesiology, and the issues relating to the state of those who have never heard the gospel, were all shaped out of a concern that WEC remained biblical and evangelical in doctrine. The various editions of *Principles and Practice* follow an obvious succession and only vary in minor technical or administrative changes. Intentionally *Principles and Practice* is not a large book so it can major on specifics that are easy to understand and embrace. With a group of people so diverse, the clear understanding on an agreed theological foundation contributed to unity and a practical trust within WEC teams and the whole organisation. Because of this agreement there have been minimal theological controversies over the years.

There was definite concurrence on the concept of the term 'inter-denominational' and what it means in a mission like WEC. All who wanted to join WEC or serve in its ranks needed to fully embrace WEC's basis of faith and avoid any insistence on very strong denominational emphases, such as exclusion of women from ministry or leadership, 'closed' communion services, speaking in tongues as 'initial evidence' and baptismal regeneration. This agreement avoided unnecessary polarisation and allowed all to function upon the same basis. In addition it contributed to the development of new kinds of experimental church structures as a result of the working of this multi-denominational missionary band.[335] Sometimes this caused confusion—in Java those with Brethren tendencies worked alongside those with paedo-baptist practices, and in the Congo ordination developed differently from the position held by the WEC-founded churches in Thailand—yet it paved the way for the ecclesiological studies carried out by Patrick McElligott, Alastair Kennedy and Brian Woodford and the freedom enjoyed by local Christians to develop the church in cultural ways that 'seemed good to them and the Holy Spirit' (Acts 15: 28).

The 'Spiritual Gifts Statement' was hammered out initially at the 1969 conference and concluded satisfactorily in 1978. During the full flush of the charismatic movement, WEC could have fallen apart if it had taken a strong emphasis on one side or the other. The outcome of the balanced declaration was a stroke of spiritual genius and removed the ground for possible disagreement.

## CT Studd's radical appeal still works

CT Studd's radical life made a powerful impact.[336] His motto for WEC was 'If Jesus Christ be God and died for me, then no sacrifice can be too great for me to make for him' and still remains the driving force of the mission. Helen Roseveare has said, 'The ringing words of that motto have spurred many of us, not only to join the team but also to keep going when the way seemed impossible or lonely or frustrating or dangerous or even pointless.'[337] Studd may have been misunderstood or vilified but his passion was real and honest and this has been taken on board by people who have joined WEC. The

129

appeal was radical in that it led individuals to embrace a sacrificial lifestyle, trust God for daily living with all its uncertainties, work with people from all round the world for purely spiritual objectives, be willing to go to the most insecure locations, and face the possibility of death.[338] There is no place for political, purely human or selfish manoeuvring. Studd's approach still has powerful drawing power today, as it speaks to integrity of life, acceptance of Christ's humble mode of service and commitment to his cause in achieving spiritual outcomes.[339]

### Stress on holiness remains

The holiness emphasis stressed by the Keswick Movement, Wesleyan associations, Moody's conferences and writings, several of the faith missions and growing Pentecostalism all formed the mid-20th century background in which Studd's radical teaching and Grubb's devotional writings could flourish.[340] There was a hunger worldwide for this kind of holiness spirituality. WEC had members who were good exponents of principles of personal spiritual development; WEC also provided platforms where they could minister freely. People were attracted to WEC as they experienced their own needs met through teaching that stressed holiness of life. Revival events in WEC's history, especially in the Congo and Indonesia, gave unique illustrations that stirred the hearts of the Christian public. Those who prayed for and supported WEC, and those who joined the mission, learned to be accountable to God and to be sensitive to each other as they sought to walk in ways of holiness.[341] Godliness was personally enriching and a means whereby workers walked humbly in fellowship with each other. When team members were 'close to God' things ran smoothly and the work produced results.

### The Core Values document was an agreed basis for action

Spiritual values shared by WEC leaders and delegates in some of the most recent international conferences showed that leaders remained true to founding principles of WEC and were keen to encourage others to embrace them also. The devotional ministry given in international conferences in 2002, 2004, 2006 and 2010 was illustrative of the values held dear within the mission: André Wenk spoke about God's control in spite of the terror and suffering; Ronaldo Lidorio stressed that the key to church planting was godly character; Maurice Charman focused on discipleship as intimacy with Jesus; and Hans and Rosi Schutze gave illustrations from Romans 16 of Paul's fellowship concerns and ministry secrets. The continued aim was to be practical, biblical, timely and relevant in the situations where WEC is working. WEC remains a 'values-based mission.'[342]

## Life of faith emphasis was effective

The whole 'life of faith' emphasis has been a noteworthy way of ensuring WEC's survival and of keeping mission and workers on track with commitment to its charter and objectives. People have to be very sure of their foundation for living if they work on the basis of only asking God rather than people for support. Living by faith has given each person and his/her prayerful community a growing and meaningful catalogue of instances that demonstrated God's personal involvement in their lives. The books of Len Moules, Robert Mackey, Helen Roseveare and Stewart Dinnen illustrated how God has honoured faith and provided resources and answers in remarkable ways. These events continue today. Stanley Davies, former Executive Director of the UK Evangelical Missionary Alliance, has affirmed, 'WEC's philosophy of faith in God for all things including finance has enabled it to sustain its vision even at times when other missions have been adversely affected by hard times financially.'[343]

## Fruitfulness of the ministry has been demonstrated

The work worldwide has been fruitful. People have been won to Christ, discipled and formed into churches which have continued to develop and multiply with or without expatriate involvement. Today the work begun by WEC in Uruguay, Canary Islands, the Congo, Ivory Coast, Indonesia, Equatorial Guinea, Burkina Faso, Ghana, Colombia, India, Kashmir, Liberia and Venezuela is in the hands of local churches with little or no foreign presence. In Thailand, the Gambia, Senegal, Chad, France, Spain, Guinea-Bissau, Italy, Japan and some restricted countries the churches handle their own affairs but WEC teams work to extend the frontiers of gospel outreach and provide specialist ministries. The examples of fruitfulness have provided an incentive and encouragement to the workers and mission that their work is achievable and their 'labour is not in vain in the Lord' (1 Corinthians 15: 58). One leader wrote,

> We remember arriving in Ziguinchor in 1988 and there were few Senegalese pastors, now there is local leadership in place in all the churches, there is a growing missionary vision amongst the leadership and it is a thrill to see how the churches are reaching out to their communities in different ways.[344]

The original objectives remain possible and are being fulfilled.

### A wide range of personalities contributed to the survival and development of WEC

It has often been said 'WEC is people' and 'You are WEC.' Diverse personalities ensured the survival of WEC as they shaped the style of the mission, developing a culture of leadership by example and a sense of family. There are hundreds of illustrations within WEC of the spirit of sacrifice, commitment and devotion to the Lord and his calling. A multitude have ensured the survival of WEC, achieved the mission's objectives, made new workers feel at home and passed the baton on to them.

Strong leaders set high standards and exemplified a disciplined way of life. No-one who has known them could fail to remember CT and Priscilla Studd, Jack Harrison, Norman Grubb, Len and Iris Moules, Stewart and Marie Dinnen, Dieter and Renate Kuhl, ByungKook and BoIn Yoo, Neil Rowe, Rosifran Macedo, André Wenk, Phyllis Kilbourn and Alec Thorne.

Gentle leaders shared vision, humble ways and pastoral care for their workers. Alfred Buxton, Jim Grainger, Robert Mackey, Ken Booth, Elwyn Palmer, Colin Nicholas, Jean Moulds, Alastair and Helen Kennedy, Tineke Davelaar, Detmar Scheunemann, Mike Dwight, Huib Wierda, Mike O'Donnell and Bob Harvey are representative of a great company.

Unforgettable radical characters abound in all the decades of

WEC's development. Many tales have been told of Bessie Brierley, Bruce Rattray, Lily Searle, Helen Roseveare, Elliott Tepper, David Block, Peter Pikkert, Annie Davies, Dore Schupack, Ronaldo Lidorio, Stewart Moulds, Don Rowley, Werner and Else Jahnke, Edith Moules and 'Gunpowder Mary' Rees.[345]

Martyrs from the WEC ranks stand as examples of faithfulness. The deaths of Fenton Hall, Ron Davies, Congo and Vietnam team members and several in recent years have all kept the mission focused on the task and its cost. Added to those were the ones who died suddenly while in active service through disease and accident. At the 2002 and 2010 international conferences the displayed photos of the martyrs graphically portrayed the challenge under the slogan 'Lord whatever it takes' as an incentive to continued faithfulness.

Women were free to serve as equals throughout the fellowship and the churches. In fact the slogan 'the woman is the man for the job' has always been popular in WEC.[346] From the time of Priscilla Studd, women were welcomed into leadership roles and exercised respected ministries. People like Linda Nagel, Elizabeth Stewart, Pauline Nicholas, Maria Robelein, Flora Gibson, Heather Wraight, Helga Meinel, Anne Kelland, Annette Botting, Truus Wierda, Win Sulley, and Iris Moules are examples of capable and active leaders.

Those that finished well have been models of faithfulness. So many have concluded their service well beyond forty or fifty years. A few of them are Violet Edson, Ivor and Rose Davies, David and Chrissie Batchelor, Fred Woodward, John and Nellie Lewis, Pat and Ellen Symes, Myrtle Whitehead, Leslie Brierley, Elizabeth Battley, Bill Lapworth and Valborg Esping.

There were and are abundant ordinary members who have served unstintingly in challenging environments. Maud Kells, Toshiko Kawashima, Joeky de Wolf, Chandra Kaliammah, Bee Cheng Ong, Ross and Avrille Campbell, Isobel Cochrane, Keith Bergmeier and Junior and Sue Damasceno are part of a long roll call of faith.

**The place of research has been honoured and well managed**
'WEC has been willing to learn from its researchers and other visionary leaders. It has also recognised the need to refocus from time to time to sharpen its vision.'[347] On key occasions WEC

reviewed progress and in so doing brought new life into the mission by adding new goals and new workers and by rejuvenating its existing ministries. Patrick Johnstone has shown how times of refocusing and renewal correlate with the increase of personnel.[348] The focus at Intercon 2002 on the need of 150 viable church planting teams and 88 prayer mobilisers for each of the agreed people groups is already moving the mission forward. By 2010 there were 199 teams of which 88 were regarded as viable and in place.[349]

### Decision-making structure and organisation of WEC

WEC's constitution, as enshrined in *Principles and Practice,* set out the parameters by which WEC would operate. The structure called for all members to be involved in decision-making and policy direction. Each field and sending base remained independent and self-governing, able to elect its own leaders, make its own decisions and set its own policies within the framework of *Principles and Practice.* Fields could make changes to policies if agreed at their annual conference. The determination to make unanimous decisions forced each team member to listen to God, to share quality time with each other and to persist until unity was achieved. Members therefore own their policies and decisions rather than have them dictated by executives or from external committees.

Instead of being top-down, WEC has been described as organisationally flat, with power vested in the rank and file, and executive leadership shared among all leaders. Three-yearly elections have been developed as a useful way to appoint or re-appoint leaders. Members of a field choose their own leaders and thus keep them accountable. Seniority is respected but not mandated for effectiveness. Giftedness and spirituality are the criteria for leadership responsibility.[350] As a result of this structure, a sense of family nearness in WEC and ownership of the present and future structure of the mission has developed, which has made leadership tightly accountable, and rank and file closely involved.

### Decisive moments

Deeply significant steps were taken when Studd obeyed God's call to the Congo, his small team underwent the 'DCD experience' and

Grubb was appointed to home leadership of the struggling mission. Beyond these, strategic milestones in WEC included Leslie Brierley setting up the International Research Office, the decisions of the 1961 and 1984 advance-oriented international conferences, the appointment of Regional Advisors/Directors, translation of the scriptures into local languages instead of only trade languages (as had been done initially in the Congo), the invitation to Patrick and Jill Johnstone to be International Research Secretaries, the choice of the Kuhls to be International Secretaries, the willingness of WEC to tackle the restricted/Creative Access Nations, and the fresh commitment to evangelism and church planting in 2002.[351] All of these steps have been crucial in re-energizing the mission, reviving the membership and bringing in enthusiastic new workers.

## Catalytic ministries

A range of ministries have had a catalytic effect on the ministry WEC was set up to accomplish. Prayer groups in the UK, New Zealand, Germany, Korea and Australia gave strong support to WEC work, but were also a fertile ground for recruitment of those younger people who attended. Betel proved to be an effective 'rescue shop' for drug addicts but also developed a pattern of church planting that would bless the church in many countries. Gospel Literature Worldwid became a mass media movement for disseminating the Christian message to people who would not normally have the opportunity to have an understandable presentation. The missionary training colleges attracted many to join WEC and provided productive soil for potential future WEC leadership.

# Are there historical developments that need to be monitored?

## The role of leadership

Foolish actions by leadership have the potential to jeopardise ground won and lose the heart support of the mission's caring community. Harold Fuller stated (2006) that 'Many mission-minded people admired the abandon of WEC but perceived it sometimes disorganised if not reckless.' Also he said, 'Conservative Christians do not always know where to place WEC in the charismatic spectrum – although they commend missionary reliance upon the Holy Spirit.'[352] From Fuller's comments it would seem there is not enough awareness of what WEC believes and practices.[353] CT Studd caused great upset through his 'irascible dogmatic and condemnatory attitude to those … whose lives did not reveal the same white-hot intensity of lifestyle that he had.'[354] Structures are now in place in WEC to give balance and responsibility. The management styles of successive international leaders proved that WEC had competence in its leadership which could keep the mission on track. Many, who were respected locally and internationally for their gifts and qualities, held other areas of leadership and responsibility in and outside of WEC. The three-yearly election or re-election process has proved effective in keeping leadership fully accountable; any abandonment of this could raise the spectre of autocratic leadership similar to that of CT Studd. The remaining need to ensure that wise leadership is nurtured has been encouraged through a policy on accountability.

### An over-obsessive bureaucracy
Rules-based central organization could stifle the vitality and self-governing heritage of WEC. Norman Grubb's willingness to take many risks and allow individuals to move forward paid off. WEC has a long history, and learnt that things can go wrong and accusations can stick. This could mean that structures set up to counter previous problems could now inhibit momentum. As a result, reliance on WEC's traditions rather than its spirit may well become a chain rather than a springboard for action. 'This is really felt here in Latin America and several good folks have passed us by because we are too slow as an agency to respond … red tape stuff.'[355] The post-modern world calls for 'the ability to make decisions and adapt much more quickly.'[356] Newer bases serving non-western countries find ponderous and pedantic movement can inhibit cultures used to decisive action.[357]

### Shortening the Candidate Orientation courses
It remains to be seen what the effect of 2004 decision to reduce the

length of the Candidate Orientation course will have on the understanding of and long-term commitment to the agency's Core Values. From an Australian survey conducted in 1998 by Kath Donovan and Ruth Myors, their conclusion was that WEC had a unique anti-attrition weapon in the long orientation course and that WEC should 'resist any pressure to move away from having less emphasis on the mission's ethos.'[358] Jonathan Chamberlain however has advised that by mid-2008 most Candidate Orientation courses had reverted to periods longer than 8 weeks, maintaining the agreed components but feeling they did need more time to do things well.[359]

## Prayer influence

Serving together cross-culturally, facing the pressures of spiritual warfare, coping with political and religious opposition, and seeing people won and discipled to Christ are all foundational concerns that move the Christian worker out of his/her comfort zone.[360] Much prayer is required to support any work which declares the gospel and develops and organises the church. Preparing the church to thrive and multiply without its spiritual parents and mentors also requires WEC workers to have strong prayer partners. Sending bases (apart from Korea) state that their prayer networks need strengthening. Pauline Nicholas has affirmed, 'Where prayer groups die, WEC influence dies.'[361]

## Lack of adequate preparation in WEC-founded churches

Was WEC too cautious and unprepared for the growth and organisation of the churches? Alastair Kennedy stated that 'WEC did not prepare the overseas churches we founded for the financial side of the missionary task.'[362] It seems expatriate workers did not train all the churches in financial management, lay involvement, use of spiritual gifts, generational issues, preparing to embrace the worldwide outreach task themselves, or coping with out-of-culture concerns. Many WEC workers were inadequately prepared and inexperienced in church strategies — they were still learning themselves. WEC ecclesiology studies took place long after some of the key churches were founded, but they produced useful insights and resources.[363] As WEC continues to be heavily involved in evangelism and church planting, new workers need to be made aware of these resources. In addition, with the increased emphasis on church planting, the potential remains of fixed ideas developing about training, ordination, style of church government and the ramifications of church life. These should be held in very gentle hands, leaving to God and local believers the outworking of the future shape of the church.[364]

## The danger of ignoring the need to share the compassion of Christ with a needy world through involvement in holistic ministries

The world is being transformed at a startling pace. Uncertainty of oil supplies, environmental changes, water and food shortages, socio-political events, natural disasters, human crises, religious intolerance and potential pandemics all compete for attention. Christian associations cannot ignore the world around them but, at the same time, those who major on evangelism and church planting must reconcile the twin needs — sharing the gospel of salvation and responding to the vast social appeals all around. As Guthrie has said, 'Holism is a force to be reckoned with in the new millennium, one that is unlikely to go away.'[365] Can WEC forsake its commitment to promote 'the compassion of Christ for a needy world'? Does it have a commission only to preach the gospel or has it a responsibility to share economic, medical, agricultural, literary and educational resources? As Henry Bell has said, 'Every act of compassion has evangelistic implications, and every evangelistic act has social results.'[366]

Within WEC today, medical and educational services are already in place; rescue services for children in crisis have been started; and many workers have already become involved in acts of kindness and mercy, as doors to living and working meaningfully in particular places. The way God has used Betel, which while exercising a relevant drug rehabilitation work has become a viable church-planting structure, is a living illustration of the power of holistic ministries set in an evangelistic context. WEC does not need to fear overbalance but should continue to stress that mercy ministries are a necessary part of the church-planting scene.

## Are there significant principles which need continued articulation for the benefit of present and future members of WEC and a wider public?

### The radical emphasis in a biblical context

Norman Grubb at the Kilcreggan Conference 1961 urged the whole mission to 'get back on to the old path of complete abandonment to Jesus symbolised in the days of CT Studd by the current saying of the Tommies (British soldiers in World War I) that they "didn't care a damn" for anything ...'[367] This is a key to a true understanding of the radicalism at the heart of WEC, not the use of the DCD terminology — which had and would cause unnecessary offence — but an embracing of 'the spirit of utter abandonment and sacrifice ... [to] care for nothing but the glory of God and the salvation of souls.'[368] To achieve WEC's objectives members have to embrace the example of Barnabas and Paul — 'men who have risked their lives for the name of our Lord Jesus Christ' (Acts 15:26). This is not to be a stupid thoughtlessness and belligerence, but a Christ-like obedience to the will of the Father in a spirit of humble respect to all, showing that God's way is a good way and that trusting Christ for salvation brings with it a life of freedom and wholeness.

### A continued promotion of personal and corporate spirituality

Spirituality that is understood, taught, seen and shared must be maintained. As has been observed through the history of WEC, godliness in leaders and in rank and file is a means to consistency and fruitfulness. The principles of holiness and fellowship are essential spiritual foundations for transparency and good relationships. The workers need to be spiritual people to complete their mission and survive the rigours of their vocation; leaders must maintain their spirituality to provide strategic and humble servant leadership; field members have to conduct all their activities in a spirit of grace so they can make wise and united decisions; and all need to live in godliness so the disciples they mentor and the churches which come into being are believable and biblical examples.

The crucial foundations in biblical spirituality laid by CT Studd,

Norman Grubb and others since, are a strong recipe for wholeness and effectiveness. However it is not helpful to aim for a new crop of Grubb 'grubblets' or Dinnen 'doubles' but people in tune with the Spirit. From a study of WEC's history it would appear that relevant spiritual emphases should continue to take vital space within WEC ministry, public activities and conference times. The life of the mission depends on the spirituality of the membership. The foundation principles and purposes of WEC are spiritual in essence, and so a growing personal delight in God must be facilitated by giving time to listen, meditate, worship and enjoy life. Therefore it falls on the leadership to ensure that the emphases being fostered in orientation and in corporate activities are not primarily organisational and administrative but follow the well-trodden paths of the past.

## Treasuring WEC's Core Values

Research has shown that most WEC leaders believe that a clear understanding and grip of the Core Values of WEC must be maintained[369]. These values have been developed in the serious realities of international and interdenominational experience in more than seventy countries and over many years. *The Objectives* need to be regularly re-emphasised to keep the mission on track and to provide united aims. *The Lifestyle* has important value to give spiritual underpinning. The Four Pillars have been shown to be important when they are held together in balance and interpreted in everyday dress. *The Convictions* are practical lessons which were proven as realistic keys for organizational effectiveness. For a mission that continues to grow in size and diversity, there is an urgent call to maintain a current analysis of the common values and to remind all of their relevance.

## Preserving the outward-looking thrust and the research to fuel it

WEC has no room for complacency because its key objective is 'To fulfil as quickly as possible the command of our Lord Jesus Christ in Matthew 28:18-20 and Acts 1:6-11 by a definite attempt to evangelise the remaining unevangelised peoples of the Earth before His return.'

The current emphasis on training in evangelism, discipling and church planting is commendable, and needs to be broadened to make it suitable for all fields and areas of ministry.[370] Training has been developed and is critical for the effectiveness of all workers. Recent seminars have provided valuable practical input and guidance to both older and fledgling church planters. In each stage of WEC's history this focus on evangelism has been seen as a continuing link. WEC has a long history of research. The dismantling of the International Research Office followed by the short-lived IDEA department left WEC dependent on the *Operation World* team, and happily in 2010 this area is being remedied because WEC requires an effective research structure to keep the society alert to genuine needs.[371]

To be true to its founding and core objectives, WEC cannot give up the diligent effort to embrace Paul's intention in Romans 15:20, 'It has always been my ambition to preach the gospel where Christ was not known.' Even a place like Europe, with its grand history of Christian movements and Christianised nations, now stands in sore need of a re-conversion to Christ. As Louis Sutton declared, 'There is a new push from ... the present workers in Europe to renew excitement and commitment to reach Europe for God's glory. We are not alone. A brief overview of current mission publications will show similar awareness; God is on the move for a much needed renewal in Europe.'[372] Also in those places where WEC has already served, but the work has not been finished, it cannot abandon ship. The goal is not a token presence in a country, but a deliberate attempt to find the remaining unevangelised peoples and reach them with the gospel.

## The life of faith as practised by the members of WEC has worked and God can keep providing for all needs

The evidence is all around the world: thousands of Christian workers have been trained, made journeys to their fields of service, lived in different places, pursued their calling, and seen their families and work provided for, without any appeals for finance. People unaware of or opposed to the Good News of Jesus Christ have come to faith, and churches, including networks of churches, have come into existence through obedience to Christ's commands and simple trust in God's promises. Permissions have been granted, properties purchased, ministries started and maintained, transport bought and kept running, bills paid on time and all of this in answer to the prayers of God's people. Budgets have not determined advance, but rather the belief that God was guiding and he would provide what was needed.[373] This confidence has not been misplaced. Scriptures like Matthew 6:33 and Philippians 4:19 remain relevant for future members of WEC.

## Multi-culturalism must be cherished and fostered

The association has maintained momentum, due to the rapid increase of some non-western members, at a time when western recruitment has slowed.[374] With the increasing growth of non-western membership in WEC, constant attention must be paid to the way that all nationalities are given orientation, and that good communication and relationships flourish. All nationalities must be seen and treated as equal, for western membership has to acknowledge that its day of dominant influence is fast slipping away. Opportunities for misunderstanding are distinctly possible. Steve Sang-Cheol Moon has said that 'Agencies need to learn and adapt local cultural traits and to maintain a spirit of and philosophy of multi-culturalism embracing both the global and the local.'[375] The difficulty for an organisation like WEC is that national concerns of its members can become opposed to the universal needs of all.[376]

The non-western world has also to carve its own way, learning from the West but not being cowed by it or copying its fads. Descriptions like 'post-Christian' and 'post-modern' are western viewpoints and the non-western members of WEC have to be given space to learn and lead in their God-given ways. Careful steps must be taken to strengthen the unifying factors and discern the issues that would tear the agency apart. Traugott Böker has said, 'In the end what is crucial is the heart attitude of members and leaders from all nations to each other. What rules and regulations cannot do can be achieved by a spirit of love and respect for each other and our differences.'

# CONCLUSION
## A FABULOUS VISION

When the Church Missionary Society (CMS) re-evaluated its work among the indigenous peoples of Australia, the reviewer described their efforts with the words 'We wish we'd done more.'[377] The CMS circumstances were greatly different to those encountered by WEC; they were only dealing with one country, beneath the spotlight of one government, under close supervision of a church which had far different origins to the indigenous peoples but now had taken a dominant role in their country. However their historian recorded that, although their workers had succeeded in many areas, they were humble enough to recognise their failures, their inability to read into the future, to learn local languages, to trust the locals with interpretation of their own culture and to give them their own leadership much earlier.

Compared to the huge churches of some partner agencies in Africa, WEC has founded churches which are in the main quite small. The numbers of WEC workers have not matched the large memberships of Youth With A Mission (YWAM), Wycliffe Bible Translators or Operation Mobilisation (OM).[378] WEC's Rainbows of Hope ministry has not achieved its possible influence; some fields and ministries have never reached their full potential; others have progressed uncertainly; yet others have continually struggled for lack of workers. There were cases of moral failure among workers; shortages of available leadership candidates; tragic breakdowns of fellowship on fields, and some people resigning from the mission through dissatisfaction.[379] Unfortunately the pressures of responding to exciting new ventures robbed growing fields of necessary and experienced personnel, and in some cases left them struggling. In several cases it was only political necessity which forced the expatriates to hand over control to the local church.

Yet my research has shown that WEC has a rich and remarkable history. From Studd's clarion call and radical example the mission developed explosively, leading to Grubb's taking up the reins in its darkest hour and extending its influence and foundations. A succession of gifted international leaders guided WEC as it grew in personnel, with an administration that generally ran smoothly and with an increase in places of service and representation. Unique structures, competent leadership, quality membership, willingness and ability to embrace challenges and change, commitment to organisation and spiritual depth have all become foundations for long-range stability. Radicalism has been tempered by wisdom and independent leadership, and self-governing fields have been schooled in accountability. Fruitfulness has blossomed from deliberate strategies. Churches today give dramatic testimony to the sacrifice and faith of their founding parents. However WEC too could have done better.

Unanswered questions remain, among them are:

How can WEC solve the challenge of producing culturally competent and experienced leaders while coping with the reality of increasing short-term service and more rapid changes of ministry?

Can the churches founded by WEC be adequately partnered and more intentionally drawn into the worldwide commission of reaching the remaining unevangelised peoples?

Today the mission is positioned by God at the threshold of a new adventure. WEC includes hundreds of workers of all ages from a broad cultural mix and represents a microcosm of the whole church taking the whole gospel to the whole world. Workers are better educated than previously. The organisation has a heritage of workable guidelines developed out of necessity and experience. Older WEC fields are now phasing out, as the churches take over total responsibility and newer fields ministering in Creative Access Nations are in the full flush of their activities.

When analysing the challenge before WEC, the real driving force comes from ordinary people who face the daily tests of living for God in the modern world, like Timothée Paton who has said,

*When I arrived in Cambodia in 1999, I knew nobody, had never been to Asia, and I knew not a single word of Khmer. But I had a passion burning in my heart for the children at risk living on the streets of Phnom Penh. At that time there were 15-20,000 street children. What got me started and kept me going was passion. You can have money, years of training in children's work and a big network of Christian friends back home. But if you don't have passion for the poor and the lost, you won't last. Money cannot buy passion. It comes from God. It will get you started and keep you going in the worst of times and the darkest of places.*[380]

What has become of the church's passion to reach the world? The task is not complete.[381] For instance 'The Bedouin need to know a loving God who longs to come near to them, a God who once walked the dusty byways in the Middle East.'[382] Then think of 'In Greece only two percent of the population is in church on an average Sunday,'[383] and 'Close your eyes and picture this: children in crisis experiencing loss, exploitation and trauma. Children without hope.'[384] Apostolic agencies and churches have to be remade by God's grace in a truly international shape to meet the challenges of the future.[385] Final breakthroughs for the Gospel among other major religions, re-evangelisation of the West and purification of Christianity call for dynamic partnerships between transformed agencies and a renewed worldwide church.

WEC has experimented at length and shown that the task can be achieved, change embraced, unity preserved and objectives maintained. Starting as a British mission in the pith-helmet era, it is now an international family pushing forward in the age of information technology, space travel and a gloriously multi-faceted worldwide church. Church planting, leadership training and multi-cultural service are all shared in Christ's name. Crucial lessons from WEC's experience are valuable and can be embraced by its new members, the church community and other missions.

Huge steps are being taken as the worldwide church and many organisations join hands in service to the world. There has never been such a time when travel and communication is so easy, access to most countries is possible, knowledge of the world and ways to reach it are widely available, the church of Christ is growing at a staggering pace and global teams can present an international face. But more must be done; the task is not finished.

The hope and promise for the future remains: 'The earth shall be filled with the knowledge of the glory of the Lord as the waters cover the sea.' [386]

# APPENDIX A
## ACTIVITIES

This is a supplementary category of Activities contained in WEC's constitution, *Principles and Practice*, explanatory to the list of WEC's Objectives.

Prayer is our first priority and the basis of every other WEC activity. Recognising this, we seek to meet our objectives by:

1   evangelising, discipling and planting churches that seek to multiple both nationally and cross culturally;

2   using every means to proclaim Christ by word and by demonstrating His compassion in our lifestyle and ministries. This may include ministries that meet people's felt needs such as medical work, education, rural development, social relief, business activities, media, ministry to children at risk and in crisis, Bible correspondence and study programmes;

3   training local leaders and pastors, empowering them to give godly leadership to their churches;

4   assisting local churches in special tasks as requested, such as Bible training, leadership training, cross-cultural outreach, translation work and medical training;

5   researching and distributing information about areas of need and worldwide mission activity;

6   presenting the need of the unevangelised world and challenging Christians and churches with their responsibility before God;

7   recruiting and sending out workers who will commit themselves to make the evangelisation of the whole world the main objective of their lives;

8   recruiting part-time workers who share the same spirit of faith and sacrifice as full-time workers;

9   establishing national sending bases and mobilisation centres;

10  developing missionary training colleges (MTCs) and other orientation facilities for the equipping of workers for service

with WEC International and other missions;

11    working together with churches and other agencies that have a similar vision;

12    providing infrastructures (as needed) to support field operations. These may include schools for workers' children, language learning centres, business agencies and retirement facilities.

(*Principles and Practice* 2005, pp. 5-6)

# APPENDIX B
## INTERNATIONAL LEADERS OF WEC INTERNATIONAL

### Superintendent / President
| | |
|---|---|
| 1913-1931 | Charles T and Priscilla Studd |
| | General Secretary (International and UK) |
| 1931-1965 | Norman P and Pauline Grubb |
| | International Secretaries (and UK) |
| 1966-1974 | Leonard J and Iris Moules |

### International Secretaries
| | |
|---|---|
| 1975 | Heini and Jo Schnyder (Acting) |
| 1975-1983 | Robert and Isobel Mackey |
| 1983-1987 | Stewart R and Marie K Dinnen |

### International Directors
| | |
|---|---|
| 1986-1998 | Dietrich and Renate Kuhl |
| 1999-2004 | P Evan W and Jenny M Davies |
| 2005-2011 | Trevor and Jen Kallmier |
| 2011- | Louis and Susan Sutton |

### Deputy International Leaders
| | |
|---|---|
| 1976-1984 | Alastair and Helen Kennedy |
| 1985-1987 | Patrick and Sarah McElligott |
| 1988-1992 | Patrick and Jill Johnstone |
| 1993-1998 | Evan and Jenny Davies |
| 1999-2005 | Jonathan and Linda Chamberlain |
| 2000-2005 | Flora Gibson |
| 2005- | Traugott and Hanni Böker |
| 2005- | YoungChoon and Elaine Lee |

# APPENDIX C
## MISSIONARY TRAINING COLLEGES DEVELOPED BY WEC

### Current colleges
**Australia**
Worldview Centre for Intercultural Studies,
PO Box 21, St Leonards, Tasmania 7250
**T** (0)3 6337 0444
**F** (0)3 6337 0494
**E** admin@worldview.edu.au
Founded: 1956; graduates by 2008: 1199; student body: 31

**Brazil**
**MTC Latino Americano,**
CP 289, CEP 39400.970, Montes Claros, Minas Gerais
**T** (0)38 3223 3696
**F** (0)38 3223 3742
**E** mtc@connect.com.br
Founded: 1984; graduates by 2008: 208; student body: 20

**Canada**
Gateway Missionary Training Center,
21233 32nd Avenue, Langley, BC V2Z-2E7
**T** 604 530 4283
**F** 604 530 7192
**E** info@gatewaytraining.org
Founded: 1995; graduates by 2008: 126; student body: 12

**New Zealand**
EastWest College of Intercultural Studies,
21, College Drive, RD1, Taupiri 3791
**T** (0)7 824 3417
**F** (0)7 824 3418
**E** office@eastwest.ac.nz
Founded: 1996: graduates by 2008: 202; student body: 40 (plus 5 part-time students)

**Netherlands**
Cornerstone Centre for Intercultural Studies,
Hagelkruisstraat 19, NL-5835 BD, Beugen
**T** (0)485 369 130
**F** (0)485 369 131
**E** administration@cornerstone-mtc.com
Founded: 1989; graduates by 2008: 340; student body: 35

**Mexico**[387]
Centro de Capitacion Transcultural,
El Monte, Ticuman, Morelos, Mexico
Postal: Apdo Postal 92, 62731 Yautapec, Morelos, Mexico
**T** 734 341 7161;
**E** cct.elmonte@gmail.com
Founded: 2006

**Former training centres**
**United Kingdom**
Missionary Training Colony, London 1921-1939 [388]
Missionary Training College, Glasgow 1949-1977
Missionary Orientation Centre, Gerrards Cross, Bucks 1977-1990

**South Africa**
Natal 1965-1969

**Hong Kong** 1996-2005[389]

# APPENDIX D
## SENDING BASES AND INTERNATIONAL MINISTRIES OF WEC, THEIR FOUNDERS AND YEAR OF ENTRY/FOUNDING

| Sending bases | Commenced | Founder |
|---|---|---|
| UK | 1913 | Priscilla Studd |
| USA | 1920 | Constance Brandon, restarted 1938 by Alfred Ruscoe |
| Australia | 1922 | Constance Brandon and Priscilla Studd, settled as a full-time base in 1941 by Arthur and Lilian Davidson |
| New Zealand | 1922 | Constance Brandon and Priscilla Studd, settled as a full-time base in 1953 by Alec Thorne |
| Canada | 1924 | Rev Roadhouse, but restarted by Olive Ashton in 1931 and then Alfred Ruscoe in 1936 |
| Switzerland | 1947 | David and Chrissie Batchelor |
| China | 1948 | Horace and Margaret Williams (closed 1950) |
| Holland | 1948 | Jack and Diny Perkins |
| France | 1950 | David and Chrissie Batchelor, started as a full-time base in 1997 by Martin and Jeanne Walser |
| Scandinavia (Sweden) | 1951 | Wilhelm and Margaret Bergling (closed) |

| | | |
|---|---|---|
| South Africa | 1955 | Will and Rhodie Dawn |
| Formosa/ Taiwan | 1955 | Horace and Margaret Williams; after a gap of several years the Taiwan field recommenced a sending base ministry under Violet McMaster |
| Germany | 1958 | David and Chrissie Batchelor |
| Brazil | 1977 | Bob and Bev Harvey |
| Singapore | 1980 | Maurice and Ruth Charman |
| Hong Kong | 1986 | NanPin and Eleanor Chee |
| Indonesia | 1991 | Stewart and Jean Moulds |
| Korea | 1997 | ByungKook and BoIn Yoo |
| Mexico | 2006 | Ricky and Ivy Choy |

| International ministries | Commenced | Founder or first office-holder |
|---|---|---|
| Research Office | 1961 | Leslie Brierley (UK) |
| Editor the WECCER | 1965 | David Batchelor (UK) |
| International Resources Office | 1974 | Stewart Dinnen (Aust) (discontinued) |
| Word Worldwide | 1978 | Marie Dinnen (Aust) |
| Schools for Missionaries' Children | 1970 | *Ivory Coast* John and Del Gunningham (US), Doreen Riches (Aust) (closed) |
| | 1980 | *Senegal* Iain and Linda Williamson (UK), Lena McCallum (UK) |

# WHATEVER HAPPENED TO CT STUDD'S MISSION?

| International ministries | Commenced | Founder or first office-holder |
| --- | --- | --- |
| Candidate Directors' Coordinator | 1986 | Evan Davies (Aust) |
| MK Education Advisor | 1990 | Joan Roberts (NZ) |
| IT Computer/ Security Consultant | 1990 | Ian Case (Aust) |
| Consultant-at-Large | 1992 | Leslie Brierley |
| Media Secretary | 1994 | Andrew Bowker (UK) (discontinued) |
| Rainbows of Hope | 1996 | Phyllis Kilbourn (US) |
| Medical Advisor | 1999 | Gisela Schneider (Ger) |
| CAN Business Consultancy | 1990s | Neil and Jeanie Young (Aust) |
| Member Care Advisor | 2000 | Tom Marks |
| International Department for Equipping and Advance | 2002 | Richard and Evelyn Hibbert (Aust) (discontinued 2008) |
| Webmaster | 2002 | Jerry Reszke (Aust) |
| Recruitment Consultant | 2003 | Wayne and Miriam Cowpland (UK) |
| WEC Latino | 2005 | Patty Toland and Cheryl Keiper |

| International ministries | Commenced | Founder or first office-holder |
|---|---|---|
| Information Technology and Web Coordinator | 2008 | Bob Harvey |
| Director for International Mobilization | 2009 | Byung Kook and Bo In Yoo |
| Consultant for Missiology and Church Planting | 2009 | Ronaldo Lidorio |

# APPENDIX E
## SPIRITUAL GIFTS IN WEC

**This statement was approved at the International Leaders' Conference in 1978.**

1    WEC is an interdenominational Fellowship whose members are from a broad spectrum of churches in many lands. It reflects therefore in the fellowship of its members something of the moving of the Holy Spirit in their respective countries.

2    We are aware that significant movings of the Holy Spirit are taking place in many parts of the world today. That these are genuine visitations from God is evidenced by deep conviction of sin, transformed lives, burden for souls and zealous witness which have accompanied them. We also recognise that some of these visitations have been marked by various gifts of the Holy Spirit.

3    While it is not our purpose to go into all the implications of the scriptural doctrine of spiritual gifts we feel constrained to emphasise certain principles which may serve as guidelines for the Mission worldwide, and be consistent with our God-given commission.

   3.1   The Spirit's gifts include every power and capacity given by God's grace to fit His people for service (Romans 12:1-8; 1 Corinthians 12; Ephesians 4:7-13; 1 Peter 4:10-11).

   3.2   We believe that speaking in tongues is one of the gifts of the Spirit (1 Corinthians 12:10). However, we do not accept the teaching that tongues is the initial or conclusive evidence of the 'fullness' or 'baptism' of the Spirit. To accept this position leads
   to grave division in a body of believers. Nor do we believe that all Christians will receive the gift of tongues any more than all will be given gifts of faith, healing, teaching, et cetera.

   3.3   In view of our interdenominational position we do not

encourage the expression of demonstrative gifts in our public[390] meetings.

3.4 Although there may be occasions when there is an expression of the Spirit in tongues in a WEC meeting under the conditions governed by 1 Corinthians 14:26-28, we believe that the preserving of the unity should take precedence over the individual 'right' to exercise or restrain this gift (Ephesians 4:3).

3.5 All members of WEC are responsible to judge the use of any of the gifts in order to approve what is of God and to challenge what appears to be false, knowing that there are demonic and carnal counterfeits (1 Thessalonians 5:19-21; 1 John 4:1-3).

3.6 To hold or propagate a forceful pro-charismatic or anti-charismatic position is totally unacceptable within WEC.

4 Each member of WEC is responsible to contribute to the upbuilding of the whole Body, and should avoid any emphasis in doctrine or experience to the neglect of the all important outworking of the fruit of the Spirit.

5 We affirm that only by a personal knowledge of the Holy Spirit in His fullness, the power of the Spirit for worldwide witness, the anointing of the Spirit in times of special need, and the fruit of His indwelling presence being displayed daily, can we fulfil our commission from God.

(*International Leaders' Conference report 1969*, pp. 28-30; *International Leaders' Conference report 1978*, pp. 25-27)

**An additional statement was made in view of the worldwide impact of the 'Toronto Blessing'.**

The Leaders' Conference 1996 strongly affirmed:

1 Our commitment to the authority and teaching of the Word of God;

2 Our commitment to our 1978 Statement on Spiritual Gifts and its practical outworking on fields;

3 The importance of leaders faithfully upholding our WEC

position on these and related issues, in order to strengthen fellowship between workers, preserve the confidence of supporting churches and maintain our unity in Christ and in WEC;

4    The importance of the International Office and Regional Directors' being informed of significant spiritual manifestations on any field so that they may be monitored, encouraged or contained as the situation demands.

(*Intercon report 1996*, pp. 20-21)

# APPENDIX F
## CORE VALUES

**These values were agreed to at the 1996 International Leaders' Conference in Germany.**

**1    Our Commission**

To bring the gospel of our Lord Jesus Christ to the remaining unevangelised peoples with the utmost urgency.
To demonstrate the compassion of Christ to a needy world.
To plant churches and lead them to spiritual maturity.
To inspire, mobilise and train for cross-cultural mission.

**2    Our Lifestyle**

We trust God completely to meet every need and challenge we face in His service.
We fervently desire to see Christ formed in us so that we live holy lives.
In dependence on the Holy Spirit we determine to obey our Lord whatever the cost.
We are committed to oneness, fellowship and the care of our whole mission family.

**3    Our Convictions**

We are convinced that prayer is a priority.
We uphold biblical truth and standards.
We affirm our love for Christ's Church, and endeavour to work in fellowship with local and national churches, and with other Christian agencies.
We accept each other irrespective of gender, ethnic background or church affiliation.
We desire to work in multi-national teams and are committed to effective international cooperation.
We recognise the importance of research and responding to

God's directions for advance.
We believe in full participation and oneness in decision-making.
We value servant leaders who wait on God for vision and
direction.
We promote local and innovative strategies through
decentralised decision-making.
We make no appeals for funds.

(*Intercon report 1996*, pp. 47-48)

# APPENDIX G
## TIMELINE OF WEC HISTORY

WEC has always been a church-planting mission. As the church is planted and begins to thrive, the main thrust of WEC's activity has increasingly been directed to countries where overt Christian witness is hindered. Over the past 30 years the proportion of workers ministering in security-sensitive countries has steadily increased. We call such nations Creative Access Nations (CANs). Most of these lands are in the belt of countries from North-West Africa through Asia to the Pacific. To protect the lives of workers and local Christians in such places, people working there need to keep a low profile and usually take up useful secular employment or cooperate meaningfully with non-religious NGOs. These countries are not openly listed but referred to as 'CAN1', CAN2', etc. To indicate the mission's continued interest in the least evangelised parts of the world.

| | |
|---|---|
| 1910 | CT Studd's survey visit to Sudan |
| 1912 | New organisation mooted called Heart of Africa Mission (HAM) and Christ's Etceteras |
| 1913 | HAM officially founded, CT Studd and Alfred Buxton arrive in Congo, UK base commenced |
| 1915 | First 'Principles & Practice' drawn up *'Christ's Etceteras'* |
| 1919 | Name change from HAM to WEC |
| 1920 | USA base commenced |
| 1921 | Missionary Training Colony opened |
| 1922 | Australian, New Zealand and American Councils formed, Arabia entered (closed possibly 1929) |
| 1923 | Amazonia entered (transferred in 1931) |
| 1924 | Canada base commenced |
| 1926 | India ('Little Tibet') entered |
| 1928 | Priscilla Studd died |
| 1929 | Norman and Pauline Grubb sent to the UK |

| | |
|---|---|
| 1931 | CT Studd died, Norman Grubb becomes General Secretary |
| 1932 | 'Memorial Ten' |
| 1933 | 'Memorial Fifteen'; Colombia, Spanish Guinea (now Equatorial Guinea) entered |
| 1934 | 'Memorial Twenty-five', Ivory Coast entered |
| 1936 | Senegal, Canary Islands entered (now closed), Canada & USA bases re-established |
| 1937 | UK Youth Crusade founded, Upper Volta (now Burkina Faso) entered |
| 1938 | Liberia entered |
| 1939 | Portuguese Guinea (now Guinea-Bissau) entered |
| 1940 | Gold Coast (now Ghana) entered |
| 1941 | CLC founded and developed autonomously, West Indies entered (transferred to CLC) |
| 1942 | Australia base established |
| 1944 | 'Black Spots' Survey |
| 1946 | Elms Children's Home Scotland started, China entered |
| 1947 | Thailand entered, Switzerland base commenced, Leper & Medical Crusade founded (discontinued), Glasgow MTC commenced (closed 1977) |
| 1948 | Netherlands base commenced |
| 1949 | Kalimantan (Indonesia) entered |
| 1950 | Japan entered, Uruguay entered (closed 1977), France base commenced |
| 1951 | Scandinavia base commenced (closed 1978) |
| 1953 | Revival in the Congo, New Zealand base re-established |
| 1954 | Java and Venezuela entered |
| 1955 | Formosa (Taiwan) entered, South Africa base commenced |
| 1956 | South Korea entered, Tasmania MTC commenced |
| 1957 | Brazil and Gambia entered |
| 1958 | Vietnam entered (closed 1975), Germany base commenced |
| 1959 | *Bientôt* gospel literature founded |
| 1960 | Kilcreggan Conference Centre Scotland opened (closed 1995), CAN1 entered |
| 1961 | First International Leaders' Conference, IRO commenced, *19-point programme,* IMF field and Radio Worldwide founded, CLC released to become a separate organisation |

| | |
|---|---|
| 1962 | *SOON* and *Cedo* founded, France, Chad and CAN2 entered, UK WEC Press started (closed 2001) |
| 1963 | CAN3 entered |
| 1964 | Italy entered, Congo crisis, CFOW proposed |
| 1965 | South African MTC commenced (closed 1969) |
| 1966 | Gambia re-entered, Mozambique entered, Len and Iris Moules International Secretaries |
| 1967 | Bulstrode UK base purchased |
| 1968 | Spain entered, Singapore business office |
| 1969 | Intercon, CAN4 & 5 entered |
| 1970 | CAN6 entered, VIS in Ivory Coast commenced |
| 1971 | CAN7 entered, UK Immigrant Ministry founded |
| 1972 | Hong Kong, CAN8 & CAN9 entered |
| 1973 | CAN10 entered |
| 1974 | CC conference, International Resource Office commenced (now discontinued) |
| 1975 | Heini and Jo Schnyder Acting International Secretaries, Robert and Isobel Mackey International Secretaries |
| 1977 | Brazil base commenced, UK MOC commenced (closed 1990) |
| 1978 | Intercon, Word Worldwide founded, CAN11 entered |
| 1980 | Singapore base commenced, BCS in Senegal commenced |
| 1982 | CC conference, name change to WEC International |
| 1983 | Betel founded, Stewart and Marie Dinnen International Secretaries |
| 1984 | Intercon, Portugal, CAN12 & 13 commenced, Brazil MTC commenced, STEP program |
| 1985 | CAN14 & 15 commenced |
| 1986 | CC conference, Guinea (Conakry) entered, Hong Kong base commenced, Dieter and Renate Kuhl International Secretaries, CDC appointed |
| 1987 | Fiji base commenced |
| 1988 | CC conference, Liberia church's 50th jubilee |
| 1989 | Euro MTC Netherlands commenced, Greece entered |
| 1990 | Intercon, Mexico entered, MKEA, IT & CAN Business Consultants appointed |
| 1992 | CC conference, Bulgaria and Cambodia entered, Consultant-at-Large appointed |

1993   Albania entered
1994   CC conference, International Media Secretary appointed
1995   Gateway Canada commenced
1996   Intercon, CAN16 & 17 commenced, Asian MTC (Hong Kong closed 2005) and New Zealand MTC started, Rainbows of Hope founded, RUN advance
1997   Russia entered, South Korea base commenced, France base re-established
1998   CC conference, Thailand church's 50th jubilee
1999   Evan and Jenny Davies International Directors, Medical Advisor appointed
2000   CC Conference, Member Care consultant appointed, East Timor and Belgium entered, Japan and Uruguay churches' 50th jubilee
2002   Intercon, IDEA commenced (discontinued 2008)
2003   Amazon rentered, Recruitment Consultants appointed
2004   CC conference, CAN18 & 19 commenced
2005   Trevor and Jenny Kallmier International Directors, WEC Latino commenced
2006   Intercon, CAN20 & 21, Mexico base, Mexico CT commenced
2007   CC conference
2008   CC conference, CAN22 commenced
2009   CC conference, CAN23 commenced
2010   Intercon, NGO Consultants, Security & Crisis Consultant, ESL Consultant, Short-Term Mission Coordinator, Directors for International Mission Mobilisation appointed, International Office relocated to Singapore.

# APPENDIX H
## GLOSSARY AND ABBREVIATIONS

| | |
|---|---|
| AIM | Africa Inland Mission |
| CAN | Creative Access Nations |
| CC | Coordinating Council |
| CFOW or CFO | Centres of Fellowship and Outreach (Worldwide) |
| CIM | China Inland Mission |
| CP | Church-planting |
| CO or COC | Candidate Orientation (Course) |
| CT | Common name given to Charles Thomas Studd |
| DCD | Don't care a damn |
| DID | Deputy International Director |
| EMA | Evangelical Missionary Alliance |
| FL | Field Leader |
| GLW | Gospel Literature Worldwide (SOON etc) |
| ID | International Director |
| IDEA | International Department (or Director) for Equipping and Advance |
| IDR | International Director for Research |
| IDT | International Director for Training |
| IMF | Indonesian Missionary Fellowship |
| Intercon | International Leaders' Conference |
| IO | International Office |
| IRO | International Research Office |
| LC | Leaders' Council |
| LTS | Leadership Training Seminar(s) |
| LDS | Leadership Development Seminar(s) |
| MK | missionary kid(s) (child) |
| MKEA | Missionary Kids Education Advisor |
| MTC | Missionary Training College |
| OMF | Overseas Missionary Fellowship |
| *Ps & P* | WEC's constitution, *Principles and Practice* |
| RD | Regional Director |

| | |
|---|---|
| 'Rubi' | Norman Grubb's African name |
| RUN | *Reaching the Unevangelised Now* (special outreach programme) |
| RUP | Remaining Unevangelised People(s) |
| SB | Sending Base |
| SBL | Sending Base Leader |
| SVM | Student Volunteer Movement |
| STEP | *Strategy Towards Every People* (special outreach programme) |
| UFM | Unevangelised Fields Mission |
| WEC | The letters W E C stand for Worldwide Evangelization for Christ |
| WECer | Member of WEC |

# BIBLIOGRAPHY

Adams, K R, *The Foolishness of God*, (Christian Literature Crusade, Fort Washington, USA, 1981).

Aikman, D, *Jesus in Beijing: how Christianity is transforming China and changing the global balance of power*, (Monarch Books, Oxford, UK, 2003).

Anderson, D, *We felt like grasshoppers: the story of the Africa Inland Mission*, (Crossway Books, Nottingham, UK, 1994).

Anderson, G H, 'Christian Mission in AD2000: A glance backward', pp. 275-288 (*Missiology* vol. XXVIII, no. 3, July, 2000).

Andrew, Bro with J & E Sherrill, *God's Smuggler*, (Hodder and Stoughton, London, 1967).

Ashcraft, N, *At the Scent of Water*, (Christian Literature Crusade, Fort Washington, USA, 1986).

Bannister, E, *Access Without Visa: reaching people that other methods do not reach*, (WEC Publications, Gerrards Cross, 1994).

Barclay, P, *Crocodiles, Cannibals and Cream Teas: Leslie Sutton*, (Noble Books, London, 1998).

Bargen G, *Forever on the Move: reflecting God's goodness and grace*, (Colony Printing, Underwood, Australia, 2006).

Barnicoat, J, *Missionary Kids Manual 1*, (WEC Publications, Gerrards Cross, UK, 2003).

Barnicoat, J, *Missionary kids manual 2*, (WEC Publications, Gerrards Cross, UK, 2003).

Barrett, D B, *Cosmos and Chaos: a chronology of world evangelization from creation to new creation*, (New Hope, Alabama, USA, 1987).

Barrett, D B, 'The Status of Christian World Mission in the 1990s' in *Mission in the nineteen nineties*, pp.72-73, (Eerdmans Publishing Co, Grand Rapids, 1991).

Barrett, D, TM Johnson, P F Crossing, 'Missiometrics 2008: Reality checks for Christian communions', *International Bulletin of Missionary Research*, January 2008, (Overseas Ministries Study Center, New Haven, Conn, 2008).

Bebbington, D W, 'C H Spurgeon' in T Dowley (ed) *The History of Christianity: a Lion Handbook*, (Anzea Books, Surrey Hills, NSW, Australia, 1977).

Beeson, R & R M Hunsicker, *The Hidden Price of Greatness: encouragement from the lives of well-known Christians whose suffering produced spiritual growth*, (Tyndale House, Wheaton, USA, 1991).

Böker, T, 'What will happen to those who never heard the gospel?', *Conference of the Coordinating Council May 1998, Cuidad Real, Spain: report, resolutions and recommendations, pp. 113-122, Appendix C*, (IO, WEC International, Gerrards Cross, 1998).

Böker, T, *Fostering True Integration in WEC: fostering true integration of non-Western team members, particularly those from Korea, into WEC International*, (unpublished paper, submitted to Azusa Pacific University, Los Angeles, CA, USA, 2008).

Booth, P, *Slim Fingers*, (Christian Literature Crusade, Fort Washington, PA, USA, 1976).

Booth, P, *The Fifth Dimension: living in the presence of God*, (Kingsway Publications, Eastbourne, UK, 1989).

Booth, W, *In Darkest England and the Way Out*, (Salvation Army, London, 1890).

Brierley, L, *Thy Kingdom Come*, (Evangelical Publishing House, London, 1944).

Brierley, L, *The Challenge of the Unachieved – Section 4 of World Survey*, (WEC, London, 1961).

Brierley, L, *19-Point Programme: personal notes of the 1961 Conference written at the time*, (unpublished document in the library of Evan Davies, 1961).

Brierley, L, *They are Bread for Us: continental surveys of the world mission situation*, (Evangelical Missionary Alliance, London, 1972).

Brierley, L, *Historic Background to the Black Spots Survey 1942-45*, (unpublished document in the library of Evan Davies, 1994).

Broomhall, A J, *Hudson Taylor and China's Open Century: book six; assault on the nine*, (Hodder & Stoughton, London, 1988).

Broomhall, A J, *Hudson Taylor and China's Open Century: book seven; it is not death to die!* (Hodder & Stoughton, London, 1989).

Burgess, A, *Daylight Must Come: the story of Dr Helen Roseveare*,

(Pan Books, London, 1975).

Buxton, A B, *1913-1922: the first ten years of the Heart of Africa Mission*, (Heart of Africa Mission, London, 1924).

Buxton, E, *Reluctant Missionary*, (Lutterworth Press, London, 1968).

Buxton, G, *Dancing in the Dark: the privilege of participating in the ministry of Christ*, (Paternoster Press, Carlisle, 2001).

*Candidate Commission Report*, (IO, WEC International, Gerrards Cross, 1986).

Chamberlain, J, 'Leading a happy and productive multi-national team', *Asiacon 94*, (WEC International, Singapore, 1994).

*Celebrate! 200 years of taking the gospel to the world*, (Church Missionary Society, Sydney, 1998).

Chevreau, G, *We Dance Because We Cannot Fly: from heroin to hope: stories of redemption and transformation*, (Sovereign World, Tonbridge, UK, 2002).

*Christ Alone: a pictorial presentation of Hudson Taylor's life and legacy*, (OMF, Hong Kong, 2005).

Clark, P A, *Organisations in Action: competition between contexts.* (Routledge, London, 1999).

Clarke, A, 'It all started in a beauty salon' in S Dinnen (ed), *Real Guidance: real examples of guidance to help you live your life*, pp. 91-100, (Christian Focus Publications, Fearn, UK, 2003).

Cleverdon, I V, *Pools on Glowing Sand: the story of Karl Kumm*, (Speciality Press, Melbourne, 1936).

Cliff, N, *A Flame of Sacred Love: the life of Benjamin Broomhall friend of China*, (OM Publishing, Carlisle, 1998).

Collier, R, *The General Next to God: the story of William Booth and the Salvation Army*, (Collins Fontana Books, London, 1965).

*Communications Directory 1999-2000*, (WEC International, Gerrards Cross).

*Communications Directory 2001-2002*, (WEC International, Gerrards Cross).

*Communications Directory 2003-2004*, (WEC International, Gerrards Cross).

*Communications Directory 2007-2008*, (WEC International, Gerrards Cross).

*Communications Directory 2009-2011*, (WEC International, Gerrards

Cross).

*Conference of the Coordinating Council June 1986: report, resolutions and recommendations, Fort Washington, PA, USA,* (IO, WEC International, Gerrards Cross).

*Conference of the Coordinating Council May-June 1988: report, resolutions and recommendations, Hamilton, Ontario, Canada,* (WEC International, Gerrards Cross).

*Conference of the Coordinating Council May 1992: report, resolutions and recommendations, MTC, St Leonards, Tasmania, Australia,* (IO, WEC International, Gerrards Cross).

*Conference of the Coordinating Council, May 1994, Fort Washington, USA: report, resolutions and recommendations,* (IO, WEC International, Gerrards Cross).

*Conference of the Coordinating Council May 1998, Cuidad Real, Spain: report, resolutions and recommendations,* (IO, WEC International, Gerrards Cross).

*Conference of the Coordinating Council, 1-15 April 2000, Fort Washington, USA: report, resolutions and recommendations,* (IO, WEC International, Gerrards Cross).

*Conference of the Coordinating Council 7-17 July 2007, Cornerstone, Beugen, Netherlands,* (IO, WEC International, Gerrards Cross).

*Conference of the Coordinating Council, 6-18 May 2008, Belo Horizonte, Brazil,* (IO, WEC International, Gerrards Cross).

*Conference of the Coordinating Council, 18-28 May 2009, Morisset (NSW), Australia,* (IO, WEC International, Gerrards Cross).

*Consultative Council Conference, March 1974: reports proposals and resolutions,* (Worldwide Evangelization Crusade, Kilcreggan).

Coomes, A, *The Authorised Biography of Festo Kivengere,* (Monarch, Eastbourne, 1990).

*Coordinating Council Conference June 1982: report and recommendations,* (IO, WEC International, Gerrards Cross).

Cornell, D, *The role of single women in present day mission,* (WEC, Fort Washington, PA, 1965).

Cox, J, 'What I have learned from writing "The British missionary enterprise since 1700"' in *International Bulletin of Missionary Research,* April 2008, pp. 586-87.

Crane, E, & B Allinger, *Mountain Daybreak,* (Christian Literature

Crusade, London, 1956).

*Crisis Management: Team Manual 6*, (IO, WEC International, Gerrards Cross, 2001).

Cunningham, L, *Daring to Live On the Edge: the adventure of faith and finances*, (Sovereign World, Tonbridge, 1991).

Cupit, T (ed.), *Five Till Midnight: church planting for AD 2000 and beyond*, (Home Mission Board of the Southern Baptist Convention, Atlanta, USA, 1994).

Davelaar, T & J Riemersma, 'Flexibility, frankness and freedom' in E Davies and S Dinnen, (eds.) *Straight From The Heart: a symposium by various WEC contributors*, pp. 74-75, (WEC Publications, Gerrards Cross, 2004).

Davidson, A I, *High Adventure with God*, (Living Books for All, Manila, 1974).

Davies, D, 'Nala – hidden in the forest' in L Moules (ed.), *This is no accident: testimonies of a trial of faith in Congo*, pp. 72-78, (Worldwide Evangelization Crusade, London, 1965).

Davies, D, *The Captivity and Triumph of Winnie Davies*, (Hodder and Stoughton, London, 1968).

Davies, D, *With Christ in Congo Forests: during the persecution under rebel occupation*, (WEC, Gerrards Cross, 1971).

Davies, E, 'Twenty seven unbelievable years' in S Hart (ed.), *Making a World of Difference: WEC MTC celebrating 40 years in 1996*, (Unpublished paper, WEC Missionary Training College, St Leonards, Tasmania, 1996).

Davies, E & S Dinnen (eds.), *Straight From the Heart: a symposium* by various WEC contributors, (WEC Publications, Gerrards Cross, 2004).

Davies, F, *Listening: celebrating 40 years of Radio Worldwide ministry*, (Radio Worldwide, Leeds, 2001).

Dinnen, S, *When I Say Move!* (Christian Literature Crusade, London, 1972).

Dinnen, S, (foreword): 'We are on target!' in *Report and Resolutions of the International Leaders' Conference 26 May – 18 June 1984*, (WEC International, Gerrards Cross, 1984).

Dinnen, S, *Here We Stand: foundations for effective Christian service*, (WEC, Gerrards Cross, 1985).

Dinnen, S, *Summit Living: selections from Norman Grubb's writings*, (CLC Books, Fort Washington, PA, 1986).

Dinnen, S, *All For the Best: testimonies of Christian growth*, (WEC, Gerrards Cross, 1988).

Dinnen, S, *Rescue Shop Within a Yard of Hell*, (Christian Focus Publications, Fearn, UK, 1995).

Dinnen, S, *Faith on Fire: Norman Grubb and the building of WEC*, (Christian Focus Publications, Fearn, UK, 1997).

Dinnen, S, *You Can Learn to Lead*, (Christian Focus Publications, Fearn, UK, 1997).

Dinnen, S & M, *Freedom and Fullness: the teachings and writings of Norman Grubb (1966-1993)*, (IO, WEC International, Gerrards Cross, 1999).

Dinnen, S & M, *Sacking the Frontiers of Hell*, (Christian Focus Publications, Fearn, UK, 1999).

Dinnen, S, *How Are You Doing? 25 checklists for your spiritual life*, (Christian Focus Publications, Fearn, UK, 2001).

Dinnen, S, *Learning about Union with Christ*, (Christian Focus Publications, Fearn, UK, 2001).

Dinnen, S, *Pulling back the curtain on WEC's Principles and Practice*, (unpublished paper, IO, WEC International, Gerrards Cross, UK, 2002).

Dinnen, S, *Real Guidance: real examples of guidance to help you live your life*, (Christian Focus Publications, Fearn, UK, 2003).

Dinnen, S & G Myers, *Thousands: a church is born in the Indonesian rainforest*, (WEC Publications, UK, 2010).

Dowley, T (ed), *The History of Christianity: a Lion Handbook*, (Anzea Books, Surrey Hills, NSW, 1977).

Drew, N, *Himalayan Harvest: Kashmir cameos*, (Worldwide Evangelization Crusade, London, 1966).

Dulka, E & D, *Colombian Jungle Escape*, (WEC Publications, Gerrards Cross, 1992).

*Ecclesiology Commission Report* 1986, (IO, WEC International, Gerrards Cross, 1986).

Eitel, K E, *Paradigm Wars: the Southern Baptist International Mission Board faces the Third Millennium*, (Regnum Books, Oxford, 2000).

Eley, J, *God's Brumby*, ed S Dinnen, (self-published by Joan Eley, Cleveland, QLD, Australia, 1982).

Engel, J F & W A Dyrness, *Changing the Mind of Missions: where have we gone wrong?* (Inter Varsity Press, Downers Grove, IL, USA, 2000).

Fiedler, K, *The Story of Faith Missions: from Hudson Taylor to present day Africa*, (Regnum Books, Oxford, 1994).

*Field Workers' Manual: Team Manual 5*, (IO, WEC International, Gerrards Cross, 2001).

*Finance Commission Report 1986*, (IO, WEC International, Gerrards Cross, 1986).

Garrison, D, *Church Planting Movements*, (Office of Overseas Operations, International Mission Board of the Southern Baptist Convention, Richmond, VA, USA, 2000).

Gaskin, R F, *Journey to the White Man's Grave: who'd be a missionary?* (self-published by Ross Gaskin, Ashton, SA, Australia 2004).

Grubb, K, *Crypts of Power*, (Hodder & Stoughton, London, 1971).

Grubb, N P, *Fenton Hall: pioneer and hero*, 6th edn. (Worldwide Evangelization Crusade, London, 1930).

Grubb, N P, *CT Studd – Cricketer and Pioneer*, (Lutterworth Press, London, 1933).

Grubb, N P, *Modern Crusaders: the challenge of Colombia*, 3rd edn, (Worldwide Evangelization Crusade, London, 1937).

Grubb, N P, *Penetrating Faith in Spanish Guinea*, (Worldwide Evangelization Crusade, London, 1937).

Grubb, N P, *Alfred Buxton of Abyssinia and Congo*, (Lutterworth Press, London, 1942).

Grubb, N P, *Touching the Invisible*, 3rd edn, (Lutterworth Press, London, 1942).

Grubb, N P, *Ploughing Through: a work of faith in the Ivory Coast*, (Evangelical Publishing House, London, 1943).

Grubb, N P, *Christ in Congo Forests*, (Lutterworth Press, London, 1945).

Grubb, N P, *After CT Studd: sequel to the life of the famous pioneer-missionary*, 5th edn (Lutterworth Press, London, 1946).

Grubb, N P, *The Law of Faith*, (Lutterworth Press, London, 1947).

Grubb, N P, *Successor to CT Studd: the story of Jack Harrison*,

(Lutterworth Press, London, 1949).

Grubb, N P, *A Mighty Work of the Spirit*, (Worldwide Evangelization Crusade, London, 1950).

Grubb, N P, *Continuous Revival*, (Christian Literature Crusade, London, 1952).

Grubb, N P, *Rees Howells Intercessor*, (Lutterworth Press, London, 1953).

Grubb, N P, *J D Drysdale: prophet of holiness*, (Lutterworth Press, London, 1955).

Grubb, N P, *The Liberating Secret*, (Lutterworth Press, London, 1955).

Grubb, N P, *The Deep Things of God*, (Lutterworth Press, London, 1958).

Grubb, N P, *Leap of Faith*, (Christian Literature Crusade, London, 1962).

Grubb, N P, *First the Blade: the story of WEC: with field surveys by Leslie Brierley*, (Worldwide Evangelization Crusade, London, 1963).

Grubb, N P, *The Key to Everything*, (Christian Literature Crusade, Fort Washington, PA, 1964).

Grubb, N P, *God Unlimited*, (Lutterworth Press, London, 1965).

Grubb, N P, *The Growth of WEC: with Field Survey by Leslie Brierley*, 3rd edn (Worldwide Evangelization Crusade, London, 1966).

Grubb, N P, *Once Caught, No Escape: my life story*, (Lutterworth Press, London, 1969).

Grubb, N P, *Mighty Through God: the life of Edith Moules*, (Lutterworth Press, London, 1971).

Grubb, N P, Foreword in S Dinnen, *When I Say Move!* (Christian Literature Crusade, London, 1972).

Grubb, N P, *The Four Pillars of WEC*, (Worldwide Evangelization Crusade, London, 1973).

Grubb, N P, *Who Am I?* (Lutterworth Press, Guildford, UK, 1974).

Grubb, N P, *Yes I Am*, (Christian Literature Crusade, Fort Washington, PA, 1982).

Grubb, N P, *Are We/We are Still on Target*, (Heini Germann-Edey & Christian Outreach, Nashville, 1984).

Grubb, N P, *Summit Living: selected daily readings*, compiled by

S Dinnen, (Christian Literature Crusade, Fort Washington, PA, USA, 1985).

Grubb, N P (ed), *The Spirit of Revival*, (Christian Focus Publications, Fearn UK, 2000). (Originally published in 1954 by Christian Literature Crusade under the title *This Is That*.)

Grubb, N P, *My Dear CUMB: Norman Grubb's letters to the Cambridge University Missionary Band 1922-1989*, compiled by Deedee Winter, (Author House, Bloomington, Ind, USA, 2006).

Grubb, N P, *Knight of Faith: the letters of Norman Percy Grubb*, Vol 1, ed by Deedee Winter, (Author House, Bloomington, Ind, 2006).

Grubb, N P, *Knight of Faith: the letters of Norman Percy Grubb*, Vol 2, ed by Deedee Winter, (Author House, Bloomington, Ind, 2006).

Grubb, N P, *The Japan Talks: Karizawa Japan 1954*, ed by Deedee Winter, (Author House, Bloomington, Ind, 2009).

Guthrie, S, *Missions in the Third Millennium*, (Paternoster Press, Carlisle, 2000).

Harris, J, *We Wish We'd Done More: ninety years of CMS and aboriginal issues in north Australia*, (Openbook Publishers, Adelaide, 1998).

Hart, S (ed.), *Making a World of Difference: WEC MTC, celebrating 40 years in 1996,* (WEC Missionary Training College, St Leonards, Tasmania, Australia, 1996).

Hart, S (ed.), *God Still Steps In: testimonies of Australian workers of the Worldwide Evangelization Crusade*, (self-published, Mission Publications of Australia, Lawson, NSW, 1983).

Harverson, S, *Doctor in Vietnam*, (Lutterworth Press, London, 1968).

Hastings, A, *A History of African Christianity 1950-1975*, (Cambridge University Press, Cambridge, 1979).

Hentschel, L, 'God's interfering presence' in *Whoever You Are: three ordinary women; three stories of an amazing God*, by M Vigilio, L Hentschel & J Forbes, pp. 61-83, (WEC Publications, Gerrards Cross, 2004).

Hession, R, *The Calvary Road*, (Christian Literature Crusade, London, 1950).

Hicks, D, *Globalizing Missions: the Operation Mobilization experience*, (Editorial Unilit, Miami, FL, USA, 1994).

Hildebrand, J, *History of the Church in Africa*, (Africa Christian

Press, Ghana, 1981).

Hochschild, A, *King Leopold's Ghost: a story of greed, terror and heroism in colonial Africa*, (Mariner Book, Houghton Mifflin, Boston, 1999).

*Intercon 90: report and resolutions of the international leaders' conference, held in Kilcreggan, Scotland, 23 May-18 June 1990*, (IO, WEC International, Gerrards Cross, 1990).

*Intercon 1996: report and resolutions of the international leaders' conference, held in Rehe, Germany, 11 June-2 July 1996*, (IO, WEC International, Gerrards Cross, 1996).

*Intercon 2002 Report: resolutions, reports, recommendations, Rehe, Germany, June 2002*, (IO, Gerrards Cross, Wec International, 2002).

*Intercon 2006 Report: devotions, decisions, reports*, (IO, Gerrards Cross, Wec International, 2006).

*International Conference: Kilcreggan, Scotland 18 May-12 June 1961*, (Worldwide Evangelization Crusade, London, 1961).

*International Guidelines: Team Manual 1*, (IO, WEC International, Gerrards Cross, 1998).

*International Leaders' Conference Report, June 1969*, (Worldwide Evangelization Crusade, Gerrards Cross 1969).

*International Leaders' Conference: report and resolutions 3-26 June 1978*, (Worldwide Evangelization Crusade, Kilcreggan, 1978).

Jackson, J C, *No Other Foundation: the church through twenty centuries*, (Crossway Books, Westchester, Ill, USA, 1980).

Johnstone, P, *The Church is Bigger Than You Think: structures and strategies for the church in the 21st Century*, (Christian Focus Publications, Fearn, UK, 1998).

Johnstone, P & J Mandryk, *Operation World: 21st century edition*, (Paternoster Publishing, Carlisle, 2001).

Johnstone, P, 'Seeking and Finding' in E Davies & S Dinnen (eds), *Straight From the Heart: a symposium by various WEC contributors*, pp. 85-89, (WEC Publications, Gerrards Cross, 2004).

Kennedy, A, 'After-thoughts' in *Report and Resolutions of the International Leaders' Conference 26 May – 18 June 1984*, pp. 94-96, (IO, WEC International, Gerrards Cross, 1984).

Kennedy, A, *The Church: an ecclesiology study manual*, (self-published, Abidjan, 1992).

Krueger, H, *Chosen to Go: a true story of my 52 years as a missionary in Ivory Coast, West Africa*, (self-published, Kamloops, BC, Canada, 2000).

Kuhl, D, 'Strange turns on a desert road' in S Dinnen (ed), *All For the Best: testimonies of Christian growth*, pp. 68-73, (WEC Press, Gerrards Cross, 1988).

Kuhl, D, '*Internationalization of an interdenominational faith mission: how acceptable and effective are multi-cultural teams in WEC International?*' (MA Ministry Perspective Project, Columbia International University, Columbia, SC, USA, 1996).

Kuhl, D, 'Norman Grubb and Jacob Boehme (1575-1624)' in S & M Dinnen, *Freedom and Fullness: the teachings and writings of Norman Grubb (1966-1993)*, pp. 132-141, (IO, WEC International, Gerrards Cross, 1999).

Kulesky, H J, *Travail, Triumph, Jubilee: the history of the United Liberia Inland Church*, (WEC International, Fort Washington, PA, USA, 1989).

Lapworth, B, *Derby – Dakar: a journey of faith*, (self-published, printed by Freedom Print, Holmer Green, Bucks, UK, 2005).

Latourette, K S, *A History of Christianity: Volume II: AD1500 - AD1975*, (Harper & Row, New York, 1975).

Lausanne Movement Congresses 2008, retrieved 28 January 2008, from www.lausanne.org/gatherings.html/

*Leaders' manual*, (Worldwide Evangelisation Crusade, Brisbane, n.d.).

Lidorio, R, *Unafraid of the Sacred Forest: the birth of a church in an African tribe*, (Christian Focus Publications, Fearn, UK, 2007).

Loane, M L, *The Story of the China Inland Mission in Australia and New Zealand 1860-1964*, (China Inland Mission Overseas Missionary Fellowship, Sydney, 1965).

Lyall, L T, *A Passion for the Impossible: the China Inland Mission 1865-1965*, (Hodder & Stoughton, London, 1965).

Macindoe, B, *Only One Life: the story of John Haywood missionary to VietNam*, (WEC Press, Gerrards Cross, 1968).

Macindoe, B, *Going for God: the story of Bessie Brierley*, (Hodder &

Stoughton, London, 1972).

Mackey, R, *God Steps in Again*, (Christian Literature Crusade, London, 1973).

Mackie, R C, *Layman Extraordinary: John R Mott 1865-1955*, (Hodder, London, 1965).

Macmillan, D, 'It's worth it!' in E Davies & S Dinnen (eds), *Straight from the Heart: a symposium by various WEC contributors*, (WEC Publications, Gerrards Cross, 2004).

McCasland, D, *Oswald Chambers: abandoned to God*, (Discovery House Publishers, Grand Rapids, USA, 1993).

McDermid, M (ed), *The Adventure of Working with God*, (WEC, Fort Washington, PA, USA, undated).

McElligott, P, *On Giants' Shoulders*, (WEC Press, Gerrards Cross, 1994).

McManners, J (ed), *The Oxford History of Christianity*, (Oxford University Press, Oxford, 2002).

*Media Commission Report 1986,* (IO, WEC International, Gerrards Cross, 1986).

Millard, E C, *The Same Lord: an account of the mission tour of the Rev George C Grubb, MA, in Australia, Tasmania and New Zealand,* (E Marlborough and Co, London, 1883).

Miller, B, *George Muller: man of faith and miracles*, (Bethany House Publishers, Minneapolis, Min, USA, 1941).

Mirams, S, *Twentieth Century History 1945-2000*, (Thomson Social Science Press, Southbank, Vic, Australia, 2004).

Moon, S S-C, 'The Protestant missionary movement in Korea: current growth and development', in *International Bulletin of Missionary Research*, April 2008, pp. 59-64.

Mott, J R, *The Decisive Hour of Christian Missions*, (Church Missionary Society, London, 1910).

Moules, L J, *Three Miles High*, (Christian Literature Crusade, London, 1951).

Moules, L, *Then God Stepped In: a jubilee publication*, (Christian Literature Crusade, London, 1963).

Moules, L, *Some Want It Tough*, (Christian Literature Crusade, London, 1964).

Moules, L J (ed), *This Is No Accident: testimonies of a trial of faith in*

*Congo,* (Worldwide Evangelization Crusade, London, 1965).

Moules, L, *Ascent of the Inner Everest,* (Christian Literature Crusade, London, 1971).

Moules, L & I, *Leadership Manual,* (WEC, Gerrards Cross, 1974).

Myers, G & Woodford, B (eds), *Serving Together without Falling Apart: Team Manual 3,* (IO, WEC International, Gerrards Cross, 1997).

Myers, G (ed), *Life Lessons: life-changing stories for Christian growth,* (Christian Focus Publications, Fearn, UK, 2010).

Neill, S, *A History of Christian Missions,* (Penguin Books, Harmondsworth, 1964).

O'Donnell, K (ed), *Doing Member Care Well: perspectives and practices from around the world,* (William Carey Library, Pasadena, CA, USA, 2002).

O'Donnell, D, 'Flora Gibson' in E Davies & S Dinnen (eds), *Straight from the Heart: a symposium by various WEC contributors,* pp. 101, (WEC Publications, Gerrards Cross, 2004).

Padilla, C R, 'An age of liberation' in T Dowley (ed), *The History of Christianity: a Lion Handbook,* pp. 628-645, (Anzea Books, Surrey Hills, NSW, Australia, 1999).

Paton, M & M, 'Standing and moving in faith' in S Dinnen (ed), *All for the Best: testimonies of Christian growth,* pp. 115-120, (WEC, Gerrards Cross, 1988).

Peters, G W, *Indonesia Revival: focus on Timor,* (Zondervan, Grand Rapids, 1973).

Pierard, R V, 'Shaking the foundations: World War I, the Western Allies and German Protestant Missions', in *International Bulletin of Missionary Research,* vol. 22, no. 1, 1998, pp. 13-19.

Pierson, A T, *George Muller of Bristol,* (Pickering & Inglis Ltd, London, 1899).

Piper, J, *Let the Nations Be Glad! The supremacy of God in missions,* (Baker Books, Grand Rapids, 1993).

Pollock, J C, *The Cambridge Seven,* (Inter-Varsity Fellowship, London, 1955).

*Prayer Force Handbook,* (WEC International, Gerrards Cross, 1996).

*Praying Always: prayer handbook of WEC International 1994 and 1995,* (WEC International, Gerrards Cross, 1993).

*Principles & Practice of WEC International,* (Worldwide Evangelization Crusade, Gerrards Cross, 1977).

*Principles & Practice of WEC International,* (WEC International, Gerrards Cross, 1982).

*Principles & Practice of WEC International,* (IO, WEC International, Gerrards Cross, 1990).

*Principles & Practice of WEC International,* (IO, WEC International, Gerrards Cross, 2000).

*Principles & Practice of WEC International,* (IO, WEC International, Gerrards Cross, 2005).

Purves, M, *Life of Jock Purves,* (WEC Press, Gerrards Cross, 1995).

Purves, J, *Lal Sahib,* (Stirling Tract Enterprise, Scotland, undated).

Purves, J, *The Unlisted Legion,* (The Banner of Truth Trust, Edinburgh, 1977).

Randall, I, *Entire Devotion to God: Wesleyan holiness and British overseas mission in the early twentieth century,* (The Wesley Fellowship, Lutterworth, UK, 1998).

Raymo, J with E Davies, *Meeting Jesus in Australia: life at the WEC Missionary Training College, Tasmania,* (WEC Press, Fort Washington, PA, USA, 1990).

Raymo, J, *Marching to a Different Drummer: rediscovering missions in an age of affluence and self-interest,* (Christian Literature Crusade, Fort Washington, PA, USA, 1996).

*Regional Directors' Handbook: Team Manual 2,* (IO, WEC International, Gerrards Cross, 1997).

*Renewed to Run for Jesus: devotional ministry from Intercon 2002: arranged for daily prayer,* (IO, WEC International, Gerrards Cross, 2002).

*Report and Resolutions of the International Leaders' Conference 26 May-18 June 1984,* (WEC International, Gerrards Cross, 1984).

Rieder, J & G, *Jewels for His Crown,* (Leathers Publishing, Leawood, KS, USA, 1999).

Richardson, K, *The Garden of Miracles: the story of the African Inland Mission,* (African Inland Mission, London, 1976).

Ritter, L, *Concepts that Shaped the Modern World from A–Z,* (Macmillan, South Yarra, Vic, Australia, 2001).

Robbins, S P & N S Barnwell, *Organisation Theory in Australia,*

(Prentice Hall of Australia, Sydney, 1989).

Roseveare, H, *Doctor Among Congo Rebels*, (Lutterworth Press, London, 1965).

Roseveare, H, *Give Me This Mountain: an autobiography*, (Inter-Varsity Fellowship, London, 1966).

Roseveare, H, *He Gave Us a Valley*, (Inter-Varsity Press, Leicester, UK, 1976).

Roseveare, H, *Living Stones: sacrifice, faith, holiness, fellowship: 75 years of WEC*, (Hodder & Stoughton, London, 1988).

Roseveare, H, 'Introduction' in N P Grubb (ed), *The Spirit of Revival*, pp. 7-12, (Christian Focus Publications, Fearn, UK, 2000).

Roseveare, H, 'The start and the heart,' in E Davies and S Dinnen (eds) *Straight From the Heart: a symposium by various WEC contributors*, (WEC Publications, Gerrards Cross, 2004).

Roseveare, H, *Digging Ditches: the latest chapter of an inspirational life*, (Christian Focus, Fearn, UK, 2005).

Roundhill, K, *Pages from a Diary in the Life of Faith*, (Hodder and Stoughton, London, 1975).

Roundhill, K, *Just a Thought*, (self published, Christchurch, New Zealand, undated).

Rowbotham, E, *Would You Believe It!* (Worldwide Evangelisation Crusade, Gerrards Cross, 1982).

Rowe, M, *Why on Earth a Mansion?* (WEC Press, Gerrards Cross, 1988).

Rowe N, 'A move and a miracle' in Robert Mackey (ed), *God Steps In Again*, (Christian Literature Crusade, London, 1973).

Rowe N, 'Jesus Christ running around in the messengers' in E Davies & S Dinnen (eds), *Straight From the Heart: a symposium by various WEC contributors*, (WEC Publications, Gerrards Cross, 2004).

Rowe, N, *Trusting Not Trying: finding peace in a world of stress*, (WEC Publications, Gerrards Cross, 2008).

Ruiz, D D (ed), 'The Two Thirds World: Lausanne Occasional Paper no44', in D. Claydon (ed) *A New Vision, A New Heart, A Renewed Call: Lausanne occasional papers from the 2004 Forum for World Evangelization hosted by the Lausanne Committee for World Evangelization, Pattaya, Thailand September 29 – October 2008*, pp. 115-170, (William Carey Library, Pasadena, USA, 2005).

Ruscoe, A W, *The Lame Take the Prey*, (Bethany Fellowship, Minneapolis, Min, USA, 1968).

Rusha, G, *Truth to Tell in Borneo*, (Oliphants, London, 1969).

*Salvation Army Handbook of Doctrine*, (Salvation Army International Headquarters, London, 1878).

Sanneh, L, *Whose Religion is Christianity? The Gospel beyond the West*, (Eerdmans, Grand Rapids, Mich, USA, 2003).

Scheunemann, D, *The Ministries of the Holy Spirit: studied against the background of the Indonesian revival*, (The Indonesian Missionary Fellowship (YPPII), Batu-Malang, Indonesia, 1984).

Scotland, T, *Voice From the Stars*, (T & L Scotland, Perth, Australia, 1990).

Scotland, T, *After Voice From the Stars*, (T & L Scotland, Perth, Australia, 1998).

Searle, C, *God Can*, (Worldwide Evangelisation Crusade, Arbroath, UK, 1963).

Searle, L, *Going Through with God*, (WEC Press, London, 1965).

*Sending Base Workers' Manual*, (Worldwide Evangelisation Crusade, Tasmania, Australia, 1976).

Shaloff, S, *Reform in Leopold's Congo*, (John Knox Press, Richmond, VA, USA, 1970).

Shenk, W R, *Changing Frontiers of Mission*, (Orbis Books, Maryknoll, NY, USA, 2001).

Staniford, F, *Operation Ivory Coast*, (Christian Literature Crusade, London, 1956).

Steer, R, *Delighted in God: a biography of George Muller*, (Hodder & Stoughton, London, 1975).

Street, R, *Called to Be God's People*, (International Headquarters, London, 1999).

Studd, CT, *The Chocolate Soldier*, (WEC International, London, 1912, updated ed 1989).

Studd, CT, *For the Shame of Christ*, (Worldwide Evangelization Crusade, London, est 1912).

Studd, CT, *The Heart of Africa: the launch of an assault on the devil's den*, (Self-published CT Studd, Norwood, UK, est. 1912).

Studd, CT, *The Laugh of Faith*, (Worldwide Evangelization Crusade, London, est 1912).

Studd, CT, *Quaint Rhymes for the Battlefield by a Quondam Cricketer*, (James Clarke, London, 1914).

Studd, CT, *Christ's Etceteras*, (WEC Publications, Gerrards Cross, 1915, facsimile republished 1975).

Studd, CT, *The DCD*, (self-published, printed by Graham & Heslip, Belfast, 1928).

Studd, CT, *Reminiscences of Mrs CT Studd*, (Worldwide Evangelization Crusade, London, 1930).

Studd, CT, *Some Wish to Live ... quotations from CT Studd*, (Worldwide Evangelization Crusade, Gerrards Cross, undated).

Sutton, S S, *A Vision of the Deep: uncovering the treasure of life in Christ*, (CLC Publications, Fort Washington, PA, USA, 2009).

Symes, P, *Action Stations Colombia*, (Christian Literature Crusade, London, 1955).

Tait, V G, *Attitude of Gratitude: the life of Wilfrid Watson*, (WEC Publications, Gerrards Cross, 1992).

Taylor, J, 'The future of Christianity' in J McManners (ed), *The Oxford History of Christianity*, (Oxford University Press, Oxford, 1993).

Taylor, W D (ed), *Too Valuable to Lose: exploring the causes and cures of missionary attrition*, (William Carey Library, Pasadena, CA, USA, 1997).

*The Crusade Hymns*, (WEC, Glasgow, UK, undated).

Theobald, D & B, *Battles, Bricks and Bees: letters from Don*, (Betty Theobald, WEC, Auckland, Australia, 1988).

Tiplady, R (ed), *One World or Many? The impact of globalisation on mission*, (William Carey Library, Pasadena, CA, USA, 2003).

Thorne, A, *God at Work in Spanish Guinea*, (Evangelical Publishing House, London, 1943).

Tucker, R A, *From Jerusalem to Irian Jaya: a biographical history of Christian Missions*, (Zondervan, Grand Rapids, Mich, USA, 2004).

*United We Serve: Team Manual 7*, (IO, WEC International, Gerrards Cross, 2002).

Vidler, A R, *The Church in an Age of Revolution: 1789 to the present day: vol. V. The Pelican history of the church*, (Hodder & Stoughton, London, 1961).

Vincent, E, *No Sacrifice Too Great*, (WEC Publications, Gerrards

Cross, 1992).

Walker, J (ed), *Fool and Fanatic: quotations from the letters of CT Studd*, (WEC, Gerrards Cross, 1980).

Walker, W, *A History of the Christian Church*, 4th ed, (T&T Clark, Edinburgh, 1985).

Walls, A F, *The Missionary Movement in Christian History: studies in the transmission of faith*, (T&T Clark, Edinburgh, 1996).

Walls, A F, *The Cross-cultural Process in Christian History: studies in the transmission and appropriation of faith*, (Orbis Books, Maryknoll, NY, USA, 2004).

Walters, T B, *Charles T Studd: Cricketer and Missionary*, (Epworth Press, London, 1930).

Warne, F G, *George Muller: the man of faith and the work established by him*, (Pickering and Inglis, London, undated).

Watt, E S, *Floods on Dry Ground: revival in the Congo*, (Marshall, Morgan & Scott Ltd, London, 1939).

Webster, D, *The Shimmering Heat: memories of a bush doctor in East Africa*, (S L Hunt Ltd, Rushden, UK, 2007).

WEC International website: www.wec-int.org retrieved 7 July 2006.

Winter, R D, 'The world Christian movement 950-1975: an interpretive essay' in K S Latourette, *A History of Christianity, Vol II: AD 1500 - AD 1975*, pp. 1477-1506, (Harper & Row, New York, 1975).

Winter, R D, 'The Long Look: eras of missions history', in R D Winter and S C Hawthorne (eds), *Perspectives on the World Christian Movement: a reader*, pp. 167-177, (William Carey Press, Pasadena, CA, USA, 1981).

Winter, R D, 'Fifteen changes for tomorrow's missionary', in *Mission in the nineteen nineties*, pp. 46-50, (Eerdmans Publishing Co, Grand Rapids & Overseas Ministries Study Center, New Haven, CT, USA, 1991).

Winter, R D & S C Hawthorne, *Perspectives on the World Christian Movement: a reader*, (William Carey Press, Pasadena, CA, 1981).

Woodford, B & S Dinnen, *Serving Together: a manual on inter-cultural relationships within WEC International*, (IRO, WEC International, Gerrards Cross, 1987).

Woodford, D B, *One Church, Many Churches: a five-model approach* to church planting and evaluation, (D Miss dissertation, Fuller Theological Seminary, USA, 1997).

Woodford, D B, *Prepare to Build: discovering God's plan for the church*, revised edition, (private publication, Hamilton, New Zealand, 2005).

Woodford, B, *Master Plan: Biblical foundations for living churches*, (EastWest College, Taupiri, New Zealand, 2007).

*World Missionary Conference 1910, Report of Commission 1: carrying the gospel to the non-Christian world*, (Oliphant, Anderson & Ferrier, Edinburgh & London, 1910).

Worral, B G, *The Making of the Modern Church: Christianity in England since 1800*, (SPCK, London, 1988).

Wraight, P, *On to the Summit: the Len Moules story*, (Kingsway Publications, Eastbourne, UK, 1981).

Yoo, B K, *Untold Stories of Missionary Yoo*, (WEC Publications, Gerrards Cross, 2009).

*2004 Conference of the Coordinating Council, April 2004, Seoul, Korea*, (IO, WEC International, Gerrards Cross, 2004).

### WEC magazines

*Heart of African Mission Magazine*, Worldwide Evangelization Crusade, London.

*INTO*, WEC International, Strathfield, NSW, Australia.

*IN TOUCH Singapore*, WEC International, Singapore.

*Wec.go*, WEC International, Fort Washington, PA, USA.

*World Conquest*, Worldwide Evangelisation Crusade, London.

*World Conquest: Australia edition*, Worldwide Evangelisation Crusade, Strathfield, NSW, Australia.

*Worldwide*, WEC International, Gerrards Cross, UK.

*Worldwide*, WEC International, Strathfield, NSW, Australia.

*Worldwide Thrust*, WEC International, Fort Washington, PA, USA.

# NOTES

1   A F Walls, *The Missionary Movement in Christian History*, pp. 253-254
2   P A Clark, *Organisations in Action: competition between contexts*, p. 53
3   S P Robbins, & N S Barnwell, *Organisation Theory in Australia*, pp. 25-29
4   C T Studd, Some Wish to Live, undated, p. 2
5   N P Grubb, *CT Studd – Cricketer and Pioneer*. p. 166
6   J C Pollock, *The Cambridge Seven*, p. 13
7   Now called the Overseas Missionary Fellowship (OMF).
8   *Christ Alone*, OMF 2005, p. 42; Neill S, *A History of Christian Missions*, pp. 333-334
9   J C Jackson, *No Other Foundation: the church through twenty centuries*, p. 256
10  They came to be borrowed later by the Communist Government of China as the basis for the government-controlled Three-Self Patriotic Movement church. For example, Chinese Christian leader Wang Mingdao practised the three self values long before the Three-Self Church came into being. Aikman, D, *Jesus in Beijing* (2003), p. 51
11  J C Pollock, *The Cambridge Seven*, p. 100
12  B G Worral, *The Making of the Modern Church*, p. 198
13  A J Broomhall, *Hudson Taylor and China's Open Century: book 6; assault on the nine*, p. 358
14  *ibid*, p. 425
15  The Seven went on to make their mark in the Christian world. All continued in China for several years. D E Hoste became Hudson Taylor's successor. W W Cassells was the first Anglican bishop in western China. A T Polhill-Turner served in China for forty-four years. C H Polhill-Turner after five years returned to the UK. Stanley Smith worked for seventeen years with Pastor Hsi. M Beauchamp returned to England after twenty-six years to take up a family title and responsibilities, but his son came out to China with CIM and the father died on a visit to see him in 1939. Studd worked in India and the Congo.
16  This preceded the Pentecostal movement by several years. Studd seemed to have an understanding that tongues was the gift of speaking other languages. Interestingly, during the WEC International Leaders' Conference in Scotland (1961), Donald Gee, chairperson of the British Pentecostal movement, pointed out that understanding another language spontaneously was a miracle and not the gift of tongues. L Brierley, *19-point programme*, p. 14
17  Moody started his residential Bible School in Chicago 'partly with the £5,000 CT Studd had given him for missionary work in India.' Fiedler, K, *The Story of Faith Missions*, p. 147

18      Muller claimed that in 50,000 cases he could trace distinct answers to specific prayers, A T Pierson, *George Muller of Bristol*, pp. 73, 300-302, and R Steer, *Delighted in God: a biography of George Muller*, p. 236

19      A J Broomhall, *Hudson Taylor and China's Open Century: book 7; it is not death to die!* pp. 59-60

20      *ibid*, p. 210

21      S T Tucker, *From Jerusalem to Irian Jaya: a biographical history of Christian Missions*, p. 367; NP Grubb, *CT Studd – Cricketer and Pioneer*, p135

22      E Vincent, *No Sacrifice Too Great*, pp. 55-56

23      D B Barrett, *Cosmos and Chaos*, p. 46

24      Quoted by E Vincent, *No Sacrifice Too Great*, p. 121

25      His son-in-law, Norman Grubb, explained that Studd did not hold a convinced doctrinal position but expressed a biblical truth forcefully, expecting to see a practical outworking of holiness in the individual's life. Grubb, *First the Blade: the story of WEC: with field surveys by Leslie Brierley*, pp. 52-53

26      J Walker, *Fool and Fanatic: quotations from the letters of CT Studd*, p. 36; N P Grubb, *CT Studd – Cricketer and Pioneer*, pp. 208-209; I Randall, *Entire Devotion to God*, p. 17

27      N P Grubb, *Christ in Congo Forests*, pp. 121-122

28      An old Congolese evangelist explained to me on a visit to the Congo in 1994 that he could still remember the DCD vow of actions and words in which he expressed his willingness to be killed if necessary for Jesus.

29      Studd, *The DCD*, p. 43

30      H Roseveare, *Living Stones: sacrifice, faith, holiness, fellowship: 75 years of WEC*, pp. 53-56

31      K Fielder, *The Story of Faith Missions*, p. 80

32      The Grattan Guinness family were made up of many missionaries and clergymen. The amazing story of the Guinness family of brewing and banking fame is told in *The Guinness Legend* by Michele Guinness, (Hodder & Stoughton, London, 1990). Lucy was the sister of Geraldine who was wife to Howard, the son of Hudson Taylor of CIM.

33      Kumm's original map was obtained by Leslie Brierley of WEC from the Royal Geographical Society in London and traces the journey.

34      I V Cleverdon, *Pools on Glowing Sand: the story of Karl Kumm*, pp. 90-91

35      S Neill, *A History of Christian Missions*, p. 393. With over 1,200 delegates meeting together from many missionary societies, denominations and countries to discuss missionary progress and strategy, it was recognised as the start of the ecumenical movement. R C Mackie, *Layman Extraordinary: John R Mott*, p. 41.

36      I V Cleverdon, *Pools on glowing sand: the story of Karl Kumm*, p. 92

37      Kumm wrote to Studd on 21 June 1910, shortly after the conference, bemoaning the way its spiritual impact was blunted by 'Bishops, Arch-Bishops, Presidents, Ex-Presidents, Convenors and Moderators', but noting that Kumm's own opening address was to go into the official report and

'should do some permanent good.'

38    J R Mott, *The Decisive Hour of Christian Missions*, pp. 27-29. Studd's personal copies of JR Mott's opening address, *The Decisive Hour of Christian Missions*, and *The Report of Commission 1* show extensive markings and marginal notes.

39    Grubb, *CT Studd – Cricketer and Pioneer*, p. 129

40    Vincent, *No Sacrifice Too Great*, p. 163

41    *ibid*, p. 157

42    J Walker, *Fool and Fanatic*, p. 73

43    A Hochschild, *King Leopold's Ghost: a story of greed, terrorism and heroism in Colonial Africa*, p. 272. Hochschild's book details the causes, abuses, ultimate triumph of the activists and then the campaign to suppress the truth. The lasting legacy still explains much of the Congo's troubles today.

44    Roseveare, *Give Me This Mountain*, pp. 154-155

45    A W Ruscoe, *The Lame Take the Prey*, p. 37

46    In both Anderson's book on the history of AIM (1994) and Richardson's account (1976), Studd's insistence on the separation of the UK AIM from US AIM, and his being solely in charge of the operation to the Congo, were regarded as the underlying causes of the disagreement.

47    Studd, *Christ's Etceteras*.

48    Walker, *Fool and Fanatic*, p. 18.

49    *ibid*, p. 19

50    *ibid*, 1980, pp. 17-18

51    Grubb claimed that only five were coming but Buxton named seven workers and added that Mr Bowers, one of the team of seven, had died at Yei near the Congo border. Grubb, *CT Studd – Cricketer and Pioneer*, pp. 143-144, 147; A B Buxton, *The First Ten Years of the Heart of Africa Mission (1913-1922)*, pp. 21, 24.

52    Grubb, *CT Studd – Cricketer and Pioneer*, pp. 163, 165

53    A J Broomhall, *Hudson Taylor and China's Open Century: volume 6; assault on the nine*, p. 420

54    Grubb, *CT Studd – Cricketer and Pioneer*, p. 132

55    Her story is told in *Reluctant Missionary,* (Lutterworth Press, London, 1968).

56    Buxton, *The First Ten Years of the Heart of Africa Mission*, inside jacket cover. The issue of it being a family organisation was alluded to in the magazine, when the editor said that it was only due to the whole family being committed to God. *Heart of African Mission Magazine* (1921, No. 29), p. 1.

57    Vincent, *No Sacrifice Too Great*, p. 215

58    *ibid*, p. 206

59    *HAM/WEC magazine*, (July/August 1921), pp. 18-37

60    *The Three Freds and Yield Xingu!* tell the story of the great sacrifices made by the workers as they were involved in spreading the word among the tribes. Interestingly today WEC Brazil has a field staffed by Brazilian WEC workers serving among people groups in the Amazon.

61    Letters to me from Roland Muller dated 20 September 2006 and 23 and 24 April 2008 state that the Heart of Arabia Mission continued officially until 1927

or 1929, but there is considerable evidence that several of its workers continued until 1949 and beyond. Quite remarkable fruit came from their efforts in the Middle East in church planting and literature ministries.

62 Studd, *The Chocolate Soldier*, p. 18

63 Grubb, *CT Studd – Cricketer and Pioneer*, p. 6

64 *The Chocolate Soldier, DCD, Laugh of Faith, Quaint Rhymes for the Battlefield by a quondam cricketer*, and *Christ's Etceteras* all symbolise Studd's passionate concerns in words symptomatic of that era.

65 Grubb, *Once Caught, No Escape: my life story*, p. 75  ~~former~~

66 Studd, *Quaint Rhymes for the Battlefield by a quondam cricketer*, pp. 50-55

67 Grubb, *Christ in Congo Forests*, p. 126

68 Grubb, *CT Studd – Cricketer and Pioneer*, p. 205

69 Jim Grainger once told me that Studd would personally check to see if he was comfortable at night and was keeping well. Eva Stuart Watt in her book *Floods on Dry Ground* (1939), pp. 37-38 gave a positive picture of him.

70 Dinnen, *Faith on Fire: Norman Grubb and the building of WEC*, p. 27

71 Dinnen, *Field Histories: Congo*, (IO, WEC International, Gerrards Cross, 2004)

72 Grubb, *CT Studd – Cricketer and Pioneer*, p. 220-222; R Beeson & R M Hunsicker, *The Hidden Price of Greatness: encouragement from the lives of well-known Christians*, pp. 121-125; Grubb, *Once Caught No Escape*, p. 97

73 Stewart Dinnen has written about the warm but frank correspondence years later to resolve any animosity between Norman Grubb and the leader of Unevangelised Fields Mission, which was initially composed of those who had separated from WEC. Dinnen, *Faith on Fire*, pp. 111-114

74 Grubb, *CT Studd – Cricketer and Pioneer*, pp. 5-6; Grubb, *Alfred Buxton of Abyssinia and Congo*, 1942; Roseveare, *Living Stones*, pp. 61, 65

75 The Searles were the founders of the WEC Home for Missionaries' Children in Scotland where I lived for eleven years. They often told us stories of the tough stand that CT Studd took on many issues. They agreed with him and spoke of him with warmth and respect.

76 Pioneer of WEC's work in West Kalimantan, Indonesia.

77 Founder of WEC work in Cote d'Ivoire.

78 Grubb, *CT Studd – Cricketer and Pioneer*, pp. 232-233

79 Walker, *Fool and Fanatic*, p. 80

80 Studd, *Quaint Rhymes For the Battlefield of a Quondam Cricketer*, pp. 16-19

81 In a letter to me, dated 4 July 2006.

82 R A Tucker, *From Jerusalem to Irian Jaya: a Biographical History of Christian Missions*, p. 318. Yet at the time of his death 2,000 Africans attended his funeral, the Congo church was nearly 10,000 strong, has not stopped developing since, and Studd's mission has reached out to over 80 countries of the world. These are surely evidence that his gamble paid off.

83 Grubb, *Once Caught, No Escape: my life story*, p. 94

84 Studd's theological emphasis, although a great encouragement to personal and corporate holiness, has proved to have a continuing unsettling influence in the Congo. My brother-in-law, Dr Brian Woodford and I discovered in a visit in 1994 that many of the pastors were reluctant to express certainty of personal assurance of salvation. In their desire for holiness, the African Christians would respond in repentance to get right with God during the occasional *makutanos* (inter-church teaching and preaching conferences) fearing they had fallen from grace. Further theological education in inter-denominational colleges has contributed balance and breadth of perspective to many of the senior leaders, who now have the responsibility for church direction.

85 Missionary Patty Toland wrote in a letter to me on 20 May 2008, 'If WEC did not give equal opportunity to women I do not think she would be as far as she is, nor have accomplished as much as she has in the world.'

86 Walker, *Fool and Fanatic*, pp. 119-120

87 Neill, *A History of Christian Missions*, p. 23

88 Grubb, *Fenton Hall: pioneer and hero*, p. 153

89 An interesting account of an influential tour by the Rev George Grubb through Australian and New Zealand is told by E C Millard, *The Same Lord*.

90 He held the rank of first lieutenant and was awarded the Military Cross for 'meritorious action.'

91 R V Pierard, 'Shaking the foundations: World War I, the Western Allies and German Protestant Missions', *International Bulletin of Missionary Research*, (vol. 22, no. 1), p. 13

92 R Padilla, 'An Age of Liberation' in T Dowley (ed) *The History of Christianity: A Lion Handbook* (1990), p. 642

93 A I Davidson, *High Adventure with God*, p. 173; Webster, D *The Shimmering Heat: memories of a bush doctor in East Africa*, p. 175

94 'Whereas in 1910 about two thirds of the Protestant missionaries came from outside North America, in 1960 it was the other way around.' G H Anderson, 'Christian Mission in AD2000: A glance backward', *Missiology* (vol. XXVIII, no. 3, July, 2000), p 277.

95 K Fielder, *The Story of Faith Missions: from Hudson Taylor to present day Africa*, p. 86

96 R D Winter, 'The world Christian movement 950-1975: an interpretive essay' in K S Latourette, *A History of Christianity, Vol II: AD1500 - AD1975*, p. 1477

97 Grubb, *CT Studd – Cricketer and Pioneer*, p. 245

98 The use of the phrase 'Don't Care a Damn' had caused great offence to respected evangelicals like F B Meyer and those on WEC's home committee. Dinnen, *Faith on Fire* (1997), pp. 28-31

99 Norman Grubb's book *Touching the Invisible* (1942) speaks to these issues and the importance they played in finding God's will, living in unity and seeing results in ministry.

100 A little leaflet *The Story of the Ten* was published by WEC in London in 1932.

101 Roseveare, *Living Stones*, pp. 74-75

102 Four of the new recruits had applied for these countries, stated Helen Roseveare in *Living Stones* (1988), p. 76. Norman Grubb had at the time of Studd's death issued a statement saying WEC's vision was for West Africa, Afghanistan and Indonesia. Dinnen, *Faith on Fire* (1997), p. 35.

103 Later Sir Kenneth Grubb, experienced missiologist, became Lord Mayor of London and author of *Crypts of Power*, 1971, Hodder & Stoughton, London.

104 In fact because of the DCD contention, the whole field had moved over to the Unevangelized Fields Mission. See Dinnen, *Faith on Fire*, p. 33.

105 B Woodford, *Master Plan: Biblical foundations for living churches*, pp. 34, 122. In a visit to Burkina Faso in 1996 my wife and I were thrilled to meet leaders and members of churches from different ethnic groups, especially since my eldest sister had served among the Birifors with her husband Brian Woodford.

106 B Macindoe, *Going for God: the story of Bessie Brierley*, pp. 38-39

107 Letter from Leslie Brierley to me 23 February 2006 and held in my personal library.

108 General circular letter to his friends held in my personal library.

109 Grubb, *My Dear CUMB: Norman Grubb's letters to the Cambridge University Missionary Band*, pp. 47-48, 70

110 Julia Brown of WEC, recorded in an interview with Jenny Carter, 9 Sept 2006.

111 Letter written by Leslie Brierley 23 February 2006 held in my personal library.

112 Grubb, *My dear CUMB* (2006), p. 70

113 Letter from Stanley Davies 13 July 2006.

114 1961 International Conference, p. 2

115 1961 International Conference, p. 41

116 Karl Fiedler has some intriguing references about the founding of WEC work in USA, Canada, South Africa, Australia and New Zealand in his 1994 book *The Story of Faith Missions* pp. 130-156.

117 The story of their experiences was told by Arthur Davidson in *High Adventure with God*, (Living Books for All, Manila, 1974).

118 Brierley, *19-Point Programme: personal notes of the 1961 Conference*, p. 15

119 Interview with Jenny Carter, 9 September 2006. 'Rubi' was the name given to Norman Grubb by the Africans in Congo and it stuck to him for the rest of his life.

120 Paul's apostolic team was in itself an international missionary society. Although some have said from Acts 13 that he acted under the oversight of the church at Antioch, yet it is not obvious that this was a matter of direction but of fellowship in which he shared with them, the church in Jerusalem and those other churches which he had founded.

121 Grubb, *Successor to CT Studd: the story of Jack Harrison*, pp. 67, 124-135. My father spoke of him as a careful Bible scholar and very competent leader.

122 The record of these events is told by Eva Stuart Watt in her 1938 book, *Floods on Dry Ground* (Marshall Morgan and Scott, London, 1938).

123 Grubb, *A Mighty Work of the Spirit*, pp. 62-62

124   *The Calvary Road* by Roy Hession (Christian Literature Crusade, London, 1950) shared their message of humility, brokenness and 'walking in the light' with God.

125   Norman Grubb compiled the stories of this revival in a remarkable little book, originally titled *This Is That* and later republished in 2000 by Christian Focus Publications as *The Spirit of Revival.*

126   Roseveare, 'Introduction' in Grubb (ed), *The Spirit of Revival*, p. 10

127   Ivor Davies, my father, travelled extensively in USA, Canada, UK, Australia and New Zealand over three years in the late 1950s telling the story of the Congo revival. He shared his personal experiences of that revival until his death in 1991. Two of my missionary uncles and aunts were also involved in the revival events. Their descriptions of the revival were awesome.

128   Norman Grubb's many books included *Rees Howells Intercessor, J D Drysdale Prophet of Holiness, The Liberating Secret, God Unlimited, The Deep Things of God, The Law of Faith, The Key to Everything, Continuous Revival, Touching the Invisible, Spontaneous You.*

129   Letter written by Norman Grubb to Jill Johnstone dated 9 June 1989 in my personal library. The letter focused on this double ministry to see people reached with the gospel but also to see the experience based on Galatians 4:17 become a reality. In the same letter Grubb expressed his fear that by 1989 WEC had moved away from the second emphasis. From many subsequent international conference reports and WEC magazines (eg *Worldwide*, May-June 2008), it would seem that emphasis is very much alive.

130   Dinnen, *Faith on Fire,* p. 193

131   *ibid*, p. 63

132   Bannister, *Access Without Visa* p. 15

133   Letter to me in June 2006.

134   Quoted in the foreword to Stewart and Marie Dinnen's book *Freedom and Fullness: the teachings and writings of Norman Grubb*, p. 5.

135   Dinnen, *Faith on Fire*, pp. 209-226. Grubb was regarded in some quarters outside of WEC as suspect theologically for his pan-entheism.

136   *ibid*, p. 199.

137   K Fiedler, *The Story of Faith Missions: from Hudson Taylor to present day Africa*, p. 86

138   I Randall, *Entire Devotion to God*, p. 20

139   'After his death in 1931 ... the constitution was changed and refounded on a fully self-governing basis.' Grubb, *First the Blade*, p. 9.

140   Letter by Grubb to Field Leaders in June 1953 held in my personal library.

141   Zena Gibson in an interview with Jenny Carter on 22 November 2006, recalled Norman Grubb working on Sundays – 'freedom from the law and every day being a holy day!' However Grubb would not force others to go against their convictions. Dinnen, *Faith on Fire*, p. 127.

142   This is evidenced by the way that Len Moules was to invest the later period of his life as associate pastor at Gold Hill Baptist Church, and how subsequently

the mission was blessed through many strong individual connections with churches.

143 Shord van Donge, Africa Regional Director, estimated that the WEC-founded church in the Congo (CECCA-16) in 2008 had under its area of responsibility '101 primary and secondary schools, Bible schools/institutes, a commercial training institute, a teachers' training college and a nurses training centre.' Report of a visit to the Congo 27 February-18 March 2008, p. 1.

144 Grubb allowed generous opportunity for all to share in the morning devotional sessions at the London WEC headquarters which became the pattern for many business conferences through WEC. Business matters were discussed and questions were raised about strategy, all against a study of biblical principles relevant to the issues. Dinnen, *Here We Stand* (1985), pp. 59-60. 'No time limit, never hurried – two or three hours or more' said Michael Tarrant in an interview with Jenny Carter, 9 September 2006.

145 Grubb, *The Four Pillars of WEC*, p. 70

146 Quoted by Stewart Dinnen in *Faith on Fire*, p. 125

147 Grubb, *First the Blade*, p. 7

148 'The workers themselves, the home or field staff, were the final executive voice' stated Grubb, p. 62.

149 Grubb, *After CT Studd*, p. 181

150 Moules, L, *Some Want It Tough*, p. 29

151 The story of the founder of the College was told by Norman Grubb in *J D Drysdale, Prophet of Holiness*. My mother, uncle and aunt and many other early WECers trained there.

152 P Wraight, *On To The Summit: the Len Moules story*, p. 83

153 J Hildebrandt, *History of the Church in Africa*, p. 245

154 Grubb, *The Growth of WEC: with Field Survey by Leslie Brierley*, p. 8

155 L Sanneh, *Whose Religion is Christianity? The Gospel beyond the West.*

156 His story is told with passion by Jock Purves in *Lal Sahib* (undated) pp. 49-52.

157 J McManners, *The Oxford History of Christianity*, p. 382

158 Lausanne Movement Congress 2008

159 R D Winter, 'The world Christian movement 1950-1975: an interpretive essay' in K S Latourette, *A History of Christianity, Vol. II: AD1500-AD 1975*, p. 1506

160 A Hastings, *A History of African Christianity 1950-1975*, p. 135

161 Roseveare, *Give Me this Mountain: an autobiography*. Her story was also told by Alan Burgess in *Daylight Must Come* (1975).

162 Roseveare, *Digging Ditches*, pp. 153-154, 204-212

163 Len Moules to Leslie Brierley on 11 February 1966 in my personal library.

164 In a series of letters written by Len Moules between 1968 and 1970 held in my personal library.

165 From 'Notes for a talk at Jan 1981 staff meetings' by Leslie Brierley held in my personal library.

166 He told Jim and Judy Raymo that he liked to 'stir up the bees' nest' when he came to Bulstrode. In one episode a lady candidate asked whether they could

wear trousers like other young Christian groups she saw. Grubb answered, as the local staff cringed, 'Why not?' Letter to me from Judy Raymo dated 30 July 2008.

167 Stewart Dinnen (in *Faith on Fire*, p. 208) tells of Grubb's voluminous correspondence with many in WEC encouraging and challenging them. I have a collection of personal and copy letters received from him until shortly before his death at the age of 98!

168 He had pushed his views about 'Christ in you' to an extreme, stating that a Christian is also god (cf. Ps 8:6) and so can act with authority and freedom. WEC in the end issued a statement clarifying its position about Grubb's teaching (Dinnen, *Faith on Fire*, pp. 217-218). Dieter Kuhl later wrote an article analysing Jacob Boehme's influence on Grubb's theology (D Kuhl, 'Norman Grubb and Jacob Boehme (1575-1624)' in S & M Dinnen, *Freedom and Fullness: the teachings and writings of Norman Grubb (1966-1993)* pp. 132-141).

169 Petrus Octavianus, leader of the Indonesian Missionary Fellowship, said 'After three years of trying we learned to live together as one. The Lord did a deep work in the missionaries – this was the beginning of integration.' (*International Report* 1969), p. 14

170 Letter from Len Moules to Leslie Brierley dated 11 January 1966 in my personal library. This is interesting in hindsight, for WEC has become today a truly international mission with a membership from 51 countries and sending offices in 18 separate countries.

171 The recently developed WEC Latino ministry in El Salvador is primarily working along similar lines to the FCOW concept.

172 Statistics come from an undated letter written by Violet Edson, former assistant to Leslie Brierley and secretary to Robert Mackey when he was the International Secretary. She listed WEC figures as 357 in 1950, 461 in 1955, 536 in 1960, 718 in 1965, 820 in 1970, 911 in 1975 and 977 in 1979. She said that figures prior to 1960 were taken from *Worldwide* magazines. The letter is in my private library.

173 In the 1969 *International Conference Report* (p. 30-31) and *Report and Resolutions of the International Leaders' Conference* 1984 (pp. 26, 42) it was seen that several fields had been opened soon after the adoption of the 1961 '19-Point Programme' and significant numbers of new workers joined.

174 Written to me in a letter on 26 May 2008.

175 Article 'God enabling us we go on ...' in UK *Worldwide,* (January-February, 1973), pp. 20-21.

176 Fellow WEC workers Wendy Baldwin and Flora Gibson testify to her motherly care, spiritual burden in prayer and fun-loving interest in them. This is shown in a written tribute given by them at her funeral on 28 February 2006, held in my private library from papers sent to me by Bobby Mackey, her son.

177 Letter from Renate Kuhl to me in November 2006.

178 From an interview with Jenny Carter on 9 September 2006.

179 Letter to me dated 20 September 2006.

180 From an interview with Jenny Carter on 9 September 2006.

181 See Appendix E.

182 The Brierleys continued their research ministry in a private way, but shared their findings with a worldwide audience through the publication of occasional magazines *Look, Wider Look* and *Koinonia* and a voluminous correspondence. I have several of their letters in my personal library. Their influence on spreading the message of the need and possibility of the world being reached with the Christian Gospel had profound implications, especially on non-western churches and Christian leaders.

183 *Operation World* is a country by country analysis of the spiritual needs and Christian progress with an emphasis on prayer. Patrick Johnstone says that 'in all five editions and in over 12 languages, nearly two million copies had been printed by 2000' (2001, pp. x-xi). The sixth edition was produced in 2001 and the seventh in 2010.

184 Until 2000 all of the various editions of *Principles and Practice* stated that each candidate to join WEC 'will spend a period of time in the Sending Base for fellowship and instruction in the scriptural principles and practical working of WEC' (*Principles and Practice*, 1990, p.21). The 2000 edition prescribed 'a four-month orientation' (*Principles and Practice*, 2000, p. 20) and the 2005 copy stated 'at least 8 weeks' (*Principles and Practice*, 2005, pp. 15, 20). This was then to be followed by a two-year period before workers could be regarded as having 'full member status' and ready for possible leadership availability.

185 'Patrick came into WEC with a WHOOSH with a vision of his own. WEC graciously embraced it.' Jean Barnicoat in an interview with Jenny Carter dated 8 November 2006.

186 Letter from Stanley Davies to me dated 13 July 2006.

187 Interview with Bob and Bev Harvey, 5 October 2007. Letter from Jonathan Chamberlain, 13 June 2006.

188 At the Worldview Centre for Intercultural Studies (WEC MTC) in Tasmania there is a large collection of taped addresses on file in the library including many WEC speakers.

189 L Moules, *Then God Stepped In: a jubilee publication*, p. 108; A I Davidson, *High Adventure with God*, pp. 122-123; E Rowbotham, *Would You Believe It!* pp. 84-86; *Sending Base Workers' Manual* (1976), pp. 46-50

190 Interview with Jenny Carter 8 November 2006.

191 Letter to me dated 22 June 2006.

192 *WECCER*, (April 1984), p. 3

193 Eileen Bannister's 1994 book *Access Without Visa*, tells the amazing story.

194 *ibid*, p 21

195 Letter from SOON Ministries 19 March 2008 in my files.

196 Letter from Tony Whittaker of SOON Ministries who has pioneered the Web Evangelism Guide and InternetEvangelismDay.com to promote creative ways

of using the internet in evangelism.

197 Every three months *SOON* (English) sends out 750,000 copies, *Bientôt* (French) 480,000, *Cedo* (Portuguese) 140,000, *Upesi* (Swahili) 120,000, *Badake* (Fulfulde) 22,000 and *Booyataa* (Pulaar) 5,000. This would add up to a total of 6 million per year. As well there is the German edition *Der Weg* targeting Eastern Europe and *SOON*.org.uk on the internet. This information comes from letters from Tony Whittaker of SOON Ministries on 15 March 2008 and Derek Cook of *Bientôt* on 26 March 2008.

198 Flora Davies recounted the tale in her book: *Listening: celebrating 40 years of Radio Worldwide ministry* (2001).

199 Programmes included English language, stories of travellers, hobbies, science, nature, quizzes, and Bible stories. Today Radio Worldwide works in partnership with many other organizations to produce relevant programmes in local languages. (F Davies, *Listening,* pp. 4-10).

200 Davies, *Listening,* p. 41

201 Letter from Grace McNeill dated 15 May 2008. Radio Worldwide staff members are involved in training in India, West Africa, Middle East and Central Asia.

202 From Alastair Kennedy's interview with Jenny Carter on 3 August 2006.

203 Interview with Jenny Carter, 8 November 2006.

204 K Fiedler, *The story of Faith Missions,* p. 121

205 Patrick Johnstone gave an excellent introduction to the Conference in 1984, setting out the worldwide challenge and the opportunities in countries, people groups, urban evangelism and media (*Report and Resolutions 1984*, pp. 25-28).

206 In 1975 I paid my first visit to Bulstrode, WEC's UK and International base, and during a conversation I had with Robert Mackey his passion for South-East Asia was evident.

207 In a letter held in my personal files.

208 Grubb, *Summit Living,* p. 340

209 In March-April 2008 there were 128 prayer groups still running in the UK (*Worldwide*), 23 in Australia (*Into Aus*) and 13 in New Zealand (*Into New Zealand*).

211 Mentioned in the UK *Worldwide* magazine March-April 2008.

212 Letter to me from Tom Scotland dated 20 May 2008.

213 On worldwide travels whilst based in the International Office, my wife and I met many people who were delighted to be involved in these prayer networks.

214 E Davies, & S Dinnen, *Straight from the Heart,* pp. 56-60

215 As a child being brought up in a WEC institution, and then as a member of WEC with my wife living at the WEC Missionary Training College in Tasmania for nearly 30 years, before living at Bulstrode in the UK for 12 years, we had a lot of experience in community. In our travels we have visited most WEC sending bases and fields. For us, more than forty years' experience of community has been overwhelmingly positive.

216 Letter to me on 17 May 2008.

217  Steve Bryant, MK Education Advisor, commenting on years spent living in the MK boarding school community in Senegal, in a letter to me dated 24 May 2008.
218  *Intercon 1990*, p.35
219  Patrick Johnstone in a letter to me dated 22 June 2006.
220  Mentioned in the tribute to Isabel Mackey, given by Patrick Johnstone, at her funeral on 28 September 2006, (copy held in my personal library).
221  D Kuhl, 'Strange turns on a desert road' in S Dinnen (ed), *All for the Best*, pp. 72-73
222  *Coordinating Council Conference June 1982*, pp. 14-15.
223  Stewart was still the International Secretary in June 1986 at the CC Conference in USA (Conference 1986, p. 6).
224  After a year they were replaced by Patrick and Sarah McElligott, whose involvement was recorded by Patrick in his autobiography *On Giants' Shoulders* (1994).
225  The 1978 and 1982 conferences dealt with very important matters, but did not give large place to investigation of unreached areas.
226  Foreword by Norman Grubb in S Dinnen, *When I Say Move!*
227  The remarkable story of the start of the college is contained in the book *Would You Believe It!* It was written by one of the founders of the College, Elsie Rowbotham in 1963. During the Dinnens' training most of their studies were undertaken at the Baptist College, until the WEC student numbers became too many and a schedule of lectures were set up independently by WEC staff.
228  E Rowbotham, *Would You Believe It!* (1982), p. 46
229  K Fielder, *The Story of Faith Missions*, p. 144
230  See Appendix C for further details.
231  I was there when a photo was taken of this group during the conference.
232  Dinnen, *Learning about Union with Christ*, p.99
233  Dinnen, *You Can Learn to Lead*. Michael Tarrant stated in an interview with Jenny Carter in 2006 that he was very grateful as a field leader in Guinea-Bissau to receive 'excellent teaching and very significant and needed leaflets' sent by Stewart Dinnen.
234  In an interview with Jenny Carter on 3 August 2006.
235  STEP was coined by Patrick Johnstone and stood for 'Strategy for Advance to Every People'.
236  Stuart Dinnen's Foreword 'We are on target!' in *Report and Resolutions of the International Leaders' Conference*, p. 10
237  The discussion on divorce was aimed at finding a policy dealing with the issue of divorcees serving in WEC – an issue of strong concern to many overseas churches and some fields. The result was a wise blend of biblical and practical positions, and a series of questions that could help in dealing with individual cases. *Report and Resolutions 1984*, pp. 68-70
238  A Kennedy, 'After-thoughts' in *Report and Resolutions of the International Leaders' Conference 1984*, p. 94

239   Bro Andrew, *God's Smuggler*, p. 92
240   Letter from Daphne Spraggett dated 30 January 2007 detailing this development.
241   D Kuhl, 'Strange turns on a desert road' in S Dinnen (ed), *All For The Best*, pp. 68-73
242   Letter to me dated 22 June 2006.
243   By 2009 the total of non-westerners had climbed to 652.
244   Myers & Woodford, *Serving Together Without Falling Apart: Team Manual 3*, pp. 19-22
245   Each International and Coordinating Council Report lists the people who spoke and often a summary of the ministry given.
246   Dinnen, *Rescue Shop Within a Yard of Hell*, p. 47; G Chevreau, *We Dance Because We Cannot Fly*, pp. 37-42
247   Dinnen & Dinnen, *Sacking the Frontiers of Hell*, p. 202
248   From a WEC prayer newsletter dated 8 December 2005.
249   *Prayer Force Handbook* (1996), pp. 22-25
250   Woodford, *Master Plan*, p.34
251   Grubb, *After CT Studd*, p. 113
252   H J Kullesky, *Travail, Triumph, Jubilee*, p. 3.
253   D Theobald, *Battles, Bricks and Bees*, p. 19
254   R F Gaskin, *Journey to the White Man's Grave*, p. 29
255   Lidorio, *Unafraid of the Sacred Forest*, p. 124
256   F Staniford, *Operation Ivory Coast*, pp. 19-22
257   J & G Rieder, *Jewels for His Crown*.
258   *Prayer Force Handbook* (1996), p. 36
259   *ibid*, p. 32
260   D Macmillan, 'It's worth it!' in E Davies & S Dinnen (eds), *Straight from the Heart*, p. 16
261   *Prayer Force Handbook* (1996), p. 97
262   *Intercessors for Thailand*, June 2009.
263   CC Conference 1988, pp. 7-14
264   CC Conference 1992, p. 10
265   After a cautious start, the Asian MTC in Hong Kong was closed in 2005 following the death of Dr Nan Pin Chee, the nominated Principal, during the 2003 SARS epidemic.
266   The ministry was called Rainbows of Hope (ROH) and, after a promising start and heavy involvement in several countries, most notably Sierra Leone and South Africa, it now operates in about eight fields (*ROH Prayer Bulletin*, Summer edition 2009). Some places have developed very impressive children's ministries not tied with ROH.
267   *Straight from the Heart* by E Davies & S Dinnen, 2004, was written to explain and illustrate WEC's Core Values for those not aware of what they are or mean.
268   See Appendix F.

269 *Intercon 1996* p. 47. The statement was ultimately incorporated in the section 'Activities'. (See Appendix A)

270 Ashcraft, *At the Scent of Water*, p. 232

271 Eley, *God's Brumby*, p. 187

272 In a letter dated 31 December 2007 she shared the details of many situations she was dealing with and in which she saw people set free from demonic influence. In Latin America there are major issues of people caught up with occult confusion and needing help from experienced leaders.

273 S S-C Moon, 'The Protestant missionary movement in Korea: current growth and development', in *International Bulletin of Missionary Research*, April 2008, pp. 59-62. Moon has said, 'WEC's recent progress is remarkable and can be attributed to the younger generation's preference for overseas training opportunities and its global network.'

274 As the person responsible for this process, I consulted widely and was grateful for excellent feedback in 1995 and 1996.

275 In an interview with Jenny Carter in November 2006.

276 It is interesting to note that from South Korea has come the largest number of ordained pastors from any country into WEC.

277 H Krueger, *Chosen to Go*.

278 At the College in Tasmania I estimated that up to 1990 50% of all graduates had joined WEC. I was Principal at the college from 1978 to 1991.

279 Officially 'Word Worldwide' was the main title but, as the *'Geared for Growth'* title was used very freely for the Bible Studies, it is often the name by which the movement is referred to.

280 Staff members were self-supported, and travel and accommodation costs were also their responsibility – special gifts were often received from the fields or bases visited.

281 Several very thought-provoking manuals were produced by Woodford and Dinnen (*Serving Together*, 1987), by Myers and Woodford (*Serving Together Without Falling Apart*, 1997), and by Myers and Woodford (*United We Serve*, 2002).

282 D D Ruiz, (ed), 'The two-thirds world: Lausanne Occasional Paper No.44', in D Claydon (ed) *A New Vision, A New Heart, A Renewed Call*, pp. 124-125

283 J D Sachs, 'National interests aren't what they used to be: our survival requires global solutions' in *'10 Ideas that are changing the world'*, TIME, (24 March 2008).

284 In 2003 Richard Tiplady raised these controversial topics in his book *One World or Many?*

285 J Taylor, 'The future of Christianity' in J McManners (ed), *The Oxford History of Christianity*, p. 658

286 Johnstone, & Mandryk, *Operation World* (2001), pp. 4-5

287 D Barrett, T M Johnson, & D F Crossing, 'Missiometrics 2008: Reality checks for Christian communions', in *International Bulletin of Missionary Research*, pp. 27-30

288 Johnstone, *The Church is Bigger than You Think*, pp. 114-115

289 Johnstone & Mandryk, *Operation World* (2001), pp. 314, 387-388

290 *Communications Directory* (2009), p. 8

291 Taken from a discussion paper 'State of the Company 2001' prepared by me for Intercon 2002 dated 28 August 2001 and circulated to all delegates prior to the conference.

292 My parents returned in 1954 after seven years, but we remained at the Children's Home to complete our schooling in Scotland. In more recent years WEC has set up homes and schools on the fields, to enable parents to have closer contact with their children who could then spend their holidays at home.

293 Interesting stories of the Children's Home are told in two little books – *God Can* by Charlie Searle (1963) and *Going Through with God* by Lily Searle (1965).

294 The college is now called 'Worldview Centre for Intercultural Studies'.

295 Raymo & Davies, *Meeting Jesus in Australia*, pp.16-19

296 Personal conversation with me in 2004.

297 Letter to me dated 13 June 2006.

298 Jean Barnicoat, former missionary to Ivory Coast as well as international MK Educational Advisor, in an interview with Jenny Carter, 8 November 2006.

299 Interview with Jenny Carter, 22 November 2006.

300 *Worldwide Thrust*, (Sept/Oct/Nov 2000), p. 13-14

301 Her fascinating story is told in *Whoever You Are,* 2004.

302 *Worldwide Thrust,* Dec/Jan/Feb 2000

303 J Cox, 'What I have learned from writing "The British missionary enterprise since 1700"' in *International Bulletin of Missionary Research*, April 2008, p. 86-87.

304 D O'Donnell, *Straight from the Heart,* p. 101

305 Letter to me dated 26 December 2006.

306 *Renewed to Run for Jesus,* devotional ministry from *Intercon 2002.*

307 Preface to *Intercon 2002 Report.*

308 Every three years all leadership positions in WEC were subject to re-election or a new leader had to be chosen. Any leaders after the age of 65 had to step down and could only be re-elected for one year.

309 *Intercon 2002 Report*, p. 6. My wife and I had the responsibility to share the conclusion of the discussion with the two couples. It was a remarkable outcome in a limited period and illustrated practical depths of open fellowship, strong corporate united faith, and dependence by the whole group on the Holy Spirit's guidance.

310 *wec.go*, Winter 2007-08, p.3

311 By 2009 there were 346 South Koreans in WEC and five branches throughout the country. This was second only to UK membership in WEC. The leadership passed to ChulLee and HeySook Choi in 2009.

312 A plan had developed among Chinese house churches to send out 100,000

missionaries to the countries between China and Jerusalem (Aikman, 2003, pp. 193-205). WEC was enthusiastic about this and was willing to give help in orientation and logistics to potential workers if needed.

313 From conversations with a group of older Australian WEC members, they mentioned to me that in 1942 one of them had been delayed from moving to the field for 24 months, until he was estimated to be spiritually fit enough to satisfy the Australian leadership!

314 The Leadership Training Seminars, the International Training and Resources Secretaries, International Directors for Training and printed Leadership Training Manuals, combined with the Regional Directors to provide specific help for field and sending base leaders.

315 The manuals that remained available in 2008 were *International Guidelines* (under revision), *United We Stand, Serving Together without Falling Apart, Regional Directors' Handbook, Field Workers' Manual, Crisis Management, Leaders' Manual* (under revision), *MK Manual 1 and MK Manual 2.*

316 Macindoe, *Going for God*, p. 7

317 Quoted to me by Stewart Dinnen who heard it said by Norman Grubb (cf. Grubb, *Summit Living*).

318 K O'Donnell, *Doing Member Care Well*, p. 4

319 Taylor, W D, *Too Valuable to Lose*, p. 32

320 The *WECCER* (June/July 2006), p. 6

321 As International Director I found a genuine transparency and warmth of friendship almost universally across the mission. When I came to lead Intercon 2002, I said to my wife it was like being in a group of friends, for we had met all but two and very much appreciated their contribution to the work in which we were all engaged.

322 R Beeson & R M Hunsicker, *The Hidden Price of Greatness*, p. 68

323 From a paper read out at his memorial service in 2005. His story is told in the 2008 autobiographical writing *Trusting Not Trying.*

324 *UK Worldwide* (November-December 2005), p. 7

325 T Scotland, *After Voice from the Stars*, p. 157

326 M & M Paton, 'Standing and moving in faith' in S Dinnen (ed), *All For The Best*, pp. 115-120

327 UK *Worldwide* (July-August 2007)

328 Lidorio, *Unafraid of the Sacred Forest*, pp. 41-44

329 Official Intercon 2006 Prayer Report nos 1 and 4, dated 6 April 2006 held in my personal files.

330 This discussion was centred around the interpretation of Acts 18:1-3, 26 and Romans 16:3. The 'Pauline' model was about a person serving in ministry who finds a business opportunity which enabled them to stay in a particular country. The 'Priscillan' model concerns a global-minded Christian who finds a job and then looks for ministry opportunities. WEC had previously concentrated on the 'Pauline' approach but were now investigating the 'Priscillan' concept as a way to tap into the large pool of competent and

experienced international Christians already resident and working in the restricted countries of the world.

331 *wec.go* (Winter 2008-09), p. 10

332 Report by Denise Rhodes dated 20-23 April 2008 held in my library.

333 'By constantly focussing on the unreached it [WEC] has maintained a steady determination to reach them for Christ whatever the obstacles'. (Stanley Davies, former Executive Director of the UK Evangelical Missionary Alliance, in a letter to Evan Davies 13 July 2006).

334 The Statement of Faith is in keeping with that produced by the World Evangelical Fellowship and in line with The Apostles' Creed and the Nicene Creed.

335 A F Walls, *The Missionary Movement in Christian History*, pp. 247-249

336 By virtue of the wise steps taken by Norman Grubb in 1931 to counter the worst ramifications of the DCD controversy, WEC was eventually accepted by those in Christian circles who were open to Grubb's stirring challenges based on Studd's life story and the commands of Christ. Dinnen, *Faith on Fire*, pp. 33-36.

337 Roseveare, 'The start and the heart,' in E Davies & S Dinnen (eds.) *Straight from the Heart*, p. 9

338 'There is a price tag attached to our airline ticket, a tag of sacrifice' (Cristina Grenier in *Renewed to Run for Jesus*, p. 8). She was speaking against a background of family loss, a much loved son killed in a motoring accident.

339 'For me he [Studd] stated in an encapsulated way what was in my heart.' Patty Toland in a letter to me dated 20 May 2008.

340 K Fiedler, *The Story of Faith Missions,* pp. 114-121

341 'Our advance will mean lonely places, dangers, difficulties. It will only be possible with a deepening of spiritual life.' Dieter Kuhl quoted in *Intercon 1996*, pp. 2, 11.

342 John Bagg, UK Sending Base Leader, in a letter to me dated 14 February 2008.

343 Letter to Evan Davies 13 July 2006.

344 Senegal Field Leader's communique 16 November 2007.

345 A wonderful description of Mary Rees is given by Grubb in *Christ in Congo Forests* (1945), pp. 160-164.

346 I Randall, *Entire Devotion to God* (1998), p. 22. A paper was written in 1965 by the US Sending Base Leader, Dave Cornell, showing that single women missionaries had a unique contribution to church planting in that, once a church was established they usually handed over leadership to local people much more speedily than men who tended to hold on as pastors to the detriment of the independence and cultural adaptation of the church.

347 Stanley Davies in a letter to Evan Davies 13 July 2006.

348 P Johnstone, 'Seeking and Finding' in Davies & Dinnen (eds), *Straight from the Heart*, pp. 87-90.

349 www.wec-int.org accessed 18 November 2010

350 *Principles and Practice* 2005 pp. 8-9 demonstrate the responsibilities of the

Field Leader. These call for visionary and managerial gifts, oversight of pastoral care, church relatedness and a person in tune with WEC's goals and ethos.

351 Brian Woodford said in a letter to me in March 2006, 'Church planting movements can be nurtured by wise planning and inter-agency co-operation. To my mind this is about the most thrilling and positive trend in Missions over the past forty plus years of my involvement. It has to do not so much with the growth of the organisation, but the growth of our understanding. I think it is every bit as significant as the culture awareness that has developed over roughly the same period.'

352 Letter to Evan Davies 4 July 2006. Fuller is a respected author and journalist with SIM International. At the other end of the scale is the comment by the Pentecostal leader, AS Worley, who said to Elliott Tepper, 'They [WEC] are the best missionaries in the world!' (S Dinnen, *Real Guidance*, 2003, pp. 19-20)

353 In my research I found it difficult to find many mission leaders who were able and willing to make informed comments about WEC International. This seems to bear out to me that there is a considerable level of ignorance about WEC and its operations.

354 Dinnen, *Faith on Fire*, p. 28

355 Letter from Patty Toland of WEC Latino on 14 February 2008.

356 John Bagg in a letter dated 14 February 2008.

357 Letter to me from the Korean sending base on 20 February 2008.

358 'Missions Attrition Survey: Responses of WEC missionaries' Christian Synergy Centre, dated 5 January 1998. This was part of a comprehensive survey of all Australian evangelical agencies conducted by Donovan and Myors. The commitment to WEC as an organisation scored particularly highly and was attributed to the long orientation process. However they also stated that it needed to be tempered with a 'focus on inspiring Generation X with the vision and finding new ways of strengthening their attachment to WEC'.

359 Jonathan Chamberlain was until the end of 2008 the Candidate Directors' Coordinator. In a letter to me dated 31 July 2008, Judy Raymo said when they were USA Candidate Directors, 'I don't know how many candidates mentioned to us that at first they had balked at the four month length of COC (Candidate Orientation Course), but in the end came to appreciate having that time to really get to know WEC and be bonded into the WEC family'.

360 The apostle Paul as a pioneer spelled out the challenges that stressed him out in 2 Corinthians 11:23-29.

361 Pauline Nicholas in an interview with Jenny Carter on 29 November 2006.

362 Alastair Kennedy in an interview with Jenny Carter on 3 August 2006.

363 *Ecclesiology Commission Report* (1986); Kennedy, *The Church*, (1992); Woodford, *Master Plan*, (2007).

364 Personal comment: Cell churches have proved their value in China; local church-based training is good for local developments; lack of ordained staff seems to preserve apostolic simplicity and the avoidance of erecting or

purchasing church buildings give Christian fellowships minimal financial burdens. However, as it can easily be seen, these are not the only models which have found acceptance or fruitfulness among Christians worldwide.

365    S Guthrie, *Missions in the Third Millennium*, p. 127

366    *wec.go* (Spring 2009), p. 11

367    Brierley, *19-point programme* (1961), p. 3

368    Dinnen, *Faith on Fire*, p. 34

369    See Appendx F.

370    Countries which have been entered by special doors, (eg medical), or which face serious political or religious restrictions, call for specialized types of training to fit their context.

371    Jonathan Chamberlain has said that WEC needs to redefine its 'niche in a world where mission is increasingly anywhere to anywhere', letter to me dated 13 June 2006.

372    *wec.Go* (Winter 2007-08), p. 11.

373    WEC's constitution states '... expansion and outreach are not controlled by "fixed budgets" or "closed doors" but rather by the "exceeding great and precious promises of God" in His Word'. *Principles & Practice* 2005, p. 3.

374    Korea, Brazil and Mexico have shown steady growth while Australia and the Netherlands have shown decline.

375    *International Bulletin of Missionary Research*, (April 2008), p. 59

376    'One of the big challenges in WEC today is the management of the tension between catholicity and indigenisation.' Philip Crooks in a letter to me dated 5 June 2008.

377    J Harris, *We Wish We'd Done More*, p. 500-504

378    Johnstone & Mandryk, *Operation World* (2001), pp. 745-746

379    My terms as International Director left me with some sad memories of human failures, as well as the joy and privilege of seeing God at work in delightful ways in individuals and on the global scene.

380    *UK Worldwide* (May-June 2008), p. 6

381    D Barrett, T M Johnson, & P F Crossing, 'Missiometrics 2008: Reality checks for Christian communions' in *International Bulletin of Missionary Research*, January 2008, pp. 27-30

382    *UK Worldwide* (September-October 2008), p. 9

383    *wec.go* (Winter 2007-08), p. 11

384    *wec.go* (Fall 2008), p. 14

385    Walls, *The Missionary Movement in Christian History*, p. 261

386    Habakkuk 2:14 (NIV)

387    The Mexican centre is run as a joint venture with the local Pastors' Alliance but is administered by WEC staff (information from Jenny Knight, August 2008).

388    Grubb says that it started in 1921 (1942a). According to David Harley, who wrote a brief history of All Nations Christian College, the Missionary Training Colony closed in 1939 due to World War II and did not open again afterwards.

This last information was in a note to me from Jill Brierley dated 4 July 2008. Wikipedia claims that it started in 1923 and merged with All Nations Bible College in 1962 to eventually merge with All Nations Christian College (Missionary Training Colony 2008, retrieved 5 June 2008 from en.wikipedia.org/wiki/All_Nations_Christian-College). The All Nations website says that '3 missionary training colleges combined to form All Nations Christian College at its present site in Easneye' (retrieved 5 June 2008 from www.allnations.ac.uk).

389   The college closed due to the death of the Principal, Dr Nan Pin Chee, who died in the 2003 SARS epidemic.

390   By 'public' we mean any gathering which is open to people who are not members of WEC.

Lightning Source UK Ltd.
Milton Keynes UK
UKOW050123160312

189043UK00001B/2/P